CW00602440

Palgrave Studies in Pragmatics, Language and Cognition

Palgrave Studies in Pragmatics, Language and Cognition is a new series of high quality research monographs and edited collections of essays focusing on the human pragmatic capacity and its interaction with natural language semantics and other faculties of mind. A central interest is the interface of pragmatics with the linguistic system(s), with the 'theory of mind' capacity and with other mental reasoning and general problem-solving capacities. Work of a social or cultural anthropological kind will be included if firmly embedded in a cognitive framework. Given the interdisciplinarity of the focal issues, relevant research will come from linguistics, philosophy of language, theoretical and experimental pragmatics, psychology and child development. The series will aim to reflect all kinds of research in the relevant fields – conceptual, analytical and experimental.

Titles include:

Anton Benz, Gerhard Jäger and Robert van Rooij (*editors*)
GAME THEORY AND PRAGMATICS

Reinhard Blutner and Henk Zeevat (*editors*)
OPTIMALITY THEORY AND PRAGMATICS

Corinne Iten
LINGUISTIC MEANING, TRUTH CONDITIONS AND RELEVANCE
The Case of Concessives

Ira Noveck and Dan Sperber (*editors*)
EXPERIMENTAL PRAGMATICS

Christoph Unger
GENRE, RELEVANCE AND GLOBAL COHERENCE
The Pragmatics of Discourse Type

Forthcoming titles:

María J. Frápolli (*editor*)
SAYING, MEANING AND REFERRING
Essays on François Recanati's Philosophy of Language

Ulrich Sauerland and Penka Stateva (*editors*)
PRESUPPOSITION AND IMPLICATURE IN COMPOSITIONAL SEMANTICS

Hans-Christian Schmitz
OPTIMAL ACCENTUATION AND ACTIVE INTERPRETATION

Palgrave Studies in Pragmatics, Language and Cognition Series
Series Standing Order ISBN 0–333–99010–2 Hardback 0–333–98584–2 Paperback
(*outside North America only*)

You can receive future titles in this series as they are published by placing a standing order. Please contact your bookseller or, in case of difficulty, write to us at the address below with your name and address, the title of the series and the ISBN quoted above.

Customer Services Department, Macmillan Distribution Ltd, Houndmills, Basingstoke, Hampshire RG21 6XS, England

Genre, Relevance and Global Coherence

The Pragmatics of Discourse Type

Christoph Unger

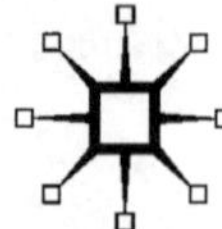

First published 2006 by
PALGRAVE MACMILLAN
Houndmills, Basingstoke, Hampshire RG21 6XS and
175 Fifth Avenue, New York, N. Y. 10010
Companies and representatives throughout the world

PALGRAVE MACMILLAN is the global academic imprint of the Palgrave Macmillan division of St. Martin's Press, LLC and of Palgrave Macmillan Ltd. Macmillan® is a registered trademark in the United States, United Kingdom and other countries. Palgrave is a registered trademark in the European Union and other countries.

ISBN-13: 978–1–4039–8533–0
ISBN-10: 1–4039–8533–2

This book is printed on paper suitable for recycling and made from fully managed and sustained forest sources.

A catalogue record for this book is available from the British Library.

Library of Congress Cataloging-in-Publication Data
Unger, Christoph, 1964–
Genre, relevance and global coherence : the pragmatics of discourse type / Christoph Unger.
p. cm. — (Palgrave studies in pragmatics, language and cognition)
Includes bibiliographical references and index.
ISBN 1–4039–8533–2 (cloth)
1. Discourse analysis. 2. Pragmatics. 3. Relevance. I. Title.

P302.U535 2007
401'.41—dc22

2006048579

10 9 8 7 6 5 4 3 2 1
15 14 13 12 11 10 09 08 07 06

Printed and bound in Great Britain by
Antony Rowe Ltd, Chippenham and Eastbourne

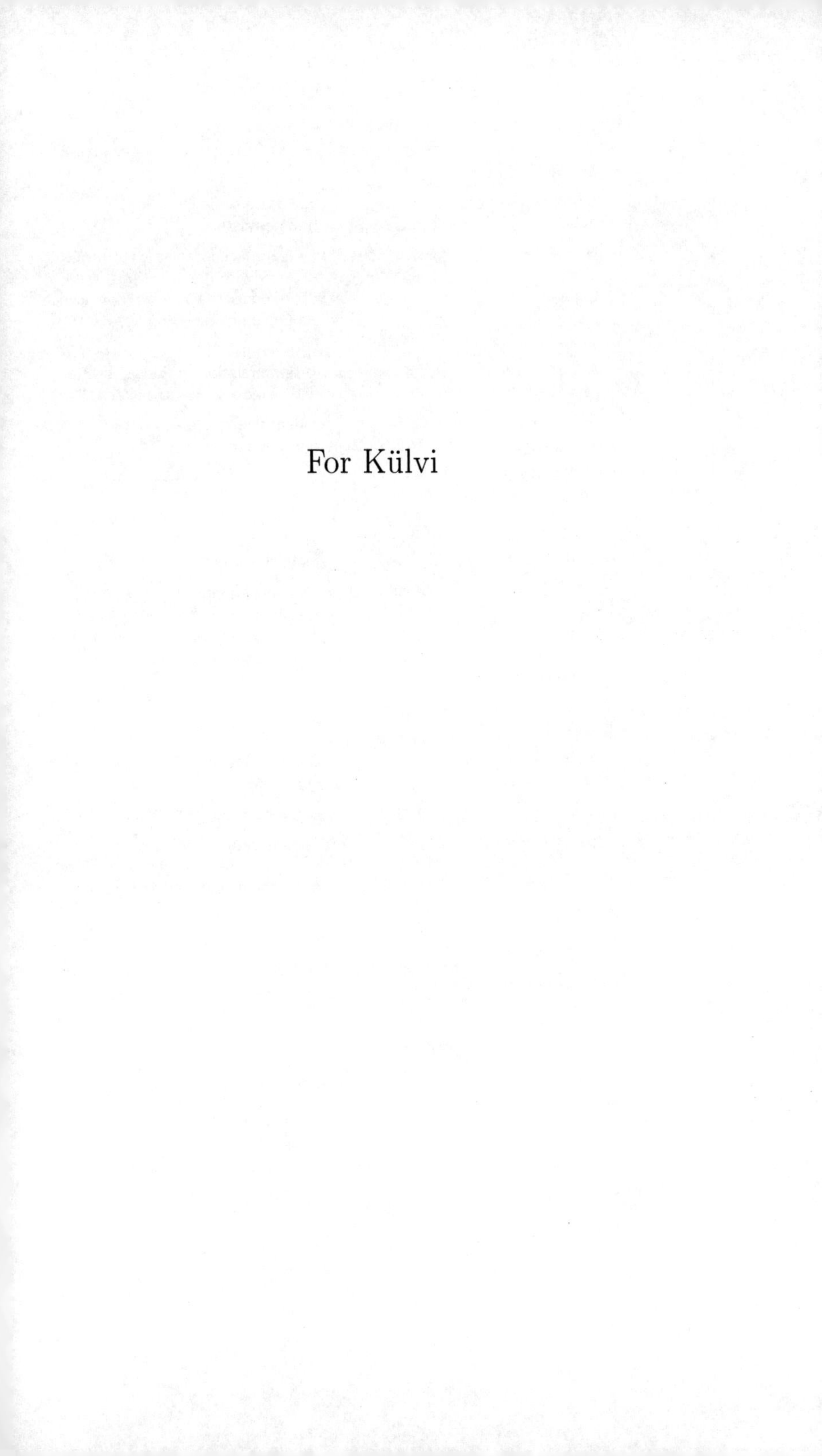

For Külvi

Contents

PART 1: GLOBAL COHERENCE AND GENRE

PART 2: EXPECTATIONS OF RELEVANCE AND GENRE

PART 3: GENRE IN INFERENTIAL THEORIES OF COMMUNICATION

Acknowledgements

First and foremost I like to thank Deirdre Wilson. She encouraged me in, and guided me through, the various stages of this project, many times beyond the call of duty, and I have profited a lot from her valuable advice. I would also like to thank Nigel Fabb and Mark Jary for very helpful comments, and Ronny Sim and Ernst-August Gutt for interesting discussions on various aspects of the topics covered in this book. Thanks are due also to Regina Blass, who first introduced me to relevance theory, and also made some valuable comments on a previous draft of this book. Above all, I thank my wife Külvi, who supported me strongly in this project, even putting up with my having to work long hours while there were little children to look after.

1 Introduction

1.1 Genre in pragmatic theory

In their book *Relevance*, Sperber and Wilson (1995) develop an explicit theory of ostensive-inferential communication. This theory is designed to explain the inferential aspects of ostensive communication: how a hearer bridges the gap between sentence meaning and speaker's intended meaning. The linguistic properties of particular utterances play an important role in constraining and directing these inferences. A large body of research has accumulated showing that relevance theory can indeed shed light on many aspects of (non-truth-conditional) semantics and pragmatics on the basis of the communicative principle of relevance and the linguistic properties of particular utterances. The theory has also been successfully applied to the study of discourse, that is of sequences of related utterances (for example Blakemore 1987, 1988; Blass 1990; Gutt 2000), and to some aspects of the interpretation of literary texts (for example Furlong 1996; Pilkington 2000; Reboul 1992).

What has not been widely studied within this framework is the extent to which the interpretation of utterances within a text or discourse may depend not only on properties of the particular utterance, but also on properties of the type of text or discourse it occurs in. Why should this be an important issue in the development of pragmatics? First, there is a widespread intuition that utterances are understood differently depending on the discourse type or genre in which they occur (for example Bex 1992; Goatly 1994). Some psycholinguistic research is designed to examine these intuitions and clarify their role (van Dijk and Kintsch 1983; Fayol et al. 1993; Copman and Griffith 1994; Hanauer 1995, 1998; Thomson and Adnan Zawaydeh 1996). More specific claims about the importance of genre in utterance interpretation have also been made in several disciplines, including linguistics, literary theory and translation theory.

In linguistics, discourse types have been claimed to affect the interpretation of linguistic forms such as tense-aspect morphemes (for example Abangma 1987; Unger 1989; Caenepeel 1995). In sociolinguistics and systemic-functional linguistics (Halliday 1978, 1985), the sociolinguistic dynamics of genre have been studied in register and genre theory (for example Goatly 1994; Eggins and Martin 1997) and claimed to play an important role in language use.

Gerhart (1989) discusses three views of genre in contemporary literary theory: the traditionalist view, the ideological view, and the deconstructionist view. On the traditionalist view, genre acts as a catalyst in the interpretation of individual texts: while genre knowledge does not determine a unique interpretation, it nevertheless facilitates understanding; in the absence of genre knowledge, a particular text would be considerably harder to understand. On the ideological view, genre is one property of language which cannot but be used in relation to the ideologies which drive writers and readers. The deconstructionst view sees texts as inevitably related to others of a similar type in a complex textual network, a semiotic system. What these views have in common is the idea that the understanding of texts depends in important ways on genre knowledge, though the precise role and extent of this dependence is seen differently in different approaches. Thus, there is general agreement in the field of literary theory that genre knowledge is crucial for understanding texts.

The importance of genre knowledge has also been emphasised in translation theory. Reiss (1981) suggests that different text types require different standards of functional equivalence. Hatim and Mason (1997) observe that there might be something like a 'text-type deficit' (Hatim and Mason 1997:133) between cultures or language communities: a certain text type may not be available in the language communities involved in cross-cultural communication. This may result in loss or shifts in certain aspects of pragmatic meaning: for example subtlety in argumentation may be lost and the translated text may seem blunt — with potentially wide-ranging consequences.[1] The question is whether the translator is permitted, or even required, to change the text type in order to preserve such pragmatic meanings.

There seems, then, to be a strong case for investigating the role of genre/text type in an explanatory theory of utterance interpretation. It might be argued that the case is not as strong as it seems. Someone might suggest that literary theory is not properly included in pragmatics. The two disciplines may use different theoretical concepts, even different concepts of genre, and there is no *a-priori* reason to expect them to cross-fertilise each other. Similarly, it might be argued that translation theory is an application of pragmatics, and as such may include non-pragmatic phenomena within its domain; so the importance of genre considerations in translation theory may be seen as coming from outside pragmatics. Arguments of this type suggest that only properly pragmatic arguments or evidence for the importance of genre knowledge in utterance interpretation should be taken into account.

But these arguments do not really go through. First, relevance theory has been shown to have interesting implications for literary interpretation (Fabb 1997; Furlong 1996; Pilkington 1992, 2000; Reboul 1992; Sperber and Wilson 1990; Trotter 1992). Moreover, some literary theorists have exploited linguistic and pragmatic theory in developing theories of genre. For example, Todorov (1990) argues that there are 'discourse speech-acts' which are systematically linked to (standard) speech-acts, and which also have to be recognised for a discourse to be understood. This suggests that while there is no *a-priori* connection between relevance-theoretic pragmatics and literary theory, relevance theory has implications for literary theory in general, and this might also be true in the case of genre. Second, Gutt (2000) has made a strong case for the claim that translation properly falls within the scope of relevance theory rather than requiring an interdisciplinary fragmentation. Thus, a relevance-theoretic account of genre might be expected to have an impact on both literary theory and translation theory, and evidence from either field may be legitimately taken into account.

Still, there is some point in the claim that literary theory and translation theory may pay attention to aspects of genre which do not directly affect linguistic or pragmatic explanation. My focus in this study will therefore be on the linguistic and pragmatic aspects of genre. Although a thorough investigation of literary and translation-theoretic aspects of genre would be of great intrinsic interest, I will not consider them in this book.

Another reason why relevance-theoretic pragmatics should be interested in genre has to do with intentionality. Relevance theory claims that the hearer's goal in utterance interpretation is to infer the speaker's informative intention on the basis of the stimulus produced. Genre theorists have argued that the intentions conveyed by a text are heavily influenced by its genre (Berger 1987 and literature cited therein). The notion of genre has also been linked to (rhetorical) purpose: genre information relates to 'conventional ways of getting things done,' and can thus be crucial to understanding the author's purpose (Swales 1990; Downing 1996; Eggins and Martin 1997). Insofar as this notion of purpose is seen as a psychological one (Downing 1996:24) the question arises of how text purpose is related to the speaker's informative and communicative intentions, and how the recognition of text purpose is linked to the hearer's method of inferring the speaker's intentions.

In the rest of this chapter I will spell out in more detail the perspective from which this discussion will be approached. In section 1.2, I will review the notions of genre and discourse (or text) type which have been used in the literature, with a view to delimiting the scope of this study. In section 1.3, I will outline the functions which genre has been seen as performing in utterance interpretation. In section 1.4 I will introduce relevance theory. Finally, section 1.5 will give an overview of the book.

1.2 The notion of genre

Texts can be sorted into generic categories in almost any imaginable way. A sample list of such categories is given in (1):

(1) Story, poem, tape-recorded story, written story, detective story, novel, science-fiction novel, fantasy novel, narrative, recipe, procedural text, non-narrative text, parable, allegory, hymn, fiction, dialogue, history text, linguistics text book, ...

Note that the individual genre labels in this list are obviously constructed on the basis of quite different criteria: thus the label *detective story* refers to aspects of what the story is about; *narrative* is connected not so much to the content of the text as to the way it is presented; *fiction* treats the logical status of a text in relation to the world as a basis for classification; *dialogue* relates to external properties of the talk exchange such as number of participants. Such generic classifications have been given different names in the literature: *genre, discourse type, text type.* Before embarking on an investigation of the role of genre in utterance interpretation, some preliminary clarification of these notions is needed.

Different terms are used in different disciplines. *Genre* is mostly used in literary theory, whereas *discourse type* and *text type* are more often used in linguistic studies of discourse. The literary-theoretic notion of *genre* often emphasises criteria based on content, whereas other classification criteria are more important in discourse studies. However, the correlation between notions of text classification and disciplines is not rigid; thus one finds literary critics such as Todorov (1990) trying to ground a literary notion of genre on linguistic foundations such as speech-act theory, and the generic distinction between narrative and non-narrative texts surfaces in both linguistic and literary studies (compare for example Longacre 1983; Todorov 1990 and Caenepeel 1995). This suggests that there is not necessarily a crucial distinction between *genre* on the one hand, and *discourse type* and *text type* on the other, at least not one which could be easily captured in pre-theoretical terms.

Discourse type and *text type* are distinguishable only to the extent that *text* and *discourse* are seen as distinguishable. While there is widespread agreement about the notion of *discourse* as encompassing spoken or written language productions in context (for example Brown and Yule 1983; Blass 1990; van Dijk 1997b), there is a certain ambivalence in the use of the term *text*. Some authors use this term in the same way as others use the term *discourse* (Blass 1990:10 refers to Lyons 1981 as using the term *text* in this way; see also the entry 'Text' in Lewandowski 1985 and more generally the literature on 'text grammar'). Others use it in a more restrictive sense, either as denoting written artifacts (van Dijk 1997b), or more generally, verbal records of the communicative act in any medium (Brown and Yule 1983; Blass 1990; Werth 1999).[2] On this latter definition of *text*, *text type* would be a purely formal notion which may become relevant to pragmatics only when texts are used in communication and therefore become *discourses*, and *text types* therefore become *discourse types*. But then it is of little consequence whether the notions of *discourse* and *discourse type* are clearly distinguished from the notions of *text* and *text type*. In this book I will therefore follow the general practice of using *discourse* and *text*, and hence *discourse type* and *text type*, as synonyms. Taken together with the above comments on genre, this means that I will use all three terms synonymously unless otherwise indicated.[3]

Turning to the classification criteria underlying different conceptions of genre, Renkema (1993) provides a useful survey of the notions of discourse type or genre most widely used in the literature on discourse analysis (Renkema 1993:86–95).

There are basically two approaches to discourse classification. One approach classifies discourse according to a small number of basic or ideal forms. This could be called a feature-based account of genre. Renkema (1993) quotes Werlich (1982) as an example of such an approach. Werlich's types are: descriptive, narrative, explanatory, argumentative, instructive, each of which is connected with a certain type of sentence structure. Each type may be further divided into subjective versus objective sub-types. Similar approaches have been put forward by Grimes (1975) and Longacre (1983), among others.

Another approach classifies discourse according to aspects of the discourse situation, such as number of speakers, social rank of the speakers, whether the theme of the discourse is fixed beforehand, and whether the theme is treated in descriptive, argumentative, or associative terms. This might be called a sociological or sociolinguistic approach. As a prime example of this type of approach, Renkema (1993) cites Steger et al. (1974).

These classifications interact with a further distinction between written and oral discourse, based on the following two assumptions. '1. Writing takes longer than speaking. 2. Writers do not have contact with readers' (Renkema 1993:86). The result is an enormous range of possible classifications and sub-classifications.

According to Renkema's survey, the distinctions most often currently used in the study of oral discourse are: monologue versus dialogue, and symmetrical versus asymmetrical discourse, where symmetrical discourse involves communicators of equal social rank, and asymmetrical discourse involves communicators of unequal social ranks. In the case of monologue and written discourse, classification is typically based on 'three categories reflecting the main goals of discourse: narration, information and persuasion' (Renkema 1993:93).

Yet another conception of genre combines aspects of different classification criteria into a prototype-based account (Swales 1990; Paltridge 1995). According to Swales, genre is mainly determined by the purpose of a text, but other classification criteria such as form, structure and audience expectations are taken into account to determine the prototypicality of a given text instantiating a particular genre.

In this book, all these various conceptions of genre will have to be taken into account. I will therefore use the term *genre* in the broadest possible sense, to cover any strategy of generic classification of texts.

It may seem that this preliminary definition of the notion of *genre* is far too broad if this book is to be of manageable size. However, I want to consider not only what genre classifications have been made, but also why they have been made. I would therefore like to consider the function of genre in a theory of genre before this investigation gets under way.

1.3 The functions of genre

A common assumption in modern linguistic theory is that generic classification is only of theoretical importance if it can be shown to have a function in utterance comprehension. The critical re-evaluation of traditional classifications is a recurrent theme. As an example, one might point to the discussion of the notion of grammatical construction (such as relative clause) in generative grammar (Chomsky 1986; Haegemann 1993). In pragmatics, Sperber and Wilson (1995) have argued that various traditional classifications have no independent function in utterance interpretation: for example, foreground versus background information, or topic versus focus (Sperber and Wilson 1995:202–17), and various types of speech-act classifications (Sperber and Wilson 1995:243–54).[4] One of the aims of this book is to critically re-evaluate claims that have been made in the literature about the functions of genre in comprehension.

Not all discussions of genre in the literature do make claims about the function of genre in utterance interpretation. Ramos (1998), for example, suggests a matrix of sixteen parameters which constitute different types of verbal-visual communication. The parameters are: whether the exchange is character-oriented (that is the communication takes place between characters, for example of a comic strip) or spectator-oriented (that is the communication takes place between the author of the discourse and the reader), whether the message is conveyed verbally or non-verbally, whether the information-transmission was intentional or unintentional, and whether the communication was maximally efficient (that is the addressee understood correctly) or minimally efficient (that is the addressee did not understand correctly). In the paper he discusses how comic strips group into different categories along the parameters he sets up, but he does not discuss which role this categorisation process is supposed to play in comprehension.

For expository purposes, it may be helpful to give an overview of the kinds of functions which genre has been — or could be — claimed to perform. These fall into four major categories. I will call them the *linguistic function*, the *hermeneutical function*, the *sociological function*, and the *historical function*.[5]

Genre is assigned what might be called a *linguistic function* in theories which see genre information as crucial to the semantic and pragmatic interpretation of particular linguistic items such as tense and aspect markers (Abangma 1987; Unger 1989; Longacre 1989a,b, 1990a,b, 1992; Hays 1995) or pronouns (Fox 1987). Here, the contribution of certain linguistic items to the information conveyed by an utterance is seen as crucially mediated by discourse-type (genre) information. For example, Longacre (1992) claims that the verbless nominal clause in Hebrew narrative discourse expresses material contributing to the setting of a narrative, that is background information, while Hays (1995) argues that in expository discourse the same construction marks foreground (or main line) information.[6]

Other theories claim that genre knowledge plays a role not so much in the interpretation of individual linguistic items as in recognising the full intended import of a text. Such theories include those which Gerhart (1989) calls the 'traditionalist view' (for example Birch 1974; Fowler 1982). Green (1995), who claims that identification of the type of talk exchange one is engaged in can influence the recognition of implicatures, provides a further illustration of this approach. Theories of this type claim that genre has what I want to call a *hermeneutical function*. Here, the contribution of genre knowledge is not so much to the recognition of explicatures or implicatures of a single utterance, but to the recognition of implicatures on the level of the text (Gutt 2000), or to constraining the type of implicatures to be expected. Such approaches make stronger or weaker claims about the hermeneutical function of genre. Thus, Green (1995) makes the weak claim that although genre may in some cases influence scalar implicatures, other types of implicatures are not so influenced. Hence genre knowledge is not always involved in utterance comprehension. Stronger claims are made in systemic-functional register and genre theory; thus, for example, Thibault (1999:557) claims that genre is always involved in the social process of 'meaning-making,' hence presumably also in comprehension. Similar claims have been made — albeit less explicitly argued — in holistic-cognitive linguistics (Paltridge 1995; Lakoff and Johnson 1980). Lakoff and Johnson (1980:83), discussing what is involved when we recognise whether we are engaged in a conversation or an argument, claim that 'we need to classify our experiences in order to comprehend, so that we will know what to do.' This need to classify extends to categories such as conversation and argument; it follows that comprehension needs to include genre recognition.

Other theories focus on sociological explanations of the role of genre (Goatly 1994; Kotthoff 1995; Eggins and Martin 1997; Downing 1996; Orta 1996 and others). Genre is seen as bound up with the way in which social realities are conveyed by a text. This is what I want to call the *sociological function* of genre. Since most of these theories do not attempt to explain communication in cognitive terms, it is not always clear if claims are being made about a cognitive function of genre in utterance interpretation. If no such claims are made, discussion of this approach falls outside the scope of this book. However, since social realities are claimed to directly affect the use of language, there is a sense in which the sociological function of genre is closely related to (and may even imply) a linguistic function (see the discussion of Eggins and Martin 1997 below). Moreover, some of the claims about the role of genre made in these non-psychologically oriented approaches can be recast so as to become relevant to questions about the cognitive role of genre in utterance interpretation. Discussion of these points will be included in this book.

Another approach to genre assigns it what I have called a *historical function*: since genres have their origin in social factors in a community, and since these factors change over time, genre changes as well, and this can be used as evidence in studying the history of (oral) traditions. This approach has its origins in the literary theory of the Romantics, and has given rise to the so-called 'form-critical' approach to Biblical exegesis (Berger 1987 and references cited therein). It is obvious that a discussion of this function falls outside the scope of this book.[7]

1.4 Relevance theory

This study of the role of genre in pragmatics takes relevance theory (Sperber and Wilson 1995) as its point of departure. As noted above, relevance theory is an inferential theory of communication, which aims to explain how the audience infers the communicator's intended meaning. The relevance-theoretic explanation of these inference processes is rooted in an account of cognition. It is because of the link this provides between communication and cognition that this book can be at the same time a study of the pragmatics of genre and of its cognitive role.

1.4.1 Communication, code and inference

An inferential theory of communication explains communication in the following terms: the speaker intends to convey some information

I, and produces a stimulus which enables the addressee to identify this information by recognising the speaker's intention to convey it. An *ostensive stimulus* is a behaviour (or the trace of this behaviour) which can only be explained on the assumption that the communicator wanted to give evidence of his intention to convey some information. It is thus a manifestly intentional behaviour. Communication involving the production of ostensive stimuli is also called *ostensive* communication.

The basic point about ostensive-inferential communication is that the communicator intentionally provides evidence that he intends the audience to arrive at certain conclusions. In other words, the communicator is attributed two intentions: an intention to inform the hearer of something, which is called the *informative intention*; and the intention to inform the addressee of this informative intention, this latter intention being called the *communicative intention.* An example of an inferential communication process is the following:

(2) I was at a conference in Spain and needed to buy a toothbrush. I didn't know Spanish, and the chemist indicated that he didn't speak English. So I mimicked the act of brushing my teeth. The chemist understood perfectly and brought a toothbrush, and so the purchase went smoothly.

In mimicking the act of brushing my teeth, I produced evidence which, together with appropriate contextual assumptions, led the chemist to entertain the conclusion in (3e):

(3)
a. Someone who walks into a chemist shop wants to buy something which he believes is sold there.
b. The customer is acting in a way similar to the act of brushing one's teeth.
c. For brushing one's teeth one needs a toothbrush.
d. Toothbrushes are sold at the chemist's.
e. The customer wants to buy a toothbrush.

By contrast, a code theory of communication — in its pure form — holds that the speaker encodes some information **I** into a signal, which the addressee has then to decode. The signal itself does not *provide evidence for the conclusion* that the speaker intended to convey this information; it encodes the information **I** itself, and the speaker's intentions are irrelevant to the identification of the intended message. An example of communication by means of a code is performed by computers exchanging information by email communication: The communicator types a natural-language sentence on the computer, which the computer encodes into a sequence of ASCII numbers. The signal, a sequence of ASCII numbers, is transmitted via the internet to the addressee's computer, which decodes the signal into the sentence displayed on screen for the addressee to read. Thus, a layer of extra encoding and decoding is added to the normal processes of verbal communication.

Is verbal communication code- or inference-based? Verbal communication surely involves a code, that is, the grammar of a particular language. However, there is reason to believe that verbal communication cannot be explained solely in terms of a code theory. In the first place, natural languages contain indexical expressions such as pronouns which do not encode their referents. Furthermore, there are ambiguous expressions in language which need to be disambiguated; it is unclear how this process could be explained in code theory terms. In other words: natural-language sentences do not fully encode the propositions they are used to express. There is evidence that the discrepancy between what is linguistically encoded in an utterance and the proposition expressed is even greater than that (Carston 1988, 1998b; Sperber and Wilson 1995, 1998). Also, slips of the tongue, that is, cases where the code is wrongly applied, are often not difficult to correct; the hearer can often recognise the speaker's intended meaning even though the coded signal does not represent it. Finally, implicatures are blatantly not encoded and yet occur frequently in verbal communication.

It seems, then, that verbal communication involves both coding and inference. In relevance theory, the relation between them is seen as follows: a verbal utterance is a stimulus which the addressee can use as evidence in inferring the speaker's meaning. The information encoded in the stimulus is treated as part of the evidence which, together with appropriate contextual information, warrants the inference of what the speaker wanted to convey.[8]

The problem for an inferential theory of communication is to explain how communicators succeed in understanding each other. After all, every single piece of evidence gained from a stimulus can be potentially interpreted against a huge range of contextual assumptions, warranting a wide variety of inferences, even mutually exclusive ones. But the fact that understanding is possible in verbal communication shows that the hearer, generally speaking, does infer the speaker's intended meaning. Sperber and Wilson (1995) argue that this is because ostensive-inferential communication exploits a general cognitive principle: that the mind tends to attend primarily to information which is relevant in a technical sense. In the following sections I will outline these aspects of relevance theory in enough detail for the purposes of this book.

1.4.2 Cognition and relevance

At every moment, the mind is confronted with much more information than it can possibly attend to. To operate efficiently, it must assign its memory and processing resources selectively, to information which seems likely to improve the individual's overall representation of the world. In other words, the mind should attend to information which enables it to achieve the general goal of the human cognitive system, which is to improve the individual's knowledge of the world as effectively as possible.

What kind of information is likely to contribute to this goal? Information which expands and builds on existing knowledge obviously does, as does information which corrects mistaken beliefs, and provides confirmation of existing assumptions. In all these cases the individual's assumptions about the world are clearly enhanced.

Conversely, consider what information is not likely to contribute to improving the individual's representation of the world. Obviously, information which the individual already has available, and which does not confirm (or strengthen) existing assumptions, does not; nor does information which is contradicted by other well established (stronger) assumptions. What about information which is new but does not connect in any way with any existing information? The cognitive system cannot assess whether it contributes to the goal, and cannot use it to modify or build on existing assumptions. So such information does not contribute to the goal of effectively enhancing world knowledge.

In short the human cognitive system — if it is efficient — should tend to pick out information which connects to existing assumptions in such a way as to improve the individual's overall representation of the world by making it richer, better-evidenced and more likely to be true. In Sperber and Wilson's (1995) terms, such information produces *positive cognitive effects*, which are of three main types: *contextual implication, contextual strengthening,* and *contextual contradiction and elimination.*

Note that the goal of the human cognitive system is to *effectively* modify the individual's representation of the world. Information which simultaneously achieves a great many positive cognitive effects is obviously effective. However, the human cognitive system can achieve such effects only by the expenditure of effort. Efficiency is a matter of balancing costs and benefits. We can thus conclude that the human cognitive system should tend to pick out and process that information which achieves the greatest positive cognitive effects for the smallest processing effort. Sperber and Wilson call this information which has this property *relevant* information and formulate a cognitive principle of relevance:

(4) *The cognitive principle of relevance*
Human cognition tends to be geared to the maximisation of relevance. (Sperber and Wilson 1995:260)

This principle states no more than a tendency: that the mind is set up in such a way that it automatically attends to the most relevant-seeming information. It takes into account the fact that the mind's mechanisms and heuristics may not always yield the best results in individual cases, and that assessments of relevance do not always produce clear-cut results (see Sperber and Wilson 1995:261–3; Sperber and Wilson 1996 for discussion). However, this principle is strong enough to have far-reaching consequences for ostensive communication. These will be discussed in the following subsection.

1.4.3 Communication and relevance

The cognitive principle of relevance has important consequences for communication. According to Sperber and Wilson, communication involves the production of an ostensive stimulus, that is, some intentional behaviour (or the trace of it) which catches the audience's attention and which the audience cannot make sense of without assuming that the communicator intended to convey some information. An ostensive stimulus in this sense can be a simple gesture, a verbal (sentential or sub-sentential) utterance, a sign or notice-board, or a complex stimulus such as an utterance accompanied by an action (for example an instructor simultaneously explaining to an apprentice and demonstrating to him how to exchange a shock-absorber in a car). Such an ostensive stimulus inevitably calls for some processing effort from the audience. However, according to the cognitive principle of relevance, the human cognition system attends only to information which seems relevant. If the communicator wants to be understood (that is, is a rational communicator), then she must produce her ostensive stimulus in such a way that it will seem relevant to the audience under the intended interpretation. Thus it can be said that every act of ostensive communication creates in the audience a presumption that it will be relevant enough to be worth the audiences's attention.

What level of relevance should the audience presume the ostensive stimulus will achieve? Certainly, at least enough relevance to make the utterance worth processing. However, since more relevant information stands more chance of being attended to and successfully understood, it can be expected that there will be cases where the level of relevance presumed is more than merely adequate relevance. On the other hand, there are all sorts of reasons why a communicator might fail to produce the stimulus which would be *most* relevant to the hearer, even though this is what he might want. In the case of a verbal utterance, the communicator may not be able to think of the best way to put it, she may be prevented from producing the simplest utterance by cultural conventions, and so on. The audience has no right to expect this kind of perfection. Nevertheless, it seems reasonable to expect speakers to produce utterances which are as relevant as possible, given their abilities and preferences. Sperber and Wilson (1995:158) call this the communicative principle of relevance:

(5) *The communicative principle of relevance*
Every act of ostensive communication communicates a presumption of its own optimal relevance.

The presumption of optimal relevance is as follows:

(6) *Presumption of optimal relevance*
a. The ostensive stimulus is relevant enough for it to be worth the addressee's effort to process it.
b. The ostensive stimulus is the most relevant one compatible with the communicator's abilities and preferences. (Sperber and Wilson 1995:270)

Recall that the basic problem in explaining how inferential communication works has to do with constraining the addressee's inferential path so that he arrives at the speaker's intended meaning. Sperber and Wilson (1995) argue that the communicative principle of relevance effectively constrains the addressee's inferences by yielding an effective comprehension procedure. This procedure will be discussed in the next subsection.

1.4.4 The relevance-theoretic comprehension procedure

According to the communicative principle of relevance, every ostensive stimulus in effect conveys to the audience the claim that it is optimally relevant. A stimulus is optimally relevant to the audience if they can find an interpretation that is at least relevant enough, without having to waste any processing effort. This motivates the following comprehension procedure: the audience should follow a path of least effort in computing cognitive effects, considering interpretations in order of accessibility, and accepting the first interpretation which satisfies their expectations of relevance. Schematically, this can be stated as follows:

(7) *The relevance-theoretic comprehension procedure*
Follow a path of least effort in computing cognitive effects:
(a) Consider interpretations (reference assignments, contextual assumptions, implications, and so on) in order of accessibility.
(b) Stop when your expectations of relevance are satisfied.

Let me illustrate how the relevance-theoretic comprehension procedure works by using an example. Mike and Sally are about to go on a week-end trip by car, and they are busy packing. Mike says to Sally:

(8) The car is open.

Intuitively, Sally will take Mike to have conveyed — roughly — the propositions that the car they own is unlocked, and that Sally should start loading it without waiting for Mike to unlock it. While the first of these (*The car they own is unlocked*) is the proposition expressed and the proposition that is explicitly communicated by the utterance — or, in relevance-theoretic terms, its *explicature* —, the second is an *implicature.* Let us see how relevance theory explains how Sally arrives at this interpretation.

First, Sally recognises that Mike has produced an ostensive stimulus: he has said *The car is open.* According to the communicative principle of relevance, Mike's utterance *The car is open* conveys the presumption that it is optimally relevant to Sally, that is, that she should be able to get at least enough cognitive effects from it (under its intended interpretation), and that it will require no gratuitous processing effort. Sally will therefore — all else being equal[9] — expect Mike's utterance to be optimally relevant. In the situation described, Sally will have easy access to the information that they own a car, that they are going on a week-end trip in it, that it is normally locked when it is parked, and so on Thus, an interpretation of (8) where *the car* refers to the car that Sally and Mike own, and where *is open* is meant to convey the idea *(It) is unlocked* is highly salient and easily accessible. From this interpretation of the proposition expressed, Sally can easily derive the contextual implication (9b) if she can supply the contextual assumption (9a) — and since this contextual assumption is arguably derivable from a cognitive scenario about packing things in a car for a trip, she can in fact access it quite easily:

(9) a. If the car is unlocked, then Sally and Mike can load the car without waiting for each other.

b. Sally and Mike can load the car without waiting for each other.

The contextual implication (9b) in turn potentially leads on to many other cognitive effects, such as the ones in (10b) and (10d), all of which seem worthy of attention in the situation.

(10) a. If Sally and Mike can load the car without waiting for each other, then loading will be faster.

b. Loading the car will be faster.

c. If loading is faster, then they will not have to start so late.

d. They will not have to start so late.

Hence, Sally is able to gain many cognitive effects for little processing effort, and the presumption that this utterance is optimally relevant to Sally turns out to be true on this interpretation. At this point, the audience can stop the interpretation process and accept the resulting interpretation as the one intended by the communicator.

Of course, there might be other interpretations which would lead to still further cognitive effects: for example that the car is open because it has been broken into. However, this interpretation is not the first to occur to Sally in following a path of least effort. Accessing it would require the rejection of a satisfactory and easily accessible interpretation in favour of a less accessible one. This step incurs extra processing effort. So even if on the effect side the resulting (second) interpretation achieved enough cognitive effects, it would have demanded more processing effort, including the gratuitous effort of constructing and then abandoning the first interpretation. Hence, the utterance will never be optimally relevant on this second interpretation. This is why the relevance-theoretic comprehension procedure licenses the hearer to accept the first interpretation which satisfies the hearer's expectations of relevance as the one intended by the speaker and stop the interpretation process at this point.

Consider again the implicatures in (9) and (10). While these all contribute to establishing the relevance of (8), and are accessible with little effort, there is a sense in which the implicatures in (9) seem stronger than the ones in (10): it is possible to imagine a whole range of other implicatures similar to those in (10), for example those in (11):

(11)
a. If loading is faster, then Sally and Mike may arrive at their destination an hour early.
b. Sally and Mike may arrive at their destination an hour early.
c. If loading is faster, then Sally and Mike may pass the major motorway junction before rush hour.
d. Sally and Mike may pass the major motorway junction before rush hour.

All these implicatures are accessible, and it is not so easy to decide which of them the speaker intended to convey and which he didn't. It is obvious that he must have intended to convey some such implicatures, but the hearer has to take much of the responsibility in deciding which ones to entertain. By contrast, the hearer can be quite sure that the speaker intended to convey something close to the implicatures in (9), for otherwise the presumption of optimal relevance could not be confirmed. There is thus a difference in the degree of responsibility that the hearer has to take in attributing different implicatures (intended implications) to the speaker: in some cases, this responsibility will be low (that is, the speaker has left the hearer little choice); in others, the responsibility is higher. Sperber and Wilson (1995) say that in the former case the implicature is *strongly* communicated (*strong implicature*), whereas in the latter it is *weakly* communicated (*weak implicature*).

To sum up, relevance theory explains ostensive communication in the following way: the production of an ostensive stimulus demands the investment of some processing effort from the addressee. Since the mind tends to allocate its resources to the most relevant information, if the communicator wants to be understood, she should produce a stimulus which is at least relevant enough to the addressee to be worth attending to. The addressee can therefore interpret the stimulus on the assumption that it will be at least adequately relevant to him. This justifies acceptance of the first accessible interpretation which satisfies his expectations of optimal relevance.

1.5 Overview of the book

In this chapter, I have introduced the basic question on which this research is focused, and have surveyed various notions of genre used in the literature. I have further argued that a theory of genre is relevant to pragmatics only insofar as it can be shown to have a communicative function. I looked at various functions which have been attributed to genre, including linguistic, hermeneutical, social and historical functions. Only the first two, and marginally the third, are relevant to this book. I also introduced the basic ideas of relevance theory, the framework in which this study of the role of genre in pragmatics will be conducted.

My argument falls into three main parts. In the first (*Global coherence and genre*, Chapters 2 to 4), I look at the connection between global coherence and genre and consider the widespread view that discourse type might interact with linguistic marking in the search for global coherence. In Chapter 2, I introduce the idea of global coherence. This chapter discusses the claim that global coherence might be analysed in terms of global coherence relations, by analogy to local coherence relations which hold between successive utterances in a text. Other notions of global coherence are discussed in Chapters 3 and 4: Chapter 3 considers various topic-based approaches to global coherence, and Chapter 4 looks at analyses of global coherence in terms of information-staging or grounding in discourse. I argue that none of these theoretical notions can be satisfactorily defined, and that research in this area has uncovered many interesting data for which there is as yet no satisfactory explanation.

In the second part of this book (*Expectations of relevance and genre*, Chapters 5 to 7), I develop a relevance-theoretic alternative to the notion of global coherence, based on the idea of management of expectations of relevance in discourse, and argue that this relevance-based account can shed new light on phenomena which have normally been attributed to global coherence, as surveyed in Part 1. Chapter 5 introduces the relevance-theoretic account of utterance comprehension as guided by expectations of relevance. It looks in detail at what this means for sequences of utterances, that is, text or discourse, and its consequences for text structure. In Chapter 6 I show how this conception of expectations of relevance in discourse accounts for global coherence and grounding, and explains the results of many experimental studies claimed to show the psychological reality of genre. Thus, many of the intuitions usually attributed to the influence of genre can be explained without recourse to the concept of genre. Chapter 7 surveys a range of linguistic data which have been claimed to reflect a linguistic function of genre, and argues that these claims are mistaken, and that these data can be better explained using the relevance-theoretic notion of expectations of relevance developed in Chapter 5.

In Part 3 (*Genre in inferential theories of communication*, Chapters 8 and 9), I extend the discussion of the role of genre in communication by considering its place in inferential theories of genre. Chapter 8 reviews systemic-functional register and genre theory, which is basically a code-based approach to genre. Advocates of this theory have argued that inference-based approaches to communication such as relevance theory need to be supplemented by an account of register and genre in systemic-functional terms. By contrast, I argue that code-based approaches to genre are inadequate, and that an adequate explanation of genre and related phenomena requires an inferential theory of communication. In Chapter 9, I consider various approaches to genre within a broadly Gricean pragmatics, that is, in inferential theories of communication. A question arising in this context is whether the essence of genre is linked to the intuitive idea of shared purposes of a group of texts, and whether these purposes can be explained as parts of the (Gricean) speaker's intention. The possibilities of incorporating some of these approaches into relevance theory are evaluated. Finally, in Chapter 10, I summarise the main contributions of this book for the theory of genre and pragmatics in general, and for relevance theory in particular.

Part 1

GLOBAL COHERENCE AND GENRE

2 Global coherence and global discourse relations

2.1 Introduction

In the first part of this book I want to investigate the claim that text types or genres have a linguistic function, that is, that the contribution of certain linguistic items to the information conveyed by an utterance is crucially mediated by discourse-type (genre) information. This claim is a central feature of coherence-based theories of discourse, where it is argued that through its influence on global coherence, knowledge of genre directly affects the linguistic interpretation of texts. A major aim of the first part of this book is to discuss various notions of global coherence and show how they might provide a basis for an explanation of genre. In this chapter I will set the scene by considering Samet and Schank's (1984) seminal article on coherence and connectivity, which discusses the nature and functions of global coherence and proposes a definition of global coherence which might provide a basis for a theory of genre (section 2.2). After discussing their notion of global coherence (section 2.3), I will look in more detail at the role of causality relations in narratives (section 2.4), which Samet and Schank (1984) use to illustrate their approach, and which plays a role in other coherence-based approaches to genre (for example Caenepeel 1995).

2.2 Samet and Schank (1984) on coherence

Samet and Schank (1984) offers a clear exposition of the idea that genre can be accounted for in a coherence-based discourse theory, which is echoed in many later accounts. In a programmatic way, Samet and Schank sketch the contents, goals and problems of a general theory of coherence. I shall therefore start with an examination of the central claims of this article.

According to Samet and Schank, intuitions of textual coherence are a by-product of our comprehension mechanisms. If they work smoothly when presented with a text, then we think this text is coherent. The comprehension mechanisms work smoothly if the representation of the text is properly formed and its parts are properly connected. Thus, connectivity is at the heart of coherence. Samet and Schank concentrate on connectivity internal to the discourse (as opposed to external connections between the discourse and the world). They restrict their data to short, simple narratives in the hope that what can be learned by investigating these can serve as the basis for a more comprehensive study of discourse coherence (Samet and Schank 1984:58).

A condition for connectivity is the existence of some form of semantic (or content) linkage between the parts of a discourse representation. Intersentential content relations such as those illustrated in (1) contribute crucially to connectivity,[1] and hence to intuitions of coherence:

(1) a. *Cause-consequence: the eventuality[2] described in the second sentence is a consequence of the eventuality described in the first.*
Mary shook the apple tree. Many apples fell off.

b. *Temporal succession: the eventuality described in the second sentence occurs after the eventuality described in the first. (This relation is called 'narration' in Fox 1987 and Lascarides and Asher 1993)*
Many apples fell off the tree. Peter picked them up.

c. *Reason-result: the eventuality described in the second sentence provides a reason for the event described in the first.*
Peter ate many apples. He likes them.

These intersentential content relations might be called *local coherence relations*, since they link adjacent units in a text. However, there is more to discourse coherence than local coherence or connectivity. Consider example (2), where every sentence is linked to its predecessor by a local coherence relation, but the resulting discourse is not intuitively coherent.

(2) Samet and Schank (1984:63), their example (11).
The heads of the city's uniformed services polished their contingency plans for a strike. Queen Wilhelmina finalized her own plans for the evening. In a nearby Danish town, two fishmongers exchanged blows. Anders, by far the stronger, had a cousin in prison. Many criminals are in prison; one might say that a good number of those individuals who have violated the penal code are incarcerated...

Samet and Schank conclude that the connectivity of discourse is not just a matter of intersentential links, but must also involve connectivity relations between the main events of the text (what one might call *global coherence relations*). In narrative texts, this global connectivity is provided by a causal chain linking the events of the story-line. More generally, an acceptable text exhibits both local and global coherence.

On Samet and Schank's account, recognition of the causal connections between the main events in a narrative is crucial for overall coherence. This is what rules out nonsense texts such as the one above, which have coherence relations between their individual sentences, but do not add up to a coherent whole. Causally connected events in narrative are usually introduced in the order in which they occurred; if not, there are principles which guide the hearer in reconstructing the intended temporal order.

The problem with the claim that discovering global coherence requires reconstruction of the causal chain underlying the events in a text is that it leads to a combinatorial explosion if the hearer has to go through all possibilities and then decide which one is acceptable. There must therefore be some cognitive mechanisms which constrain the hearer's inference processes. Samet and Schank discuss two possible mechanisms that might be used in this connection: scripts on the one hand, and plans and goals on the other. However, as I will argue below, neither mechanism can explain every aspect of story comprehension. Not all stories are organised around a script. Moreover, as Samet and Schank themselves note, stories that follow a script very closely generally seem banal. Similar points apply to plans and goals. The authors suggest that several cognitive mechanisms might work together to constrain the inference processes used in recognising the causal connections between the main events of a text. This claim will be discussed below.

Within this framework, genre affects the comprehension of texts in the following way. According to Samet and Schank, in narrative texts, as we have seen, causal connections between the events described are crucial for global coherence. In other text types, other types of connections are required. For example, in instructional texts, the key to global coherence may be the relation between various plans and goals. Thus, different types of global connectivity provide the basis for a typology of discourse types. To the extent that different cognitive processes are involved in dealing with these connectivity relations, the notion of genre has a cognitive foundation.

In the rest of this chapter, I want to examine the theoretical foundations of this approach to genre. Since it rests on the notion of global coherence, the first question must be whether this notion itself can be made precise and given a firm theoretical basis. In the next section I will turn to a discussion of this point.

2.3 On the notion of global coherence

2.3.1 Global coherence relations

According to Samet and Schank (1984), global coherence (in a narrative) is connectivity between the main events of the text. They propose that every event must be related to the causal chain underlying the narrative. These relations hold independently of the local coherence relations between discourse segments. There are thus two relational networks established in narrative: one where adjacent discourse segments are related by various formal coherence relations, and a second one where the events in the narrative are related to each other by causal relations. This second relational network accounts for global coherence. Notice that it is constituted in a way similar to the network pertaining to local coherence: formal relations hold between the elements of the network. The global coherence network differs from the local coherence network in that the elements of the latter are any discourse segments, whereas the elements of the former are events; furthermore, the network of local coherence contains many different coherence relations, whereas the network of global coherence contains only causal relations (in narratives). Global coherence is thus analysed by means of relations in a way similar to the analysis of local coherence.

The main role of global coherence is to give a common direction to the interpretation of the parts of the text. This leads to the idea that global coherence is fixed in different ways for different text types. Authors such as Samet and Schank (1984) and Caenepeel (1995)[3] assume that in narrative texts the hearer must establish the causal chain between the main events, which also relates to the temporal organisation of the text. Thus, there is one global coherence relation holding between the main events of the text: that of causality (or consequentiality). Whereas there are many possible relations on the level of local coherence, the range of relations on the level of global coherence is severely restricted.

What this amounts to is the claim that the global coherence relation is given, and that in the case of narrative, the interpretation process mainly involves finding out how the main events are causally related to each other. Similar remarks apply to other text types and their respective global coherence relation(s). Whereas on the level of local coherence the expectation is only that there are coherence relations (Charolles 1983), on the level of global coherence the expectation is more stringent: in narrative texts, the global coherence relation is that of causality (or consequentiality).

To assess the merits of this account, let's turn to considerations of discourse comprehension. According to the Samet and Schank (1984) proposal, text types differ as to which coherence relation holds on the level of global coherence. It is thus of great importance for the hearer to find out which type of text he is dealing with. Furthermore, he must do this very early in the interpretation process, preferably during the first utterance of a text. This could be done on the basis of formulaic expressions or extratextual clues (such as the fact that it is printed in a book, or written on stationery, and so on, or from information in the title or subtitle). However, not all texts, and certainly not all narratives, do have formulaic expressions or come with extratextual clues. So comprehension in such cases must be based on something else.

Another way of determining the text type would be by reference to a script associated with the text, or to plans and goals underlying it. These psychological constructs might provide information as to the basic kind of connectivity underlying the text. This can be illustrated with the following examples:

(3) John took the bus. He arrived at the office just about in time. (Narrative)

(4) Sue was hungry. She asked a passer-by where the next restaurant was. (Narrative)

(5) This proposal is not convincing. It is based on a lot of questionable assumptions. (Argumentation)

In (3), knowledge of a script TRAVEL TO WORK can help the hearer recognise the causal chain underlying this text, understanding it as a narrative. This might go as follows: the hearer can access the script about TRAVEL TO WORK, which gives access to stereotypical information of bus travel, including *Taking a bus is best for getting to work on time*; on the basis of this, the hearer can infer that John's arrival in the office on time was caused by John's taking the bus. In (4), stereotypical knowledge of the goals which hungry people have lead the audience to the assumption that Sue may want to eat something. The second sentence can be interpreted as contributing to such a goal, since restaurants are places where one can eat.

Thus, this stereotypical knowledge about plans and goals allows the audience to infer the causal chain underlying this narrative. Turning to non-narratives, (5) might be explained as follows: Stereotypical knowledge of the goals which people have who make controversial statements leads the hearer to expect that the speaker will enter into an argument, and that the connection between the sentences is not one of 'narrative causality' but of reasoning.

But as Samet and Schank note, not every text is organised around scripts, plans or goals. It is unclear in this theory how texts not organised in one of these ways would be comprehended.

Samet and Schank (like other authors, for example Mann and Thompson 1986, 1988) also suggest that some text types lack global coherence. Casual conversation or personal letters, for example, may not create expectations about global coherence at all. There is thus a dichotomy between texts which do exhibit global coherence and texts that do not, and the hearer's initial task will be to recognise whether the text creates expectations of global coherence or not. Again, the hearer will have to examine extralinguistic clues or certain (formulaic) expressions in the initial utterance to infer the text type. Only then can understanding of the following utterances proceed.

Notice, however, that the task of understanding is seriously complicated by the contention that there may be mixed text types (Samet and Schank 1984:77). This means that in principle every utterance in a text may belong to its own subtype, and this subtype must be recognised before comprehension can succeed. But this line leads to a *reductio ad absurdum* of the claim that global coherence is fundamental to discourse comprehension.

These observations on the role of text-type recognition in text comprehension suggest that a theory of discourse incorporating a notion of global coherence on the lines proposed by Samet and Schank (1984) is psychologically implausible.

2.3.2 The purpose of global coherence relations

For Samet and Schank (1984), the main purpose of global coherence relations is to help eliminate locally coherent nonsense texts. In a relevance-theoretic framework, where considerations of effect and effort are central, coherent nonsense texts are avoided by a different mechanism based on the relation between cognitive effects and processing effort. The more processing effort is needed to derive some relatively simple cognitive effects, the less justification there is for treating them as part of the intended interpretation. To see that this notion is really sufficient for the purpose of distinguishing coherent nonsense texts and acceptable texts, let us compare an acceptable text (example 6) and a coherent nonsense-text (example 2).

(6) (i) We need to begin by casting doubt on the legitimacy of the notion of literature. (ii) The mere fact that the word exists, or that an academic institution has been built around it, does not mean that the thing itself is self-evident. (Todorov 1990:1; second paragraph)

Intuitively, (i) seems to make a non-obvious, and perhaps a radical, claim, which causes the hearer to expect that the author will justify this claim. Sentence (ii) can indeed be interpreted in this way, as justifying (in part) why the author could have made the claim in (i). Thus, the hearer's expectations about how the text will unfold are satisfied with little processing effort. In other words: the reader has to invest little processing effort in realising how (ii) is connected to the previous part of the discourse. Also, the interpretation of (i) makes a difference in the interpretation of (ii), a later part of the discourse. In a coherent text, the hearer does not seem to have to invest wasted processing effort (Blass 1990:79).

In an incoherent text such as (2), things appear to be different. While the first of each sentence pair arguably makes a difference for the interpretation of the second, so that the second sentence can be interpreted with the investment of little processing effort in a context suggested by the first sentence (for example *Anders* may be one of the fishmongers referred to in the first sentence; *many criminals are in prison* can be seen as an idea standardly associated with the concept

PRISON), the first sentence of a pair does not appear to have a bearing on the interpretation of later parts of the text. The author of this text has caused the hearer to invest processing effort which does not seem to be rewarded in the end.

However, it is possible to save the text in (2) if one adds clues to how the globally incoherent part can contribute to a satisfying overall interpretation:

(7) The heads of the city's uniformed services polished their contingency plans for a strike. Queen Wilhelmina finalized her own plans for the evening. In a nearby Danish town, two fishmongers exchanged blows. Anders, by far the stronger, had a cousin in prison. Many criminals are in prison; one might say that a good number of those individuals who have violated the penal code are incarcerated...

That was what John Fox remembered from his dreams when he woke up from a healthy sleep. The last two days had been filled with unusual events and strange news. He tried to understand what was going on and wondered what would happen next.

The added paragraph makes it possible for the reader to construct an interpretation in which the previous paragraph is a meaningful contribution to the text in front of him, and the effort required to process it is not wasted. A context is now accessible in which the expectations of relevance created by this text can be satisfied. That the text in (2) can be saved in this way without any change in coherence relations or connectivity strongly suggests that 'global coherence' is not to be sought in terms of formal relations between parts (linguistic items) of texts, thus directly falsifying Samet and Schank's (1984:64) statement:

> It follows then that if connectivity is in fact at the heart of coherence, there must be some other type of relation that holds between the discrete parts of a narrative but which is not included in our tree of expository connections. On

> our view, the missing connections are the causal relations that are at the heart of the story line.

I conclude that it is not to other kinds of relations, or relations on different levels, that we must turn, but to another kind of explanation of what makes a text 'hang together' and 'make sense.' The relevance-theoretic framework fulfils this condition. In this framework, the main functions of the concept of global coherence (ruling out 'mock narratives') are fulfilled by the notion of relevance itself. There is thus no need to establish a notion of global coherence.

Notice also that a text like (7) may be typical for a novel, not for a short and simple narrative. It appears thus that the research restriction of Samet and Schank (1984) to short, simple narratives is methodologically unsound since it leads to unwarranted conclusions and excludes data from consideration which can lead to a different explanation of the phenomena in question.

The argument in this subsection was that there is reason to doubt that a notion of global coherence is needed. If this is correct, the account of genre in terms of global coherence relations as suggested by Samet and Schank (1984) is *a fortiori* called into question. My aim in the rest of this part of the book is to substantiate this claim about global coherence and to establish a relevance-theoretic account of the phenomena normally attributed to global coherence. However, before embarking on this project by considering different conceptions of global coherence in subsequent chapters, I will turn to discuss a narrower issue, that is, the claim that the global coherence of narratives can be accounted for in terms of global causal relations in the sense of Samet and Schank (1984).

2.4 Causal relations, global coherence and time

In the last section I suggested that the primary role of global coherence might be accounted for in other ways, thereby avoiding the problem of defining the notion. In this section, I want to discuss some specific problems with analysing the global coherence of narratives in the framework of Samet and Schank (1984). Recall that they see the global coherence of narratives as established by recognising a causal chain between the main events of the story, which may be used to establish the temporal relations between these events. One way of interpreting this claim is as saying that 'semantic', that is content-based, causal relations have to be recognised between the main events. There is an alternative interpretation of Samet and Schank's position: they may be claiming that causal relations between the main events have to be established, and these relations are not content-based ones but relations in an individual's representation of the world (what I may call *cognitive relations* pending better terminology). I want to argue that the first interpretation — that content-based causal relations must be established between the main events of a narrative — is not tenable, and that the second interpretation does not need recourse to notions of global coherence at all. I will also point out that there is evidence that temporal interpretation is not parasitic on discourse relations at all.

2.4.1 Content-based causality relations and the cognitive concept of causality

Coherence relations are generally thought of as intended meaning relations, that is, as part of what is communicated by a text. This is particularly clear in Mann and Thompson (1986) who use the term 'relational propositions' in explaining coherence relations, and treat relational propositions as some kind of implicatures. Their reasons for doing so are mostly connected with doubts about the role of a Cooperative Principle in monologue and in manipulative or coercive texts, monologue or dialogue (p. 79). However, in a relevance-theoretic framework there is no Cooperative Principle to abide by, and implicatures are defined as implicated assumptions which the communicator intended the audience to entertain. Since Mann and Thompson claim that these relational propositions are communicated, that is, that the communicator intended the audience to entertain them, they must be taken to claim that relational propositions are implicatures in this sense; and in Sanders et al. (1993:94), who say that coherence relations are 'conceptual relations.'

For Hobbs (1983) coherence relations are structural relations which are essential to communication; he claims that these formal meaning relations have to be recognised by the hearer in order to understand a text.

Consider now two events in the world, presented in example (8):

(8) a. [Peter shakes a branch of an apple tree.]
b. [An apple falls off the branch which Peter has shaken.][4]

If we see these two events taking place, our cognitive system automatically treats them as connected: we understand that event (8b) is caused by event (8a). This is a fact about cognition, and the causality relation involved here is a relation in the cognised world, not a meaning relation between discourse units. Now consider two utterances in sequence:

(9) (a) Peter shook a branch of an apple tree. (b) An apple fell off.

Under normal circumstances one would also infer a causal relation between the events described by these utterances. How is this to be explained? The answer is obvious and trivial: because we understand these events described by the utterances as related. However, there is a non-trivial question about how knowledge of the causal relation between eventualities described by utterances relates to the pragmatic interpretation of utterances. As noted above, many coherence theorists claim that texts are understood on the basis of formal coherence relations between their units. Thus, in interpreting (9), the hearer has to recognise an intended content relation of causality based on a prior ability to represent causality relations in the cognised world. In other words: utterance interpretation necessarily involves the recognition of causality relations which form part of the communicated content of texts.

To see how this proposal can be developed, consider the following early definitions of the coherence relation of causality:

> Segment S_0 is a Cause of segment S_1 if a causal chain can be found from the state or event asserted in S_0 to that asserted in S_1. (Hobbs 1983, 45)

> The cause relationship holds where one portion of a text presents a cause for a condition conveyed by the other portion. (Mann and Thompson 1986:65)

It is important to notice that these definitions would be circular if there were not two separate categories of causality involved: the communicated relation and a more fundamental relation on the level of world representation, as described above. If utterance interpretation — as it is claimed — necessarily involves recognition of coherence relations, then both types of causality relation have to exist.

However, the conditions in the above definitions could be fulfilled vacuously. Consider example (10):

(10) (a) Peter shook a branch of an apple tree. (b) Mike brought a bucket. (c) Mary collected plums.

A causal chain could be established from the event described in (10a) to the one in (10b): that Peter shook a branch of an apple tree could be the cause of Mike's thinking that apples will fall off, which in turn may be a reason for Mike to get a bucket to pick them up. However, it is intuitively unlikely that this text will be understood in this way.

More recent definitions of the causality relation do not advance much over these earlier attempts. Sanders et al. (1992) define the relation of causality somewhat more formally as one of the parameters used in characterising what they call basic operations:

> A causal operation exists if an implication relation $P \rightarrow Q$ can be deduced between two discourse segments, in which P is antecedent and Q is consequent. (Sanders et al. 1992:7)

P and Q stand for the eventualities conveyed by discourse segments S_1 and S_2, and Sanders et al. add the caveat that P has to be relevant to the conclusion of Q in the spirit of Anderson and Belnap's (1975) concept of relevant implication. On the face of it, this definition avoids the need to operate with two different concepts of causality. However, this definition has serious problems of its own: not all implication relations are causal. Thus, an implication relation can be established between the sentences in (11a) such as the one in (11b), but this is not a causal one:

(11) a. I'm tired. My eyes are hurting. It's time to stop working on the computer and call it a day.

b. If I'm tired and may eyes are hurting, then it's time to stop working on the computer and call it a day.

Hence, to arrive at an adequate definition of causality, one would have to add to Sanders et al.'s definition a requirement that the implication relation between the discourse segments involved must hold in virtue of causal chains between the eventualities expressed. The result would be a definition very similar to the ones proposed by Hobbs (1983) and Mann and Thompson (1986), and would share the same problems.

There is also a further problem for the coherence theory account of causality, which can be illustrated with one of Mann and Thompson's (1986:65) examples:

(12) I went riding last week. I was sore for three days.

(13) Riding caused the speaker's being sore for three days.

According to a coherence theory of the type described above, all that is necessary to establish a coherence relation between the segments in (12) is to supply a relational proposition such as the one given in (13). All that is needed to recognise the coherence relation of causality is that a (relevant) causal chain between the eventualities conveyed in the discourse segments can be established. Now there are several ways in which a causal chain for (12) can be established: the speaker might have fallen off the horse, and this may have caused him to be sore; or he was not used to the hard saddle and the movements of the horse and this caused him to be sore. According to coherence theory, recognition of the precise causal chain is not necessary, just the recognition of one or other of the possible (relevant) chains. This is apparent for example in Mann and Thompson's (1986:65) definition of causal relation quoted above: 'The *cause* relationship holds where one portion of a text presents a cause for a condition conveyed by the other portion' (emphasis mine; see also Hobbs' 1983 definition quoted above). The definitions of various subtypes of causal relations in Mann and Thompson (1988:274–6) also require the recognition of a possible causal chain. But intuitions suggest that hearers don't understand discourses like (12) in a general way, but must have a specific idea of the causal chain in mind before they feel they have understood. In view of this, the coherence theorist must admit that more is involved in utterance interpretation than recognition of the formal coherence relations; there must be inference processes which lead to an enriched understanding of the utterance. However, coherence theory (as based on coherence relations) does not explain the processes involved and must therefore be supplemented by another theory. One theory that comes to mind is the relevance theory of Sperber and Wilson (1995), which arguably presents the most detailed theory of inference in communication. In the next section I want to apply this theory to the problem of fine-tuning the inferred content relations between utterances. It will be argued that these inferences proceed without recognising a meaning relation such as the one in (13).

2.4.2 A relevance-theoretic account of causal relations

A relevance-theoretic explanation of the interpretation of example (12), repeated here for convenience and with utterances numbered (a) and (b), might run as follows:

(12) (a) I went riding last week. (b) I was sore for three days.

After processing utterance (12a), the hearer has — among others — the concept of RIDING easily accessible in memory. When it comes to processing utterance (12b), a context must be chosen for interpreting this utterance. The most cost-effective way to do this (and hence the method favoured by the relevance-theoretic comprehension procedure) is to choose contextual assumptions most easily accessible in memory and — if this fails — to extend the context stepwise in a cost-sensitive way (see Sperber and Wilson 1995 for a detailed account). In the case of (12b), the concept of RIDING gives access to encyclopaedic entries such as those listed in (14), among others.

(14) a. The rider sits on a saddle.
b. Occasionally, riders fall off their horses.

Each one of these encyclopaedic entries in turn gives access to other assumptions such as the following:

(15) a. Concept: SADDLE
Encyclopaedic entry: riders may get sore from riding on hard saddles.
b. Concept: FALLING OFF SOMETHING
Encyclopaedic entry: somebody who falls off something of a low or medium height may get sore, though not necessarily injured.

From each of these assumptions the hearer might compute cognitive effects that would make the utterance worth his attention, thus satisfying the presumption of relevance created by the utterance. These might be as follows:

(16) a. 1. Riders may get sore from riding in hard saddles.
2. Saddles are often hard.
3. If saddles are often hard then it is likely that a rider will use a hard saddle.
4. The speaker is likely to have used a hard saddle.
5. The speaker was not used to riding.
6. It is more likely for untrained riders to get sore from riding on hard saddles.[5]
7. The speaker got sore from riding on a hard saddle.
b. 1. Somebody who falls off something of a low or medium height may get sore, though not necessarily injured.
2. A horse is something of a medium height.
3. Somebody who falls off a horse may get sore, not necessarily injured.

4. The speaker got sore.
5. The speaker went riding last week.
6. The speaker may have got sore from falling of his horse.

Although, if the comprehension procedure works smoothly, the hearer will not be aware of making a choice, and will not need to consider alternative interpretations, the effect of comprehension will be that a choice between these (and maybe other) possible interpretations will be made. How is this done? According to the relevance-theoretic comprehension procedure, the hearer should follow a path of least effort in considering contextual assumptions. Which of these three routes is the most accessible to a given hearer at a given occasion will depend in part on the strength of the assumptions they contain (the stronger the assumption, the more accessible it is likely to be). In the absence of any clues from the situation or the preceding conversation, personal susceptibilities may come in. The resulting interpretation will be partly the responsibility of the hearer who arrives at it (on weak communication, see Chapter 1, section 1.4.4).

Note that this interpretation at no step relies on the recognition of a formal coherence relation of causality. Rather, the recovery of the contextual assumptions and cognitive effects needed to satisfy the hearer's expectation of optimal relevance establishes the connectivity between the utterances by providing access to contextual assumptions and/or strengthening them in turn, as is obvious from the analyses in (16).[6] Of course, a coherence relation such as the one in (13) might be inferred as a final step in the interpretation of the utterance; but this step can only be made after an interpretation of the utterance which satisfies the hearer's expectation of relevance has been found. And since this inferred relation would not lead to extra effects, there is no basis on which the hearer is justified in assuming that the speaker intended him to infer it: so according to relevance theory, the coherence relation should not be treated as communicated by the speaker.

In this section I have argued that the recovery of causality relations in discourse is not achieved through the recognition of formal coherence relations based on causality. This directly argues against a possible interpretation of Samet and Schank's (1984) proposal as entailing that narrative text type (genre) is characterised by a communicated global coherence relation of causality. The other interpretation of Samet and Schank (1984), that the global coherence of narratives is based upon inferred but not communicated causality relations in the sense explained above, is not touched by this argument; however, it was shown that an adequate explanation of the recognition of causal chains in this sense is found in relevance theory, which is thus an advance on Samet and Schank's (1984:71) contention that their theory involving scripts, plans and goals does not solve the problems involved in recognising the causal chain. The relevance-theoretic account leads to an altogether different kind of explanation of what is involved in 'global coherence,' making appeals to a technical notion of global coherence unnecessary.

Given the argument of this subsection, the (global) coherence-based account of genre must be seen as seriously defective. The problem is further compounded if we turn to an investigation of the role of coherence relations such as causality in establishing the temporal relations between events.

2.4.3 Causality and time

In discussing Lascarides and Asher (1993), Sequeiros (1995) points out several problems with accounts of temporal interpretation based on coherence relations. First, there is the phenomenon of irrelevant relations, as in example (17):

(17) ? Peter phoned Mary. Bell invented the telephone. (Sequeiros 1995:181)

The invention of the telephone might at some level be construed as a cause of Peter's calling Mary on the phone. However, the text does not seem acceptable, and considerable elaboration is needed to set up a context which might remove the unacceptability. An adequate discourse theory based on coherence relations must therefore predict that no relevant coherence relation, in particular not one of causality, is established. Nevertheless, we can infer a temporal relation between the clauses of example (17) based on our knowledge of the world. This strongly suggests that temporal relations are not necessarily derived on the basis of coherence relations.

An important aspect of the temporal interpretation of utterances is determination of the temporal interval between the eventualities in question, a problem not addressed in coherence-based accounts of temporal interpretation (Wilson and Sperber 1998; Sequeiros 1995:184–6). It is not clear how a coherence-based account of temporal relations could incorporate the differences between the following examples.

(18) Bill sat down on his couch. He opened the newspaper.

(19) Bill went to University. He became a research fellow.

The examples differ in the inferred intervals between the eventualities involved. These temporal intervals are vital for discourse interpretation: not only do they have effects on possible continuations of the text, but they may also affect the truth-conditions of utterances (Wilson and Sperber 1998:2–4; Sequeiros 1995:185–6). This is illustrated in examples (20) and (21):

(20) a. Bill sat down on his couch. He opened the newspaper. ? In between he slept a few hours.

b. Bill sat down on his couch. He opened the newspaper. ? In between he spent a year abroad as voluntary helper in a relief organisation.

(21) a. Bill went to University. He became a research fellow. ? In between he slept a few hours.

b. Bill went to University. He became a research fellow. In between he spent a year abroad as voluntary helper in a relief organisation.

In (20a) the continuation is odd because the inferred interval between the first two events is much narrower than 'a few hours.' In (21a), the inferred interval is much wider than 'a few hours.' Only a continuation like the one in (21b) is consistent with the inferred interval between the events mentioned in the first two sentences.

The claim that the pragmatically inferred time span communicated by utterances may affect their truth conditions may be illustrated with the examples in (22):

(22) a. (Peter to Mary on January 19, 1998):
I have seen 'Titanic.'[7]

b. (Peter to Mary on January 19, 1998):
??I have seen 'Titanic,' but I haven't been to the cinema within the last month.

c. (Peter to Mary on January 19, 1998):
I have seen 'Die Feuerzangenbowle.'[8]

d. (Peter to Mary on January 19, 1998):
I have seen 'Die Feuerzangenbowle,' but I haven't been to the cinema within the last month.

While the utterance in (22b) would be judged contradictory (not just inconsistent), utterance (22d) would seem perfectly consistent. For the statement *I have seen 'Titanic'* to be true, the speaker must have been to the cinema within the time-span pragmatically inferred through encyclopaedic knowledge of the concept CINEMA FILM CALLED 'TITANIC' such as *The film 'Titanic' has not yet been on TV and The film 'Titanic' was first shown in German cinemas from January 8, 1998,* which is less then a month before the indicated time of utterance, although in (22b) this is explicitly denied. The same does not hold for (22d), where the time-span associated with the first part of the utterance may be much longer: this shows that (22a) and (22c) have different truth-conditions depending on the pragmatically-inferred time-span involved.

Wilson and Sperber (1998) propose an explanation of the pragmatic processes involved in temporal interpretation in the relevance-theoretic framework. This account goes roughly as follows: utterances such as *He opened the newspaper* or *I have seen 'Titanic'* provide access to an ordered set of contextual assumptions consistent with the grammatically encoded time indication (some time in the past in the case of our examples): *He opened the newspaper a few seconds after sitting down/he opened the newspaper a few minutes after sitting down,* and so on. The more stereotypical the interval, the more accessible the assumption. Using these contextual assumptions, the hearer can compute cognitive effects, which may be increased by narrowing the time interval in various ways. The relevance-theoretic comprehension procedure entitles the hearer to accept the interpretation with at least enough cognitive effects to make it worth his attention, and which is furthermore the one that makes the utterance the most relevant once compatible with the speaker's abilities and preferences. Given standard scenarios of reading newspapers leisurely at home after working hours, the normal — hence preferred — interpretation would be that of a small interval.[9]

This relevance-theoretic explanation works without recourse to coherence relations, and Wilson and Sperber (1998) argue convincingly that this account is more successful than coherence-based approaches. There thus are strong arguments for the claim that the temporal interpretation of discourse does not involve the recognition of coherence relations. *A fortiori*, the time-line in narratives cannot be established on the basis of causal coherence relations between the (main) events of the text.

2.5 Conclusion

In this chapter I have introduced the notion of global coherence by discussing the proposal of Samet and Schank (1984). Global coherence, they argue, is that aspect of discourse connectivity which accounts for the discourse 'hanging together' as a whole, over and above the mere connectivity between adjacent parts (sentences or larger units). However, I suggested in Section 2.3 that the notion of relevance may be more successful in fulfilling this function than a notion of global coherence which is relativised to text-types. Section 2.4 raised various issues connected with Samet and Schank's account of the global connectivity of narratives, which they see as constituted by causal relations between events on the narrative time-line. The arguments of this chapter cast some initial doubt on the theoretical status of the notion of global coherence, and suggest that the intuitive data inspiring the theory of global coherence can be better explained by appeal to a relevance-theoretic account. However, both these points need considerable elaboration. This will be attempted in the following chapters.

3 Topic-based approaches to global coherence

3.1 Introduction

Though some approaches to global coherence have tried to analyse it in terms of coherence relations, by analogy to the usual treatment of local coherence, the resulting problems (outlined in the last chapter) have led some researchers to approach global coherence in terms of a notion of (discourse) topic relevance. In this chapter I want to survey four recent variants of this approach: Klein and von Stutterheim's (1987) and von Stutterheim's (1997) *quaestio* approach, Giora's (1985a; 1985b; 1988; 1997; 1998) topic-based account of global coherence, and van Kuppevelt's (1991; 1995a; 1995b; 1996) question-based theory of topic, comment and discourse structure.[1] These approaches to the notion of topic have in common that they more or less explicitly suggest an influence of genre on discourse topics.

3.2 Global coherence as topic relevance

A recent topic-based approach to coherence is that of Giora (1985a,b, 1988, 1997, 1998). In her 1985b paper, Giora argues that the coherence of texts can be explained neither by the presence of cohesive devices nor by appeal to local coherence relations (1985b:714). Rather, the coherence of texts derives from their relation to a discourse topic. In other words, the notion of coherence is largely reduced to that of global coherence.[2]

The function of (global) coherence in this sense is to account for the well-formedness of texts: 'Subsequently, I take text coherence intuitively as well-formedness' (p. 700). It is these well-formedness intuitions which a theory of coherence is designed to explain. Giora seeks the explanation of these intuitions in the notions of discourse relevance and discourse topic.

Giora's first step in elaborating on the notions of discourse relevance and discourse topic is to show that there are texts which exhibit local coherence relations but are nevertheless judged intuitively as incoherent. Her example (5), quoted here as (1), is in the same spirit as (2) of Chapter (2), but is included here for reasons which become apparent later.

(1) (a) Ronit is never home nowadays because she lives near school. (b) School, you know, is the center of the kids' social life. (c) Uri has missed school a lot this year. (d) He never showed up at tennis, either. (e) Orit too has stopped playing chess.

In order to explain the intuitive connectedness between two adjacent sentences of this text and the intuitive unconnectedness of the whole text (or even of any group of three sentences), Giora claims that connected sequences have a common topic which each of the sentences is about. For example, the first two sentences of (1) can be understood as predicating something about the topic *Ronit.* However, sentence (1c) is not about this topic any more. Still, (1b-d) can be said to share the topic *Uri's absence from school* (Giora 1985b, 703). From these observations Giora makes the generalisation that in a coherent discourse every sentence predicates something about a common discourse topic. This is the essence of her Relevance Requirement:

(2) *The Relevance Requirement*
Every proposition in a coherent text can be interpreted as being about a certain discourse topic.

The discourse topic is understood as a proposition, and is independent of sentence topics, though sentence topics can help in recovering the discourse topic (pp. 710–1). In later work, Giora claims that the discourse topic 'is a generalisation, preferably made explicit, and placed in the beginning of the discourse' (Giora 1997:22).

Giora (1985b:704) notes that the acceptability of some sentence sequences which violate the Relevance Requirement can be much improved if a linguistic digression marker is inserted, as in example (3b).

(3) a. John took the underground and got off at Tottenham Court Road. Tottenham Court Road is a good place to buy computers.

b. John took the underground and got off at Tottenham Court Road. Tottenham Court Road, by the way, is a good place to buy computers.

This is the motivation for a second requirement, which says that deviations from the Relevance Requirement (and the Graded Informativeness Condition, see below) must be explicitly marked (Giora 1985b:708; 1997:23). It is possible for a sentence sequence to conform to the Relevance Requirement and still be seen as ill-formed:

(4) John took the underground and got off at Tottenham Court Road. He followed the signs for the exit and found the elevator to the next level. Having arrived on the next level, he found a sign for the exit and found another elevator. This brought him to the ground level. There he followed another sign for the exit. He walked through the exit and reached Tottenham Court Road.

All the sentences in (4) are about the topic *Getting off the Underground at Tottenham Court Road station.* But intuitively, most of these sentences are superfluous. Giora (1988, 1997) explains this by saying that each consecutive sentence fails to add enough information. Thus, coherent texts are claimed to obey a third condition — the Graded Informativeness Condition — which says that each proposition must be at least as informative, if not more informative, than the previous one (Giora 1997:22–3).

Thus a text is globally coherent, that is, well-formed, when the Relevance Requirement and the Graded Informativeness Condition are met, or when deviations from either of these are explicitly marked. In Giora (1985a) and Giora (1997:22), these three conditions are used to explain coherence only for informative discourse; the well-formedness of texts of other discourse types is presumably to be explained by other coherence conditions. It is therefore clear how this notion of global coherence could provide the basis for a theory of genre, although Giora (1997) does not make any suggestions about how the coherence of non-informative discourse might be explained. However, it is not necessary to investigate how coherence conditions for other text-types might be isolated, for the notion of global coherence in the sense of Giora (1985a,b, 1988, 1997) is conceptually flawed even for informative discourse — or so I will argue in the remainder of this section.

Concerning the role of coherence in discourse, Giora (1997:28) comments:

> On various occasions, proponents of [Sperber and Wilson's (1995)] relevance theory (e.g. Blakemore, 1987; Blass, 1990) made the claim that the frequent occurrence of (relatively) incoherent but S & W relevant discourses attests that speakers and hearers are not necessarily constrained by the search for coherence. This claim is not problematic for a coherence-based theory. A coherence-based theory endeavours to account for and make explicit speakers' intuitions as to the well-formedness of discourses. It does not assume that coherence is the only principle that governs human communication.

As Wilson (1998:71) remarks, 'this amounts to the claim that [a (relatively) incoherent but acceptable discourse] is acceptable but ill-formed.' But if some discourses can be acceptable even though they are incoherent, that is, ill-formed, then it is no longer clear what purpose the notion of well-formedness has. It would then distinguish not between texts and non-texts, but between two types of acceptable texts. It might be claimed that even in this case the notion would do some work, for some texts are regarded as better connected than others (Giora 1997). However, discourses such as the one in (5) are not obviously harder to process or 'less-well-formed' than coherent discourses such as (6).

(5) a. Peter: Look, there is a very nice jumper over there.
b. Mary: Watch out, your purse. You are going to lose it.

(6) a. Peter: Look, there is a very nice jumper over there.
b. Mary: Yes, it has a beautiful colour which suits you very well.

It thus appears that well-formedness is not a notion which has much relevance in discourse theory.

This conclusion is reinforced by considering Giora's third condition which licenses deviations from the Relevance Requirement and the Graded Informativeness Condition by use of explicit marking. In Giora (1997:22–3), this is listed as one of the categorial conditions for discourse well-formedness. Wilson (1998:71–2) points out that it places no constraint on the number of violations allowed. Thus, under this condition, discourses such as (7) should be accepted as well-formed.

(7) Look, there is a very nice jumper over there. By the way, in the other store I saw a really awful book. Incidentally, the car at the corner has really nice colours, too. Anyway, is there a way to convert Nisus Writer files into Word documents? ...

In her reply to Wilson (1998), Giora (1998:80) responds:

> Though marking the digression alleviates the relative incoherence, a discourse containing a digression is relatively marked compared to a discourse that does not contain digressions. However, such a discourse is more coherent than discourses which do not mark their digressions.

In other words, violations of the Relevance Requirement or the Graded Informativeness Condition inevitably result in relative incoherence. Thus, the licence to violate some such requirements if the violation is explicitly marked is not really a categorial condition on discourse well-formedness. It rather amounts to the claim that sometimes incoherence does not result in unacceptability. Which again dissociates the well-formedness of discourse from its acceptability, calling into question the status of well-formedness in the theory of discourse.

In this case, it might be argued that acceptable discourses without digressions are easier to process (and hence more acceptable) than discourses with marked violations, which again are better than incoherent discourses. This is indeed what Giora (1998:80) claims. Thus, (8) should strike one as more acceptable than (5).

(8) a. Peter: Look, there is a very nice jumper over there.

b. Mary: By the way, watch out, your purse. You are going to lose it.

But this doesn't seem to be the case. On the contrary, in most situations where (5) would be natural, speakers would prefer not to use the expression 'by the way,' since it would distract from the impact of the utterance (the warning about the purse). In other words, there are incoherent discourses which are more acceptable and easier to process than equivalents which include an explicit marking of the deviation. So there is no simple correlation between the degree of licensed violation of coherence and the acceptability or ease of comprehension of discourses. It is then no longer obvious what role the distinction between well-formed and ill-formed discourses plays.[3]

In this context, it is interesting to note that many of the examples which Giora (1985b) treats as ill-formed are in fact perfectly acceptable and natural given an appropriate contextualisation. Thus, (1) could be said by the mother of Uri, Ronit and Orit in a conversation with a friend who has asked her about the children's well-being. It seems to be perfectly natural in this situation, more so than Giora's (1985b:708) own suggestion, quoted as (9), where explicit digression markers are inserted.

(9) Ronit is never home nowadays because she lives near school. School, you know, is the center of the kids' social life. Oh, by the way, I forgot to tell you that Uri has missed school a lot this year and that Orit, too, has stopped playing chess. (Giora's example 12)

Thus, there seems to be ample evidence that the notion of well-formedness has little or no role to play in an adequate theory of discourse. It is also questionable what intuitions, if any, Giora's notion of discourse well-formedness picks out: judgements of acceptability cannot be reduced to judgements of discourse well-formedness, nor do judgements of well-formedness of discourse influence comprehension in an obvious way.[4] If the notion of global coherence reduces to the notion of well-formedness of discourse, then by the same token there is no room for the notion of global coherence in an adequate theory of discourse. If global coherence is distinct from discourse well-formedness, then global coherence needs to be explained in an altogether different way from the one proposed by Giora (1985a,b, 1988, 1997, 1998).

3.3 The *quaestio* approach

Klein and von Stutterheim (1987) and von Stutterheim (1997) maintain that the principle which holds a text together — that is, which is responsible for both local and global coherence — is the *quaestio,* an implicit question which the text is designed to answer. The *quaestio* determines what is the topic and what is the focus, it determines how the individual utterances that provide partial answers to the *quaestio* are to follow each other (what the authors refer to as 'referential movement'), and what belongs to the main structure (foreground) and side structure (background). In first-person narratives, the *quaestio* is of the form: *What happened to you at* $t_1,..,t_n$ *[*t_n *after* t_1*;* t_n *in the past]?* That is, the propositions belonging to the main structure must represent activities which occur in sequence (temporal progression of narratives), and which hold the protagonist constant (the narrator him/herself).

Klein and von Stutterheim (1987:182) share with relevance theory the idea that (local) coherence is not a primitive theoretical notion: they maintain that coherence is a consequence of the fact that the utterances of a text together answer a *quaestio.* The idea has some intuitive appeal, and is worth serious investigation.

I want to argue that this notion of *quaestio* alone does not really yield a satisfactory notion of global coherence. Consider the following examples, which satisfy the conditions proposed by Klein and von Stutterheim, and yet would not generally be regarded as fully acceptable texts:

(10) *Quaestio:* What did you do on St. John's day (24 June) 1999

1. I walked out of the door.
2. A few seconds afterwards, I stood beside my car.
3. Then I unlocked the driver's door with my key.
4. I sat down in the driver's seat and shut the door.
5. Then I drove to Giessen.
6. Later I entered through the main gate of the 'Praktiker' store.
7. Afterwards I played with my son.

(11) *Quaestio:* What did you do on St. John's day (24 June) 1999

1. I walked out of the door.
2. Birds were singing in the garden.
3. It made me feel happy as
4. I walked to the car.
5. Then I unlocked the driver's door with my key.
6. I sat down in the driver's seat and shut the door.
7. The driver's seat in my car is on the left hand side.
8. This means that I had to use the right hand to move the gear shift.
9. I engaged first gear.
10. Then I drove to Giessen.
11. Having done the shopping, I drove home.
12. Afterwards I played with my son.

Both examples describe events which really happened on 24 June 1999, in chronological order. The first example contains only 'main structure' utterances, that is, utterances conveying events which advance the story and are presented in iconic order (compare Chapter 4 for discussion of the notion 'main structure'). Intuitively, the problem is that a lot of irrelevant material is included (utterances 10:1 to 10:4), whereas a lot of presumably relevant material is left out in the transition from utterances (10:5) to (10:7) (such as a mention of having driven home after shopping and before playing with my son). Notice, incidentally, that at least some of the superfluous irrelevant material and some of the missing relevant material could both be part of a schema *Going shopping.* So what is missing in the *quaestio* approach to global coherence can not be accounted for by a simple appeal to cognitive schemas or scripts.

The second example contains some further utterances pertaining to side structure. Side-structure utterances, for Klein and von Stutterheim, are utterances which do not conform to the constraints laid out by the *quaestio:* Utterances (11:2) to 11:3) and (11:7) to (11:8) conform to this (negative) definition of side structure. The problem is that they are intuitively unmotivated in the text. This means that side structure cannot simply be defined in negative terms, as Klein and von Stutterheim (1987) propose.

It is interesting in this respect to compare the *quaestio* approach to Giora's topic-based account of global coherence, discussed above. Giora's early work seems to state the Relevance Requirement in a fairly strong way, requiring that a well-formed discourse states a discourse topic in the first sentence. This provides a trivial explanation for the oddity of (10) and (11): they do not explicitly state a discourse topic in the first sentence, so the Relevance Requirement can't be met. But, as noted above, this version of the Relevance Requirement is fairly unrealistic. The *quaestio* approach does better than Giora's early work because it does not require the explicit statement of a topic discourse-initially. This requirement is treated as merely a preference in Giora (1997), so the text in (10) could be seen involving an unstated topic *This is an account of what I did on 24 June 1999.* It might then be claimed that all the propositions conveyed by the utterances in (10) are relevant to this topic. However, it is hard to argue this in detail, since Giora's notion of relevance is undefined. It could therefore be claimed that some of the utterances are not relevant to the topic: for example (10:3), since this is probably not a distinctive activity for St. John's day, and that this accounts for the unnacceptability. The result is that it is unclear whether or not text (10) conforms to Giora's Relevance Requirement. The Graded Informativeness Condition is met by all the utterances since they introduce new information on top of the old information from the previous clauses; and there are no obvious deviations from either the Relevance Requirement or the Graded Informativeness Condition, so no markers of deviation are necessary.

If this text is judged ill-formed because no topic is explicitly stated discourse initially, then the same judgement should apply to all first-person narratives of personal experience, even acceptable cases such as the one in (12):

(12)
1. On St. John's day 1999 I had breakfast at the usual time with my family.
2. Then I went shopping in Giessen.
3. I drove to the Praktiker-store.
4. There I bought some wooden parts for a bed for my son which I am building.
5. After this I went to another store.
6. Back at home, I played with my son.

On the other hand, if text (10) is judged as satisfying the Relevance Requirement by virtue of an *implicit* topic, then it should be (wrongly) predicted as a well-formed text.

So the only way to account for the 'ill-formedness' of (10) on Giora's account is to say that it violates the Relevance Requirement because not all its constituent utterances are relevant to the implicit topic *This is an account of what I did on St. John's day 1999.* The problem is that the notion of relevance employed in this requirement is not defined. If we were to claim that (10:2), for example, is not relevant to the topic because it is not a distinctive activity for the time frame in question, then the same should apply to (12:1). It appears, then, that neither the *quaestio* approach nor Giora's account can explain the oddity of text (10).

3.4 Questioning in discourse, topic, and discourse structure

Another recent attempt to define topic in a formal way has been put forward by van Kuppevelt (1991, 1995a). Van Kuppevelt has applied this theory of topic to several problems of discourse analysis such as discourse structure, discourse typology (1995a), grounding (1995b) and implicature (1996). His theory of topic therefore deserves detailed discussion in this book, especially since many of the questions van Kuppevelt discusses are relevant to a discussion of genre.

3.4.1 Van Kuppevelt's theory of topic and discourse structure

Van Kuppevelt (1991, 1995a) argues that discourse coherence is an effect of the internal, hierarchical topic-comment structure of texts (van Kuppevelt 1995a:109). A topic is defined as the set of discourse entities such as persons, objects, places, events (among others) at which the discourse is directed, which are 'in the focus of attention' (van Kuppevelt 1995a:112). Thus, the notion of topic adopted in this framework is one which sees the topic as what the discourse is about. This notion of topic is defined for discourse units, which may be sentences or larger discourse segments. In this way it is hoped that a uniform notion of topic can be defined for sentences, discourse segments and whole discourses.

Van Kuppevelt's concern is mainly with the identification of topics, and for this purpose the above definition is insufficient. He therefore presents an operational characterisation of topics based on the observation that discourse segments may contextually induce questions, which may be explicit or implicit in the discourse and are answered subsequently. The assumption is that topics and comments are related to these contextually-induced questions: what is being questioned in such a contextually-induced (explicit or implicit) question is a topic, whereas the answer (found subsequently in the discourse) is the comment (van Kuppevelt 1995a:113).

In fleshing out this hypothesis, van Kuppevelt (1995a:117–8) notes that his research program aims only to account for the hierarchical structure of expository monologues and dialogues, and for the way this structure is related to (contextually-induced) WH-questions and questions derived from them. The assumption is, though, that this account can be generalised to other discourse types (van Kuppevelt 1995a:117).

Against this background, van Kuppevelt develops his framework by addressing in more detail the ways in which topic-constituting questions can be induced, how these questions may be related, and what happens when a question is answered. Questions may be contextually induced in discourse in one of two ways: they can be raised as a result of so-called feeders (utterances or non-linguistic events such as the bang of a door being slammed), or as a result of an unsatisfactory answer to a preceding question. In the first case, the question constitutes a topic; in the second, it constitutes a sub-topic.

Subquestioning is regulated by two principles. The Principle of Recency says that every subquestion that arises in well-formed discourse is asked as the result of the most recent unsatisfactory answer (van Kuppevelt 1995a:129). The Dynamic Principle of Topic Termination says that after a satisfactory answer of a (sub)question, no further question is raised (explicitly or implicitly) and in consequence the topic ceases to be actual in discourse (van Kuppevelt 1995a:131). It is easy to see that these two principles in conjunction impose a hierarchical structure on the topic-comment structure of discourse.

In the light of these considerations of topic identification, van Kuppevelt (1995a:137) extends his definition of topics to cover discourse topics as well:

> Definition
> A discourse topic DT_i is defined by the set of all topics T_p that are constituted as the result of one and the same feeder F_i ($\mathrm{DT}_i = \mathrm{T}_p | \mathrm{T}_p$ constituted a.r.o. F_i). As such DTi is a set of main, higher order topics usually hierarchically comprising lower topics. (van Kuppevelt 1995a:137)

The topic of a sentence or other discourse segment was defined as the set of discourse entities which the segment is focally about. These are the entities questioned in topic-constituting questions which arise explicitly or implicitly in discourse. The discourse topic is then defined as the union of the sets of discourse entities which discourse segments are about, as long as the topics of these entities relate to questions arising from one and the same feeder.

Based on this definition of discourse topic, it is possible to distinguish discourses which have a single discourse topic from those which do not. An illustration of the latter class is van Kuppevelt's (1995a, 120) example (10), given here as (13):

(13)F_1 A: Mary is on holiday.

Q_1 B: When did she leave?

A_1 A: Yesterday.

F_2 A: Tomorrow, after many years, George will again apply for a job.

Q_2 B: Why?

A_2 A: A competitor of the company he works for has invited him to apply for the position of assistant manager.

Van Kuppevelt calls such discourses discontinuous discourses.

There is another property of discourse topics which yields a distinct, but related, typology of texts. This can be illustrated with a further example, van Kuppevelt's (1995a, 138) example (21), given in (14):

(14)F_1 A: Yesterday a jury of investigation came to the conclusion that the 31 casualties of the fire in the King's Cross London underground station died as the result of an accident and not as the result of negligence.

Q_1 B: How did people react to the outcome of the investigation?

A_1 A: Relatives of the victims rejected it.

Q_2 B: Why?

A_2 A: They are of the opinion that the jury did not do their job well.

Q_3 B: What is the consequence of this outcome?

A_3 A: The consequence is that further prosecution of the officials of London Regional Transport is ruled out.

Question Q_3 in (14) is not a subquestion, but a further question resulting from the feeder F_1. Thus, there is one discourse topic, but it is defined in two production steps: as a result of two topic-constituting questions. Van Kuppevelt (1995a:139) calls such discourses free or unbound spontaneous discourses. These contrast with discourses whose discourse topics are defined in one production step, and which are called bound discourses (van Kuppevelt 1995a:139). Examples are narratives and task-oriented dialogues. Concerning narratives, van Kuppevelt (1995a:139) cites Klein and von Stutterheim (1987), who treat narratives as answering one implicit question, the *quaestio* (see above, section 4). Task-oriented dialogues, on the other hand, closely follow the structure of the task, which can be subsumed under one leading or programmatic question: for example 'How can I replace the spark-plugs of my car?' (van Kuppevelt 1995a:140).

Note that discourses can be both discontinuous (that is, have several discourse topics) and free, as in the case of (13). This yields a four-way typology of discourse with the logical combinations *bound, continuous*; *bound, discontinuous*; *free, continuous*; *free, discontinuous.* The combination *continuous, free discourse* is impossible. All the other three feature combinations are realised: *bound, continuous* discourses such as narratives or task-oriented dialogues; *bound, discontinuous* discourses as in (14); and *free, discontinuous discourses* as in (13). Notice that bound, continuous discourse is defined so that the only main structure (other terms: foreground, backbone; see Chapter 4, van Kuppevelt 1995b) contains a single discourse topic established in one production step. There may be side structures such as explanations, or background segments which involve a temporary topic shift (van Kuppevelt 1995a:140).

The notions of discourse topic, topic, and subtopic are thus hierarchically defined, implying through the Principle of Recency and the

Dynamic Principle of Topic Termination that discourse is hierarchically structured in units corresponding to these hierarchically ordered topics. However, the structural hierarchy of topics and the discourse units related to them can be complicated by topic shifts. Various types of topic shifts are possible. First, as in (14), a topic may shift under the same feeder. Second, topics may shift under different feeders, and this in three different ways (van Kuppevelt 1995a:142–4). First, an answer to a question may be a satisfactory answer, thus closing the topic constituted by the question and then functioning as a new feeder. This happens in two different but related kinds of topic shifts: associated topic shifts, and topic descending shifts. The details of these need not concern us here. The third type of topic shift is illustrated in (13), where new feeders are introduced which are not conditioned by the discourse so far:

> In contrast to an associated topic shift, a non-associated topic shift results from the introduction of a new feeder 'from outside' so to speak, as when a newsreader on radio or TV starts a new topic, switching from one crisis to another. (Van Kuppevelt 1995a:143)

3.4.2 A critical discussion of van Kuppevelt (1995a)

In order to evaluate van Kuppevelt (1995a), it is helpful to get an overview of the claims made in this paper. There are claims about the notion of topic, and claims about discourse:

Claims about topic

1. Topic is to be defined in terms of 'aboutness.'
2. Topic is to be characterised as a set of discourse entities which are the focus of explicit or implicit questions in discourse. Thus, topics are not always stated explicitly or equated with sentences.
3. Topics result from specific questions.

Claims about discourse

1. Discourse coherence comes from the topic-comment structure of discourse.
2. The organisation of discourse units corresponds to the topic-comment organisation of the discourse.
3. The topic-comment structure of discourse is hierarchical.

In this section, I will discuss van Kuppevelt's claims about discourse, and have little to say about his claims on the notion of topic. The claims about discourse are the most relevant ones for this book, as they relate the notion of topic to that of global coherence, by way of arguing for an explanation of discourse connectivity and organisation in terms of a general theory of topics.[5]

Consider the first claim about discourse: 'the central hypothesis is that a discourse derives its structural coherence from an internal, mostly hierarchical topic-comment structure' (van Kuppevelt 1995a:109). Though van Kuppevelt doesn't say so explicitly, the notion of topic is usually taken to account for global coherence (Giora 1985a,b, 1988; Duszak 1994; Giora 1997; Lenk 1998). As noted in Chapter 2, the main function of global coherence is to rule out locally coherent mock narratives such as the one given in Samet and Schank (1984) and used as example (2) in Chapter 2. Furthermore, the notion of global coherence must also account for the acceptability of the rescued version of this text in (7) in Chapter 2. How are these issues handled in van Kuppevelt's (1995a) approach?

The unacceptability of example (2) in Chapter 2 might be traced to a lack of discourse topic. To establish this, one would have to show that a discourse must have at least one discourse topic. Given this, there are two reasons why example (2) in Chapter 2 could be said to lack a topic: either there is no topic at all, since no question raised by any feeder is answered, or there are many topics, and none of them is closed off. Suppose we claim that this example lacks a discourse topic. It should follow that the acceptability of example (7) in Chapter 2 could be explained in the same way: the added section provides a topic. However, this would amount to a licence for acceptable texts to contain any kind of topic-less sub-section, which is clearly not adequate. Consider example (15), where the topic-less subsection is set in italics:

(15) ? Tuning a piano is a straightforward procedure. Some pieces of felt are used to dampen two of the three strings of the note which is to be tuned. A special tuning key is then used to turn the pins which hold the strings. *Low humidity is bad for plants. Turning the heat down will save costs. The sun doesn't shine that much in winter.* However, this process must be done with care, as the pins need to be turned only very slightly and the force on the string may amount to several kilos. Furthermore, the equal temperament of the intervals needs careful listening and experience. Of course, this task can nowadays be eased by using electronic tuners.

On this approach, then, it is only possible to account for the unacceptability of example (2) in Chapter 2, but not for the acceptability of example (7) in Chapter 2.

If we claim instead that there are many topics in (15) and none is closed off, that is, satisfactorily answered, the acceptability of example (2) in Chapter 2 can be explained: the text does have at least one topic, that is, the dream of John Fox, which is introduced in the last paragraph. But there are many more topics raised: 'some fishmongers exchanged blows,' 'criminals are in prison,' etc. As far as I can see, there is no requirement in van Kuppevelt's theory that topics must be closed off. So, as long as there is at least one topic raised, the text should be acceptable. But then there is no explanation for the unacceptability of example (2) in Chapter 2.

Yet another possible way of explaining the acceptability difference in the above examples using van Kuppevelt's theory might run as follows: in the acceptable text, the 'coherent nonsense-part' as a unit functions as a feeder raising the question: *Why did the writer write this?* This question is implicitly answered in the text: *The author wrote this because he intended to describe the thoughts of John Fox in a state where he is not thinking in an orderly way.* The topic would be the author's purpose or intention in writing — perhaps a fairly implausible suggestion about the topic of this text.

However, all attempts to account for the unacceptability of example (15) are undermined by the claim that there is free, discontinuous discourse. The fact that free, discontinuous discourse is possible means in essence that there can be implicit feeders 'from the outside' (van Kuppevelt 1995a:143; see quote above). So in principle, every sentence of this example could be a response to its own feeder, resulting in a free, discontinuous discourse. As long as there are no constraints on the development of this type of discourse, any discourse which fails to show principled topic progression can be treated as falling into this discourse type. As a result, the unacceptability of this example remains unexplained.

It is evident from discourses such as (15) above that there should be some constraints on the development of free, discontinuous discourse. Discourse of this type can only be seen as natural in a narrowly defined context, such as when a phone conversation has reached the stage where the caller is asking for news of the answerer's friends; or, as van Kuppevelt (1995a:143) points out, in a news broadcast, where the presenter switches from crisis to crisis. Outside these narrowly defined contexts, discourses such as (13) are odd indeed. Thus, there must be some constraints on the development of free, discontinuous discourse. However, there is no obvious way of formulating them in van Kuppevelt's theory.

It seems, then, that van Kuppevelt's theory of topics does not yield a notion of global coherence which might fulfil the function assigned to it by Samet and Schank (1984). It is impossible to account for the unacceptability of (2) in Chapter 2 because free, discontinuous discourse is allowed, and there is also no meaningful account of the acceptability of (7) in Chapter 2.

Let us turn now to van Kuppevelt's second claim about discourse: that the organisation of discourse units corresponds to the topic-comment structure of the discourse. Consider the following example:

(16) a. John came home from school.
b. (What happened next?)
c. He had his lunch.
d. (What did he eat?)
e. On the menu was a home-made lasagne.

f. (1. What else did he eat?)
(2. Did he like it?)

g. There was a big ice-cream dessert to follow it,
that made him like the lunch better.

(16g) might be an answer to either question ($16f_1$) or ($16f_2$). Both these questions may be implicitly raised by (16e). ($16f_1$) is a subtopic-constituting question, which arises because the hearer did not judge (16d) satisfactorily answered. ($16f_2$), on the other hand, would be a topic-constituting question. In other words, there is an ambiguity about whether (16e) induces a topic-constituting question or a subtopic-constituting question. In fact, as the discourse proceeds, it must be inferred that both questions were raised; at least, both questions are answered in (16g). Thus, this segment should have topics both subordinate and coordinate to (16e). Clearly, these cannot both be reflected in the single discourse unit (16g).

One might try to avoid this conclusion by arguing that only one of the questions in (16f) had to be anticipated by the author. In that case, the prediction will be that the discourse structure of the text (16a.c.e.g) is ambiguous — a prediction which is unlikely to be confirmed by intuitions. Example (16) thus provides evidence that there is no necessary relation between the topic hierarchy and discourse structure.

Another argument against the attempt to link discourse structure to topic-comment structure comes from examples which show that the interpretation of texts can be changed in subtle ways just by changing the paragraph indication (for example in a written representation), yielding interesting interaction with particle scope. The following example is from a written narrative, a biography, presented first as one paragraph unit:

(17) Poverty and ill fortune seemed to dog the family's footsteps. By this time Will had lost almost all his hearing. He attributed the cause to a rebounding plank that had bounced off his chin back in Colorado. A prize calf swallowed Cam's first store-bought necktie and choked to death. Produce from the tenant farm brought hardly enough income for the family

to exist on. But Will's stubborn, keep-trying, hard-work philosophy made an indelible impression on his children. ... (Hefley, J. and M. Hefley, 1981: *Uncle Cam.* Milford: Mott Media, p. 14. Modified layout)

In this example, the connective *but* in the last sentence can be understood to have either global or local scope: in the former case, Will's philosophy of life made an impression on the children despite all the odds mentioned from the first sentence onward. In that latter case, Will's philosophy of life made an impression on them in spite of the produce from the farm bringing hardly enough income (that is, what is expressed in the preceding sentence alone).

(18) Poverty and ill fortune seemed to dog the family's footsteps. By this time Will had lost almost all his hearing. He attributed the cause to a rebounding plank that had bounced off his chin back in Colorado. A prize calf swallowed Cam's first store-bought necktie and choked to death. Produce from the tenant farm brought hardly enough income for the family to exist on.

But Will's stubborn, keep-trying, hard-work philosophy made an indelible impression on his children. ... (Hefley, J. and M. Hefley, 1981: *Uncle Cam.* Milford: Mott Media, p. 14. Original layout)

Here, the global-scope reading of the connective *but* is the preferred interpretation, while the local-scope reading is hardly recognisable at all. Now consider a final variant of the same example:

(19) Poverty and ill fortune seemed to dog the family's footsteps. By this time Will had lost almost all his hearing. He attributed the cause to a rebounding plank that had bounced off his chin back in Colorado. A prize calf swallowed Cam's first store-bought necktie and choked to death.

Produce from the tenant farm brought hardly enough income for the family to exist on. But Will's stubborn, keep-trying, hard-work philosophy made an indelible impression on his children.

In this case, the local-scope reading of *but* in the last sentence is the preferred interpretation. Since the sentences in these examples do not change, the topic-comment structure as defined by van Kuppevelt (1995a) does not change in these examples and yet the preferred interpretations are different in the different paragraph layouts. This provides further evidence that discourse organisation is not directly linked to the topic hierarchy of discourse.

Furthermore, consider the case of multiple-topic paragraphs, discussed in Unger (1996). These occur often in transitional paragraphs in scientific writing. However, such paragraphs occur in other genres, too. Here is an example from narrative:

(20) It was a singular spot, and one peculiarly well suited to the grim humour of my patient. From the windows of our little whitewashed house, which stood high upon a grassy headland, we looked down upon the whole sinister semicircle of Mounts Bay, that old death-trap of sailing vessels, with its fringe of black cliffs and surge-swept reefs on which innumerable seamen have met their end. With a northerly breeze it lies placid and sheltered, inviting the storm-tossed craft to tack into it for rest and protection. Then comes the sudden swirl round of the wind, the blustering gale from the south-west, the dragging anchor, the lee shore, and the last battle in the creaming breakers. The wise mariner stands far out from that evil place.

On the land side our surroundings were as sombre as on the sea. It was a country of rolling moors, lonely and dun-coloured, with an occasional church tower to mark the site of some old-world village. In every direction upon these moors there were traces of some vanished race which had passed utterly away, and left as its sole record strange monuments of stone, irregular mounds which contained the burned ashes of the dead, and curious earthworks which hinted at prehistoric strife. The glamour and mystery of the place, with its sinister atmosphere of forgotten nations, appealed to the imagination of my friend, and he spent much of his time in long walks and solitary meditations upon the moor. The ancient Cornish language had also arrested his attention, and he had, I remember, conceived the idea that it was akin to the Chaldean, and had been largely derived from the Phoenician traders in tin. He had received a consignment of books upon philology and was settling down to develop this thesis, when suddenly to my sorrow, and to his unfeigned delight, we found ourselves, even in that land of dreams, plunged into a problem at our very doors which was more intense, more engrossing, and infinitely more mysterious than any of those which had driven us from London. Our simple life and peaceful, healthy routine were violently interrupted, and we were precipitated into the midst of a series of events which caused the utmost excitement not only in Cornwall, but throughout the whole West of England. Many of my readers may retain some recollection of what was called at the time 'The Cornish Horror,' though a most imperfect account of the matter reached the London Press. Now, after thirteen years, I will give the true details of this inconceivable affair to the public.

I have said that scattered towers marked the villages...
(Arthur Conan Doyle, 'The adventure of the Devil's foot,' in: *The Case Book of Sherlock Holmes.* Wordsworth Classics, Ware, Hertfordshire: Wordsworth 1993)

Consider the second paragraph of (20). It seems that this paragraph is centred around two topics: *The description of the country side where Sherlock Holmes and Dr. Watson went for relaxation,* and *The occurrence of a case for Sherlock Holmes to solve.* Notice that the paragraph cannot be easily separated in two so that each would have its own topic:

(21) On the land side our surroundings were as sombre as on the sea. It was a country of rolling moors, lonely and dun-coloured, with an occasional church tower to mark the site of some old-world village. In every direction upon these moors there were traces of some vanished race which had passed utterly away, and left as its sole record strange

monuments of stone, irregular mounds which contained the burned ashes of the dead, and curious earthworks which hinted at prehistoric strife. The glamour and mystery of the place, with its sinister atmosphere of forgotten nations, appealed to the imagination of my friend, and he spent much of his time in long walks and solitary meditations upon the moor. The ancient Cornish language had also arrested his attention, and he had, I remember, conceived the idea that it was akin to the Chaldean, and had been largely derived from the Phoenician traders in tin.

? He had received a consignment of books upon philology and was settling down to develop this thesis, when suddenly to my sorrow, and to his unfeigned delight, we found ourselves, even in that land of dreams, plunged into a problem at our very doors which was more intense, more engrossing, and infinitely more mysterious than any of those which had driven us from London...

That the second paragraph is actually designed as one unit rather than an orthographic accident can be seen by the fact that inserting a paragraph break before the sentence *He had received...* would require further changes: the pronoun *He* would have to be replaced by a noun phrase (*my friend; Holmes;* or the like), and the sentence would have to be split up in this way:

(22) ...The ancient Cornish language had also arrested his attention, and he had, I remember, conceived the idea that it was akin to the Chaldean, and had been largely derived from the Phoenician traders in tin. He had received a consignment of books upon philology and was settling down to develop this thesis.

Then, suddenly, to my sorrow, and to his unfeigned delight, we found ourselves, even in that land of dreams, plunged into a problem at our very doors which was more intense, more engrossing, and infinitely more mysterious than any of those which had driven us from London....

The second paragraph of (20) is, then, a paragraph containing two topics. This is a case where obviously the discourse organisation does not directly reflect the topic structure of the text. This shows that discourse organisation is not always a reflection of topic-comment structure. It also falsifies the assumption that 'a topic shift implies a transition from one discourse unit to another' (van Kuppevelt 1995a:141). This conclusion receives additional support from the observation that the first topic of this paragraph (*The description of the country side where Sherlock Holmes and Dr. Watson went for relaxation*) is actually shared by the preceding paragraph, and yet the author decided to insert a paragraph break at the place where he did. This paragraph division reflects the sub-topic shift *The description of the sea side of the countryside where Sherlock Holmes and Dr. Watson went for relaxation* and *The description of the land side of the country side where Sherlock Holmes and Dr. Watson went for relaxation.* So, in one case the paragraph division is responsive to sub-topic change under the same topic, whereas in the other there are two unrelated topics developed in one paragraph. Again, discourse organisation does not match the topic structure of the discourse.

The correct conclusion seems to be that the organisation of discourse units does not correspond to the topic-comment structure of discourse. An immediate consequence is that even if it could be maintained that the topic-comment structure of discourse is mostly hierarchical, it does not follow that discourse is hierarchically organised. Notice at this point that even if it could be confirmed that the topic-comment structure of discourse is hierarchical, it would be of no consequence for the connectivity and organisation of discourse, and hence will not account for global coherence. Therefore I will not discuss this third claim of van Kuppevelt's about discourse here, but see Unger (2001:93–5) for more details.

In summary, van Kuppevelt's theory of topic does not yield an adequate account of connectivity in discourse, as it can not account for both the unacceptability of (2) and the acceptability of (7) in Chapter 2. Furthermore, it does not account adequately for discourse organisation, as there is evidence that discourse organisation does not always match the topic structure of discourse, and that the discourse structure itself is not always hierarchical. Since an adequate account of global coherence would have to account for both connectivity in discourse and discourse organisation, it must be concluded that van Kuppevelt's theory does not provide an adequate account of global coherence.

3.5 Conclusion

In this chapter I have surveyed four recent theories of global coherence in terms of discourse topics and argued that none of these provides an adequate notion of (discourse) topic. Thus, the notion of global coherence cannot be adequately defined by recourse to the notion of discourse topic. It follows that the effect of genre on comprehension cannot be explained in terms of a topic-based approach to global coherence.

That the notion of (discourse) topic is difficult to define has been pointed out elsewhere in the literature (Brown and Yule 1983; Levinson 1983; Lenk 1998). It has even been suggested that we abandon topic in favour of more flexible notions which stand a better chance of shedding light on the intuitions of topicality: Brown and Yule (1983:75) argue that the notion of topic should be replaced by the notion of a *topic framework,* by which they mean a contextual framework within which several descriptions of what the text is about can be articulated (that is, which contain the persons, objects and eventualities which the text is about), a set of contextual assumptions which are required for interpreting a text; Lenk (1998:24 footnote 14) abandons the pursuit of an adequate definition of topic in favour of operating with a more intuitive and flexible definition of *conversational topic* as that which participants in a conversation talk about at any given time, such as 'persons, events, states, objects, etc.' (Lenk 1998:25). By contrast, Sperber and Wilson (1995:216–17) reject the notion of topic as a primitive of pragmatic theory not replacing it with a different one, but to explain the intuitions underlying topicality as a result of processing discourse following the relevance-theoretic comprehension procedure. Since relevance is a well-defined technical notion in relevance theory (Sperber and Wilson 1995:118–71; see Chapter 1 of this book, Section 1.4), this approach appears to be more promising as a candidate for an explanatory account of the intuition underlying notions of topicality in particular, and of global coherence in general, than Brown and Yule's (1983) and Lenk's (1998) proposals. In Chapters 5 and 6 I will take up Sperber and Wilson's suggestions to develop a relevance-theoretic account of the intuitions underlying theories of global coherence, as a basis for an account of genre.

There thus seems to be converging evidence not just from the argumentation in this chapter, but also from writers such as Brown and Yule (1983) and Lenk (1998) for the view that the notion of (discourse) topic cannot be adequately defined and should therefore be abandoned as a primitive of pragmatic theory. This has obvious consequences for the theory of global coherence: it cannot be explicated in terms of discourse topic. However, there is still another way to conceive of global coherence: information staging in discourse, that is, that the relative 'salience' or 'importance' of information may lie at the heart of global coherence. These issues will be taken up in the next chapter.

4 Global coherence and grounding in discourse

4.1 Introduction

One approach to global coherence assumes that the overall well-formedness of discourse depends on the way information is distributed over it in terms of varying importance or prominence. This position was originally developed for the study of narratives: early accounts distinguished 'storyline' information from 'non-storyline' information (Labov and Waletzky 1967) or 'backbone' information from supportive information (Grimes 1975). Later studies extended these notions so as to include other discourse types, and introduced the terms 'foreground' and 'background' (for example Hopper 1979; Hopper and Thompson 1980; Longacre 1983; Reinhart 1984; Hooper 1998). The basic idea underlying these approaches is that the distribution of information in well-formed texts is staged in such a way that the hearer can relate supportive material to more important information. Levinsohn (1992) argues that it is this ordering of information according to communication-functional principles rather than structural principles of paragraph organisation that govern the organisation of discourse.

While grounding theory (that is, a theory using notions of foreground and background) has not normally been described by its proponents as dealing with global coherence, it does have implications for the study of global coherence. For example, one might explain the oddity of texts such as (2) in Chapter 2 by claiming that they violate the principles of information staging because it is unclear what sentences are foreground and what are background. It is for this reason that I discuss theories of grounding as approaches to global coherence.

4.2 Defining 'foreground'

Various attempts have been made in the literature to give the intuitive notions of 'foreground,' 'storyline,' and so on some theoretical substance. In this section I will review the main proposals.

4.2.1 Storyline and temporal succession

The earliest attempts to define 'storyline events' referred to the temporal relations of events in narrative (Labov and Waletzky 1967; Labov 1972; compare Fabb 1997:169–71). It was recognised that storyline clauses are presented chronologically in iconic order, that is, events narrated earlier precede events narrated later. If this order is reversed, the temporal interpretation changes. This is illustrated in example (1) (Fabb 1997):

(1) a. I hit him. He hit me.
    b. He hit me. I hit him.

(1a) suggests a different interpretation from (1b). This property was taken by Labov and Waletzky (1967) to be definitional for storyline clauses. By contrast, non-storyline (or background) clauses can be shifted around in the text without changing the temporal interpretation, as is shown by the positioning of *I was angry* in (2):

(2) a. I was angry. I hit him. He hit me.
    b. I hit him. I was angry. He hit me.
    c. I hit him. He hit me. I was angry.
    (Fabb 1997)

This definition of 'storyline' appears to rest on a firm criterion whose results can be formally tested. However, the definition is clearly narrative-specific, and it is not obvious whether it can be generalised to other discourse types. If it can't be generalised, then it is doubtful whether it can be treated as foundational for discourse analysis in general (compare van Kuppevelt 1995b).

In fact, the intuitions underlying this definition are not as robust as they appear. For example, while it is possible to interpret (2a-c) as temporally equivalent (that is, in each case *I hit him because I was angry*), (2c) also has another interpretation: *I hit him because he hit me, and after he hit me* (Fabb 1997:171). Fabb (1997:171) also makes a further objection:

> Similarly, consider a situation in which a sequence of clauses describes a location; while in most cases these would be interpreted just as orienting clauses, if these are instead interpreted as the sequential perceptions of the hero, then they might also be interpreted as storyline clauses.

So the definition of 'storyline' clauses in terms of temporal order is not entirely satisfactory.

4.2.2 'Foreground' as forward movement in discourse

Another proposed definition involves the metaphor of forward movement: foreground clauses are clauses which 'move the story further' (Grimes 1975; Longacre 1989b, 1990a). Fleischmann (1985:858) calls this the criterion of 'causality:' foreground is — in Aristotle's sense — causal, that is, important for the development of the plot. This definition, while taking its inspiration from narrative, may be generalised to other discourse types by applying the metaphor 'moving the discourse forward' in appropriate ways. For the most part, however, it has been proposed with respect to narrative. Thus, Longacre (1989b:417) defines foreground (that is, storyline) in (English) narratives as follows: 'The storyline is here a broad term to include a variety of *punctiliar, sequential happenings* which advance the narrative' (italics as in the original). This definition has two major components: one which appeals to the intuitive notion of 'forward movement' or 'advancement' of the story, and the other relating the notions of aspect, time, and predicate type to foreground and background respectively.

This definition is still fairly intuitive, and it is not obvious how the idea behind it can be stated non-metaphorically. If the metaphor of 'moving/advancing the story forward' is understood in terms of sequentiality, that is, as saying that the storyline consists of sentences describing eventualities in sequence and in iconic order, it does not really differ from the definition in Labov and Waletzky (1967) considered above. If the idea is more abstract, and intended to allude not only to temporal sequence, but to something like the 'quality' or 'salience' of the forward-movement of the story, it is not clear how this can be made precise.

4.2.3 The foreground-background distinction as a taxonomy of linguistic markers

Another approach to the definition of foreground (and background) may be seen as an elaboration of the original definition based on temporal ordering (subsection 4.2.1), but with the advantage of being rooted in independently observable facts. Instead of relying on the criterion of temporal order alone, the idea is to define foreground clauses by appeal to linguistic markers such as word order or aspect marking. Hooper (1998:123) explicitly adopts this approach, saying: 'foreground is the sequence of narrated events PRESENTED AS FOREGROUND, that is with the characteristic syntax of narrative clauses.' Other work on the same lines includes Hopper (1979); Reinhart (1984); Longacre (1989b, 1990a).

Here is a sample analysis of foregrounding in a specific language using this approach:

(3) a. After breakfast, we got ready to drive to grandmother's place. *We loaded our luggage into the car and seated the children well in their safety seats. Then we set out on our journey.*

b. After breakfast, we got ready to drive to grandmother's place. After having loaded our luggage into the car and having seated the children well in their safety seats, *we set out on our journey.*

According to criteria of content alone, all the sentences except the first one in (3a) are foreground ones. (The foreground sentences are italicised.) However, it is generally assumed (with some qualifications) that subordinate clauses in English contain background information (Longacre 1989b; Reinhart 1984). In (3b), some successive events are encoded in a subordinate clause; hence, if foreground clauses (or sentences) are defined as ones which present the events as foreground, then the two successive events in the subordinate clause in the second sentence are to be regarded as background, for they are presented as background, that is, with linguistic forms which normally encode background information (even though by content criteria alone the information presented in this subordinate clause must be regarded as foreground information, just as in (3a).

This approach assumes that notions such as 'foreground' actually are linguistically marked in natural languages. Even if this assumption turns out to be true, it could only be established by appeal to some independent definition of foreground, for example a semantic and/or pragmatic one. It seems, then, that the researcher investigating a language must start from an intuitive definition (such as the one in section 4.2.2) in order to arrive at tentative analyses of foreground markers. As a result, this approach loses much of its objective appearance.

Furthermore, the assumption that grounding is marked in natural language would have to be justified. Much depends on how 'linguistic marking' is understood. One way to interpret it is to see it as referring to linguistic encoding. However, linguistic forms can also be used to guide the pragmatic interpretation process in more 'natural' ways. Thus, Sperber and Wilson (1995) have argued that the information conveyed by contrastive stress need not be encoded or grammaticalised; rather, this natural highlighting device interacts with syntactic and semantic information to guide pragmatic interpretation. Given this, foreground status might be *linguistically indicated* by use of forms which do not encode anything relating to the notion of foreground.[1] There is then no *a priori* reason why linguistic markers of grounding as such should be expected in natural language, and the definition of foreground (and related notions) in terms of linguistic marking is inadequate.

4.2.4 Grounding defined in pragmatic and psychological terms

Hopper and Thompson (1980:280) define grounding in general terms which are not intrinsically linked to a particular discourse type:

> Users of a language are constantly required to design their utterances in accord with their own communicative goals and with their perception of their listeners' needs. Yet, in any speaking situation, some parts of what is said are more relevant than others. That part of a discourse which does not immediately and crucially contribute to the speaker's goal, but which merely assists, amplifies, or comments on it, is referred to as BACKGROUND. By contrast, the material which supplies the main points of the discourse is known as FOREGROUND.

Notice that in this attempt to define grounding independently of discourse type, Hopper and Thompson call upon such pragmatic notions as 'relevance' and 'the speaker's goal.' In essence, their definition says that foreground information is that information which is most relevant to the speaker's goal at the current state of the speech exchange. Put in this way, the closeness in spirit of this definition to Gricean pragmatics is obvious.

However, it is also obvious that this definition relies on a number of vague or undefined notions: in particular, one would have to clarify what it means that some information 'immediately and crucially contributes to the speaker's goal.' This is just the question of how to define relevance, for 'immediately and crucially contributing to the speaker's goal' is meant to explain what it is to be 'relevant to the speaker's goal.'

In illustrating their definition of foreground and background, Hopper and Thompson use only examples from narrative discourse, relying on the intuitive notion of 'backbone' or 'skeleton' of the text to explain the points of their examples (Hopper and Thompson 1980:281). So, unfortunately, the value of their genre-independent definition is much reduced.

4.2.5 Grounding as a scalar notion derived from several criteria

Fleischmann (1985, 1990) suggests that the foreground-background distinction should be understood not as binary but as a scalar notion. Several different factors combine to determine the level of grounding of some information in discourse, on a continuous scale between foreground and background. Four parameters contribute to determine the grounding level. The first is Labov and Waletzky's (1967) definition of foreground as the sequential, temporally successive events in narrative. The second involves 'what is humanly important,' that is, salience or goal-relevance in discourse (much in the spirit of Hopper and Thompson 1980). The third parameter defines foreground as those events which are pivotal to the development of the plot of the story. All three definitions (functioning in Fleischman's account as parameters) are reviewed above.

A fourth parameter concerns the unpredictability or unexpectedness of information in a given discourse context. The more unpredictable or unexpected the information, the more foregrounded it is. This can be illustrated with the following example:

(4) (a) Sam came home from school, (b) put his bag into the corner, (c) stormed into the kitchen (d) and sat down quietly onto a chair. (e) Then he told his mother about all the trouble they had at school today...

Every clause expresses a bounded event in the past in iconic order and can be regarded as foreground clauses in a narrative. However, the information in (4b) corresponds closely with expectations about what children do when they arrive home from school. While it is then expected that after putting down his bag the child moves on, the particular manner is not quite expected, so (4c) is in a way more foregrounded than (4b). That a child sits down quietly on a chair after having stormed into the kitchen is indeed rather unexpected, so that (4c) is even more foregrounded. It seems, then, that foregroundedness is a matter of degree, determined by several factors including, but not exhausted by, temporal movement (in narrative) and script predictability. These factors relate in a non-obvious way to produce intuitions of foregrounding.

Thus, on the face of it there is much to favour Fleischmann's (1985) approach. However, it is also obvious that this account of grounding inherits the problems of the individual parameter definitions as discussed above. Moreover, while some of these parameters may be generalised to non-narrative discourse types, others cannot, with the consequence that there are fewer criteria available for checking the grounding level of information in non-narrative discourse types. The advantages of this cluster-concept approach will thus diminish in non-narrative discourse, particularly since the criteria relevant for these types — *importance* or *goal-relevance,* and *expectability* and *predictability* respectively — are among the least precisely defined of the criteria suggested.

4.2.6 Grounding in discourse as a pragmatic principle

Hopper (1979) observes that the distinction between foreground and background in narrative is linguistically marked in some way in many languages. The most common devices for marking foreground in narrative are tense-aspect forms (French, Russian), word order (Old English) and voice or mood alternations (Malay, Tagalog). Hopper relates these devices to properties of foreground and background in a systematic way: foreground clauses in narrative are those which are narrated in the same order as they occur in the world, that is, in iconic order. Background clauses do not enter into this sequence, but may have different temporal relations with foreground material and with other background material. This is the definition of foreground and background introduced by Labov and Waletzky (1967) and Labov (1972). Hopper derives several further properties from it: first, foreground clauses describe sequential events. This favours the use of punctiliar verbs with perfective aspect marking.

Second, sequential events are likely to be dynamic in the sense of focusing on the action expressed, creating an expectation that the focus in foreground clauses will be the predicate (or the verb), while in background clauses, the focus should fall more readily on entities in preverbal position (topic changes, new information). Third, only foreground clauses, strictly speaking, narrate events. Hence, foreground clauses should favour the more 'assertive' modalities such as the (positive) indicative, whereas subjunctive, optative and irrealis moods, along with negatives, should be more expected in background clauses. Clearly, these properties relate to the types of linguistic markers of grounding surveyed in Hopper (1979). Hopper claims that the foreground-background distinction is a universal discourse feature which is indicated differently in different languages. Ultimately, the tense-aspect system, word order and voice and mood systems find (at least part of) their explanation in the discourse function of grounding.

Hopper and Thompson (1980) take this idea about the relation between grounding in discourse and morphosyntactic features in language a step further, claiming that grounding underlies transitivity effects in grammar. They start by examining the notion of transitivity. The traditional notion of transitivity is understood, they claim, 'as a global property of an entire clause, such that an activity is "carried-over" or "transferred" from an agent to a patient.' (Hopper and Thompson 1980:251) They isolate ten parameters which explain what it means to say that an activity is 'carried over' from one participant to another (compare Fabb 1997:174–5):

1. *Number of participants:* the basic distinction is whether there are two or more participants referred to in the clause, or only one. In the former case, the parameter is specified for high transitivity, and in the latter for low transitivity.

2. *Kinesis:* this is about the type of eventuality described. If the clause describes an action, the parameter is set for high transitivity; if it describes a state, the parameter is set for low transitivity.

3. *Aspect:* when the action has an endpoint, transitivity is high; when it doesn't have an endpoint, transitivity is low.

4. *Punctuality:* when the action expressed in a clause takes place at a moment (punctiliar), the clause is high in transitivity. Otherwise, the transitivity value is low.

5. *Volitionality:* when an action is carried out on purpose, the clause describing it is high in transitivity, and low in transitivity otherwise.

6. *Affirmation (Polarity):* an action described in the affirmative is higher in transitivity than one which is described in the negative. *I threw the ball* is higher in transitivity than *I didn't throw the ball.*

7. *Mode:* an action actually happening in the world is higher in transitivity than one that is presented as happening in a possible world (including a fictional one) other than the actual one.

8. *When agent and cause coincide* — that is, when the action is caused by the agent — the clause is higher in transitivity than when the action is caused by someone or something other than the agent.

9. *Affectedness of the object:* if the object of an action is totally affected by it (for example *Peter ate all of the cake*) the clause is high in transitivity. Otherwise, the transitivity value of this parameter is low (for example *Peter ate just two pieces of the cake*).

10. *Individuation of the object:* this parameter is set for high transitivity when the object is highly individuated, and low when it is generic.

Hopper and Thompson (1980:255) then formulate the 'transitivity hypothesis:'

> If two clauses (a) and (b) in a language differ in that (a) is higher in Transitivity according to any of the features [1–10], then, if a concomitant grammatical or semantic difference appears elsewhere in the clause, that difference will also show (a) to be higher in Transitivity.

According to this thesis, if a language obligatorily marks some of the features 1–10 (for example telicity and punctuality), and in a clause one of these features (say, telicity) is set for high transitivity, then the other feature(s) are also set for high transitivity (for example every verb marked for telicity must be marked for punctiliar aspect in a language where both telicity and punctuality are obligatorily marked). Hopper and Thompson give many examples from a number of typologically and genetically distinct languages to support their hypothesis.

All this raises the question of why the transitivity hypothesis should hold at all. According to Hopper and Thompson, it is grounded in discourse principles, and more precisely in the foreground-background distinction, where the foreground is the material which supplies the main points of the discourse, and which is mostly relevant to the speaker's goal in the speech situation at hand, while the background material supports or elaborates on the foreground.

Hopper and Thompson (1980:284–8) observe that the features of transitivity correspond with the features of foregrounding in narrative: thus, typical punctiliar, sequential events will normally contain an agent and a (non-human) patient, have a definite endpoint (otherwise they could not strictly speaking be sequential), and so on. Notice, though, that this correlation is plausible only for narratives, where the 'main points of the discourse' are the temporally successive (pivotal) events. The justification goes roughly as follows: narratives are crucially about events, and typical events involve the transfer of action from an agent to a patient in the sense described above. So clauses which are highly transitive are most appropriate for the mainline of the story.

In hortatory texts, by contrast, the 'main points of the discourse' may be exhortations like *Listen to the advice of wise men:* here the predicate is neither telic nor punctiliar, and the foreground clauses are low in transitivity (at least according to some parameters). It is interesting that Hopper and Thompson (1980) choose a definition of grounding which is independent of discourse type, and even devote a whole section (section 4.2) to the discussion of different discourse types, suggesting that conversation may be a more central genre, in which grounding phenomena may appear first and only later be generalised to narrative and other discourse types; however, they switch back to tacitly equate 'grounding in discourse' with 'grounding in narrative' in the rest of their paper. But the whole argument that the features of transitivity correspond closely with the features of foregrounding turns crucially on the restriction to narrative discourse.

In other words: the discourse feature of grounding provides a plausible explanation for the transitivity hypothesis only in the case of narrative discourse. Should the transitivity hypothesis hold also in other discourse types (which is apparently Hopper and Thompson's intention), then there is no explanation for this generalisation to be found in the discourse feature of grounding.

As for narratives, there is indeed a strong correlation between foreground clauses and highly transitive clauses in languages such as English: Hopper and Thompson report that they found in a sample of English texts that 78% of clauses identified as foreground came out as marked for high transitivity on all ten parameters, whereas only 39% of background clauses had these parameter settings. However, this is a probabilistic characterisation, not a deterministic one. It is thus obvious that the foreground-background distinction is not encoded by any one of the morphosyntactic means of reflecting transitivity.

According to Hopper and Thompson, in some languages, such as Tagalog and Malay, foreground seems to be statistically very closely related to the morphosyntactic marking of individual transitivity parameters, rather than to a combination of all ten parameters. In these languages, a passive construction is routinely used in foreground clauses. This can be explained on the assumption that in some languages the foreground-background distinction is sensitive to transitivity marking of selected parameters only, not to the whole cluster of settings. In Tagalog, the important parameter is that of object individuation, as the so-called 'passive' construction (Hopper and Thompson 1980 call this also the 'goal-topic' construction) is originally used only with definite objects. Since these clauses are usually foreground clauses in narrative, the construction has become specialised for, and re-interpreted as indicating, foregrounding, and has even been extended for use in foreground clauses with indefinite objects. Thus, the 'passive' construction in Malay and Tagalog is seen as signalling foreground material in narrative discourse (compare Fabb 1997:176). But this construction can not signal foregrounding in narrative by way of *encoding:* the relation between the 'passive' construction and foregrounding breaks down in other discourse types. So either the relation between the 'passive' construction and foreground interpretation is a thoroughly inferential one across discourse types, or there must be a decoding-*cum*-inference account for non-narrative discourse which runs roughly like this: when the hearer recognises that the discourse is not narrative, he will activate inferential processes to override the encoded meaning 'narrative foreground.' Hopper and Thompson's observations thus strongly suggest that grounding of information in discourse is a purely pragmatic phenomenon: it is not encoded in language but rather inferentially determined.

This conclusion, that grounding is an inferential, pragmatic phenomenon, is further strengthened by the fact that in some texts, usually highly-planned literary texts, the relation between linguistic signals and their usual association with grounding is broken, as in example (5):

(5) The door slammed while she dashed out of the room in anger.

Subordinate clauses are normally expected to carry background information. In this example, however, the woman's dashing out of the room is the main event on the narrative line, but it is presented in the subordinate clause. Likewise, the door's slamming is a concomitant event of the woman's dashing out of the room, but it is presented in the main clause. 'Such subtleties are a complicating factor in discourse studies, but one which becomes problematic only if texts of a highly-polished "belletristic" sort are chosen,' comment Hopper and Thompson (1980:285), and similar remarks have been made for example by Reinhart (1984:796–7) and Fleischmann (1985:861). But surely pragmatic explanations have to be valid even for highly literary texts. If there were a coding relation between main clause and foreground information, then the reader of (5) would have to recognise that this example was part of a literary text, which knowledge would then trigger an inferential process undoing the association between main clause and foreground, and subordinate clause and background. But the fact that even isolated utterances such as (5) can be correctly understood with respect to grounding militates strongly against such a modified code-based account.

The fact that grounding is linguistically signalled in one way or another in many languages suggests to Hopper and Thompson that

> at a higher level of explanation, some psychological limitation in processing discourse may be involved; language users apparently need to attach overt morphosyntactic signals to those parts of the discourse which are to be stored for immediate sequential processing, as opposed to those parts which are to be stored for future reference or concomitant access. (p. 282)

However, Hopper and Thompson do not pursue this line further. In a later chapter I will develop an account of grounding which sees it as a reflex of cognitive and communicative principles (much in the spirit of this quote), and which explains the thoroughly inferential relation between linguistic 'signalling' devices and grounding effects in discourse.

4.2.7 Foreground and topic-constituting implicit questions in discourse

In the last chapter, I reviewed approaches to topicality based on the intuition that clauses in discourse can be seen as answering questions explicitly or implicitly raised as the discourse proceeds. This intuition has also been used as the basis for an explanation of grounding in discourse. Approaches on these lines bring together issues connected with (discourse) topicality and those connected with grounding in discourse, underlining the importance of grounding as a concern in the investigation of global coherence.

An early approach defining foreground by appeal to (implicit) questions in discourse can be found in Labov (1972). The suggestion is that foreground clauses in narrative are those which answer the question *What happened next?* A more elaborated approach is developed in Klein and von Stutterheim (1987) and von Stutterheim (1997): here, foreground sentences are those which contribute directly to an answer to the *quaestio* of the text (see above, Chapter 3). Consider (6):

(6) (a) Tuning a piano is a straightforward procedure. (b) Some pieces of felt are used to dampen two of the three strings of the note which is to be tuned. (c) A special tuning key is then used to turn the pins which hold the strings. (d) However, this process must be done with care, as the pins need to be turned only very slightly and the force on the string may amount to several kilos. (e) Furthermore, the equal temperament of the intervals needs careful listening and experience. (f) Of course, this task can nowadays be eased by using electronic tuners.

The *quaestio* of this text is something like *How does one tune a piano?* However, only sentences (b), (c) and arguably (d) directly contribute to answering this question and they constitute the foreground of this text. Sentences (a), (e) and (f) have a more supportive role: sentence (a), while not answering the *quaestio*, provides a 'starting point' for the text. Sentences (e) and (f) elaborate on some of the difficulties that might arise in tuning a piano and how to approach them. These constitute the background of the text.

Van Kuppevelt (1995b:812) finds fault with both these approaches. To Labov's proposal, he objects rightly that it relates only to narrative discourse, and therefore fails to provide a general definition of foreground. To Klein and von Stutterheim (1987), he objects that the approach cannot handle information which doesn't directly answer the *quaestio* but intuitively makes an important or supportive contribution to foreground information. An example of what he means can be seen in (7):

(7) Van Kuppevelt's (1995b:825) example (9)′:

A: Whatever happened to RJ?

B: (a) Six years ago, she mysteriously disappeared. (b) Though the authorities had a suspect, their investigations stalled. (c) A spokesman confirmed that they had missed the final link. (d) Two years later her body was found in a North Coast grave. (e) It was found near Eureka. (f) Now [the] authorities have a chilling new theory about what might have happened to her.

According to van Kuppevelt, sentences (a), (b), (d) and (f) provide the sequential temporal material which constitutes the narrative, that is, these are the foreground sentences. However, he does not classify (c) or (e) as background material, because he feels that they are intuitively important to the foreground material: (c) confirms that the investigations did indeed stall (as opposed to having continued in secret), and (e) makes the location of the grave more precise.[2] Therefore, he argues, these sentences should not be classified as background, that is, side structure, but as substructure, regarded as something in between foreground and background.

Van Kuppevelt (1995b) proposes a theory of grounding which is designed to avoid these shortcomings. Recall that the basic assumption of this theory is that discourse is organised by its topic-comment structure. Implicit or explicit questions raised by the discourse constitute topics on various levels of the hierarchy (see Chapter 3 above). There are three types of topic-forming questions: main questions, which constitute the discourse topic(s), subquestions, which result from unsatisfactory answers to other questions, and side questions, which arise from previous answers but shift the theme of the discourse in a different, though related direction, leaving the original topic open. Answers to main questions constitute the main structure, that is, the foreground of the discourse. For example, in (7) above, there is an explicit main question, asked by A. Sentences (a), (b), (d) and (f) successively answer this main topic-constituting question. Answers to subquestions also help to answer the main question, but in a more indirect way. These answers also contribute to the main structure — that is, foreground — albeit in a more supportive manner, which is called sub-structure in van Kuppevelt's approach. Thus, (c) is an answer to the question: 'why do you think that their investigations stalled (and were not, e.g., continued in secret)?' (van Kuppevelt 1995b:825). This question is designed to make the answer to the main question qualitatively more precise (as opposed to introducing an aside or opening another topic). Finally, answers to side questions constitute side-structures, that is, background information. (Van Kuppevelt 1995b:827) illustrates side structure with the following variant of (7) above:

(8) Van Kuppevelt's example (9)″:

A: Whatever happened to RJ?

B: (a) Six years ago, she mystériously disappeared. (a)′ She was a nice person. (b) Though the authorities had a suspect, their investigations stalled. (c) A spokesman confirmed that they had missed the final link. (d) Two years later her body was found in a North Coast grave. (e) It was found near Eureka. (f) Now [the] authorities have a chilling new theory about what might have happened to her.

Sentence (a)′ in (8) answers the question *What kind of person was she?*, which cannot be construed as a subquestion of (A), the main topic-constituting question.

Both main structure and sub-structures imply a continuation of the main topic, so they both belong to the foreground. Moreover, 'if the coherence and goal of the text are to be preserved, the former substructures [which help to answer the main topic-constituting question; CU] are the only ones that cannot be deleted.' (van Kuppevelt 1995b:813) This idea that foreground sentences cannot be deleted if one wants to shorten the story and yet be faithful to its content has also been proposed in Grimes (1975).

In evaluating this theory, I will first consider whether the question-based approach to discourse can be generalised to all discourse types. For example, to what extent can poetry be seen as raising and answering (implicit) questions. This idea does not seem to be straightforwardly applicable to many poems, especially those involving parallelism or chiasmus. Consider example (9):

(9) The sun shone. The acacia bloomed. And the butcher slaughtered. (Haim Nachman Bialik: *The city of slaughter;* Giora's (1985b:706) example 9).

Giora (1985b:706) comments on this example as follows:

> [(12)] can be interpreted as a comment on the world's attitude to man's suffering. What question is it possible to construct for it? Would a question such as "what happened" do? Or, "what happened during the pogrom?" In other words, would the question be the "question under discussion" in the sense that this is the topic discussed?

It appears to be clear that no such question would be able to capture the 'topic' of the text, and for this reason Giora (1985b) rejects question-based analyses of topic. It appears that van Kuppevelt's (1995b) theory falls under the same sort of criticism. Thus, van Kuppevelt's approach is not as general as it is claimed to be.

Second, the definition of side structure rests on an approach to topic digression which is rooted in the idea that a statement can function as a feeder having already functioned as an answer. I argued above (Chapter 3) that this idea undermines the whole approach to discourse organisation, since it offers no explanation for the oddity of mock-narratives such as (2) in Chapter 2. In other words, the definition of background is rooted in the weakest part of the theory. Thus, the definition of background, and *a fortiori* that of grounding in general, within van Kuppevelt's approach is questionable on theoretical grounds.

Finally, this approach presupposes that some given information belongs either to the main structure or to the side structure. Other researchers have been led to posit a much more fine-grained scale of grounding levels (Longacre 1989a,b, 1990a,b), some even proposing a continuum, as we have seen above (Fleischmann 1985, 1990). In light of these proposals, an approach which does not easily allow for the possibility of a continuous scale from foreground to background is in need of more justification.

The inadequacy of van Kuppevelt's three-way scale of grounding in discourse can be illustrated using example (6) above. The main question which this text is designed to answer is *How does one tune a piano?* Sentences (b) and (c) undoubtedly help to answer this question. For sentence (d) the answer is not so obvious. It does not introduce another procedure, but rather elaborates on the one previously mentioned (the turning of the tuning key). It is an intuitively 'important' elaboration, as is typical with exhortations to be careful with certain tasks. Thus, this sentence might be an example of sub-structure in van Kuppevelt's terms, answering a question such as *Is there anything special about turning the pins?* Problems arise with the analysis of sentence (e): the information conveyed by this sentence is no longer directly related to the procedure of turning the pins, but it does not function as an aside (witness the connective 'furthermore'). It therefore doesn't appear to fall squarely into either the category of sub-structure or the category of side-structure. The same is true of (f).

Similar remarks apply to (7) (see note 3 to this chapter): sentences (c) and (e) are both claimed to be sub-structures, since they are in some way important to the foreground. However, while it could be argued that (7c) is 'important' to the foreground in the sense of providing evidence for it, it is hard to see how (7e) is 'important' for the foreground: it merely specifies a location, and the narrative will not suffer if this information is left out.

This, and the observations made in subsection 2.5 above with regard to examples (5), (6) and (7), suggests that an adequate theory of grounding cannot be based on a simple, discrete system of classifications such as the one proposed in van Kuppevelt (1995b). The conclusion must be that van Kuppevelt's (1995b) definition of main structure and side structure does not yield a viable account of grounding in discourse.

4.2.8 Other approaches to grounding

Apart from these widely-accepted definitions of grounding, other suggestions have been made. For example, Reinhart (1984) approaches grounding from a *Gestalt* psychological point of view. Grosz and Sidner's (1985; 1986) theory of discourse intentionality has been seen as implying a certain distinction between foreground and background information (van Kuppevelt 1995b). In this sub-section I want to discuss these approaches.

Reinhart (1984) accepts the definition of foreground in narrative in terms of temporal succession, following Labov and Waletzky (1967) and Labov (1972). However, she argues that this defining characteristic of foreground (that is, that foreground sentences in narrative contain temporally successive events in iconic order) has a deeper explanation in terms of *Gestalt* psychology. Her argument runs roughly as follows: first, it is pointed out that temporal criteria for making the foreground-background distinction in narrative are the most important ones proposed in the literature. There are three kinds of such temporal criteria: 'narrativity,' punctuality and completeness. 'Narrativity' means that only textual units which convey successive events in the order in which they occur (in the real or fictional world) can serve as foreground sentences. The punctuality criterion says that foreground sentences usually convey events in punctiliar aspect. Similarly, the completeness criterion says that foreground sentences tend to convey completed events. These criteria can be illustrated in examples (10) to (12).

(10) Reinhart's (1984:799) example (18); italics as in original, marking background information in subordinated clauses

a. The host was telling another joke. *Having already heard this joke many times before,* Rosa started to yawn.

b. [?] The host was telling another joke. *Starting to yawn/having started to yawn,* Rosa has/had already heard this joke many times before.

(11) My example (3) from page 75, repeated here for convenience:

a. After breakfast, we got ready to drive to grandmother's place. We loaded our luggage into the car and seated the children well in their safety seats. Then we set out on our journey.

b. After breakfast, we got ready to drive to grandmother's place. After having loaded our luggage into the car and having seated the children well in their safety seats, we set out on our journey.

(12) a. After breakfast, we got ready to drive to grandmother's place. We loaded our luggage into the car and seated the children well in their safety seats. Then we set out on our journey. After an uneventful journey we finally reached our goal and we got out of the car. *The birds were singing;* it was lovely.

b. After breakfast, we got ready to drive to grandmother's place. We loaded our luggage into the car and seated the children well in their safety seats. Then we set out on our journey. After an uneventful journey we finally reached our goal and we got out of the car. *The boy ran to his grandmother;* it was lovely.

In (10b) there is an attempt to make information which is not on the story time line (*Rosa has/had already heard this joke many times before*) which refers to times in the past outside the span of the narrative (which is presumably the story of a party) into foreground by presenting it as a main clause; likewise, it attempts to present an event which is on the narrative time line (*Rosa started to yawn*) as background, subordinating it under the main clause expressing information off the storyline. In other words, a reversal of the foreground-background relation (by content criteria) is attempted. The oddity of (10b) shows that this cannot be done, in conformity with the 'narrativity' criterion. While in (11a) the information in the second sentence may be construed as foreground or as background, as in (11b), the information in the first sentence (*We got ready to drive to grandmother's place*) cannot be construed as foreground. Notice that *Getting ready* is not a punctiliar event, in contrast to *Loading luggage, Seating children in the car,* and *Setting out on the journey.* Example (12) illustrates the completeness criterion: while the italicised clause in (12a) cannot easily be interpreted as foreground, the italicised clause in (12b) can. The latter, but not the former, expresses a completed event.

The second step in the argument is to show that these temporal criteria for the foreground-background distinction in narrative are closely parallel to the principles proposed by *Gestalt* psychologists to explain spatial perception. The laws in question are the Law of Good Continuation, the Law of Size and Proximity, and the Law of Closure. The Law of Good Continuation says that spatial perception tends to give priority to continuous shapes. In identifying a figure, it is difficult to break up a contour. This is the most robust principle of Gestalt perception, and Reinhart (1984:803) argues that it parallels the 'narrativity' criterion of foregrounding: the temporal succession of events is the narrative's 'contour,' so to speak. The Law of Size and Proximity has it that spatial perception tends to identify smaller areas as foreground, rather than larger ones, which are usually seen as background. According to Reinhart, this law of spatial perception parallels the punctuality criterion of narrative foreground: punctiliar events can be said to (metaphorically) occupy less space on the time line than non-punctiliar events or states. Hence, the condition that foreground sentences express punctiliar events can be compared to the Law of Size and Proximity. However, this law is not as robust as the Law of Good Continuation, and can more easily be overridden in context. Finally, the Law of Closure says that the more closed areas are easier to perceive as figure. Reinhart links this law to the criterion of completedness in narrative: completed events have similar properties to closed areas in spatial perception.

This account of the foreground-background distinction in narrative is interesting as far as it goes. However, the account doesn't get quite far enough to account for grounding for discourse in general: first, it only concerns the definition of foreground and background in narrative discourse. Nothing is said about foreground and background in other discourse types. Furthermore, it only concerns the temporal criteria for grounding levels in narrative. Reinhart lists four other criteria for the foreground-background distinction which have been proposed in the literature, modality: Hopper (1979); Hopper and Thompson (1980); causality: for example Samet and Schank (1984); Caenepeel (1995); semantic load; genre or convention, and notes that though some similarities may exist between some of these criteria and the *Gestalt* theory of spatial perception, the similarities are not as striking as in the case of the temporal criteria (Reinhart 1984:803). In other words: the *Gestalt*-psychological explanation of foreground in narrative is not complete, it relates only to some of the criteria which are said to define foreground and background in narrative discourse. It is apparent that foreground and background in discourse are complex notions which can only partially be explained by recourse to *Gestalt* psychology, at best. Thus, the attempt to find a more general definition of the foreground-background distinction for discourse in general on the basis of the *Gestalt* theory of spatial perception cannot in principle be successful.

Grosz and Sidner (1986) propose a theory of discourse which distinguishes three basic description levels: the discourse segment structure, the intentional structure, and the attentional state of the discourse participants. The discourse segment structure is the result of the linguistic grouping of utterances into segments. Every discourse segment has its own discourse segment purpose, which is the intention with which the communicator standardly uses this segment in discourse.[3] These discourse segment purposes (or intentions) enter into dominance relations with one another: if the fulfilment of the intention of discourse segment B contributes to the fulfilment of the intention of discourse segment A, the purpose (intention) of discourse segment A is said to dominate the purpose (intention) of discourse segment B. The dominance relations between discourse segment purposes are independent of the discourse segment structure itself.

The discourse segment purpose is often the intention that the audience believes some proposition **P**. For example, the discourse segment purpose of the second last paragraph ('This account of the foreground-background distinction in narrative is interesting as far as it goes ... Thus, the attempt to find a more general definition ... cannot in principle be successful') is that the audience believes that P, where P is something like *The Gestalt-psychology account of foreground and background in narrative of Reinhart (1984) is defective.* In other words: the discourse segment purpose may be something like a summary of a segment; it may furthermore be directly stated somewhere in the text, or implied by the utterances of the segment. Grosz and Sidner's notion of intentional structure could be seen as contributing to a theory both of discourse topic and of grounding in discourse, though they themselves explicitly address only the connection between intentional structure and topic (Grosz and Sidner 1986:191–2). Foreground material in discourse would be — on this theory — that material which contributes directly to establishing the discourse segment purpose, and background material would be that material which is extraneous to the discourse segment purpose. However, I don't know of any worked-out theory of grounding based on Grosz and Sidner's account of discourse structure in the literature, and van Kuppevelt (1995b:811) comments likewise that 'while not making an explicit distinction between foreground and background, [Grosz and Sidner's account] does implicitly provide a general criterion that implies a broader concept of the main structure of a discourse.'[4] Therefore it does not seem to be advisable to dwell more on the possible implications of Grosz and Sidner's account on grounding in discourse. Suffice it to say that the move to a pragmatic account of grounding in terms of intentions is a positive one, and the pragmatic account of grounding effects in discourse to be developed in Chapter 5 in terms of expectations of relevance is quite in line with this suggestion. However, to achieve adequacy, such an account must take the notion of intention seriously as a psychological one, not as a property of discourse segments *per se*.

There are also still other views on the foreground and background distinction expressed in the literature. Thus, Bailey and Levinsohn (1992) distinguish between storyline clauses or 'backbone' information and foreground in the sense of 'highlighted information.' In their view, continuity in discourse is what characterises storyline information, whereas 'foreground' has to do with importance or salience.[5] This resonates somehow with Reinhart's (1984:787) observation that storyline information is not always 'foreground' information in the literary theory sense of information which is important for the plot of the story. While Reinhart opts to retain the term 'foreground' and use it in the sense of 'storyline,' (basically because of the similarities of storyline information to the concept of figure in the *Gestalt* theory of spatial perception), Bailey and Levinsohn (1992) seem to opt for the opposite solution: reserve the term 'foreground' for important (salient) information, and use 'backbone' or 'storyline' for the staging (or grounding) of information in discourse. These considerations about the different use of the terms 'foreground,' 'storyline/backbone,' and 'importance/salience' provide additional support for the claim, alluded to above in the discussion of Reinhart (1984), that the staging — or grounding — of information in discourse is a complex phenomenon. However, there is no adequate definition of foreground and background found among the accounts surveyed in this section.

4.2.9 Evaluation

The conclusion that emerges from this survey of a wide variety of approaches to defining foreground and background information must be that van Kuppevelt's (1995b:810) comment is still valid: 'there is still no adequate, generally accepted, formal definition that provides an identification criterion for this distinction in both complex narratives and other discourse types.' What the research on grounding in discourse leaves us with is a wealth of interesting cross-linguistic data which have not yet been adequately explained. Attempts to explain the phenomenon of global coherence in terms of grounding have also failed. There are two possible responses: one is to look further for a better definition of the notions of foreground and background. This does not look very promising, since there are few possibilities (if any) which have not been investigated in the literature. I prefer, then, to opt for a second approach: to reject the notions of foreground and background as primitives of pragmatic (or semantic, or linguistic) theory, and assume that observations about grounding in natural languages find their explanation in a deeper pragmatic notion. A further reason for choosing this approach is that there is some evidence that grounding is a purely pragmatic phenomenon, and that whatever relation linguistic markers may have to grounding, it is not one of coding. Grounding appears to be an 'unencodable' notion, which is to be expected precisely if it is not a primitive of pragmatic theory or discourse analysis. In a later part of this book I will argue that the deeper notion which can explain grounding effects is relevance in the sense of Sperber and Wilson (1995). This explanation is in line with hints given by Hopper and Thompson (1980), that foreground somehow relates to relevance, and that grounding in discourse may have a deeper explanation in psychology. Before embarking on this argument, I want to take a step back and survey the ways in which grounding has been seen as sensitive to discourse type.

4.3 Grounding in discourse and discourse type

Throughout my survey of approaches to grounding in section 2, it was clear that one of the main questions raised by attempts to define the foreground-background distinction is how to generalise observations about narrative texts to other discourse types. All the approaches surveyed appear to agree on a basic assumption: the essential content of the foreground-background distinction is independent of discourse types, but manifests itself in different ways in different discourse types. This may be seen in patterns of linguistic marking, most typically word order or tense-aspect marking. In other words: discourse type has a linguistic function in the sense adopted in this book (Chapter 1), which is mediated through information staging — that is, grounding — in discourse. In the rest of this section I will survey the main claims about grounding and discourse type made in the literature.

4.3.1 Grounding scales, linguistic marking, and discourse type

Probably the strongest claims about the influence of discourse type on linguistic marking are made by Longacre (1989a,b, 1990b, 1992) and by researchers following his tradition (for example Hays 1995; Abangma 1987). Longacre claims that the verb system in any language is sensitive to discourse type: in each discourse type there is a complex multiple-layered hierarchy of grounding levels, each characterised by a certain verb construction. Thus, the verb system can only be described with respect to the different discourse types. An example of this approach may be seen in Longacre's description of English in Longacre (1989b:416):

(13) *Rank scheme for English narrative texts*

Band 1: Storyline

1.1 Past (S[ubject]/Agent) Action, (S/Agent/Patient) Motion

1.2 Past (S/Experience) Cognitive events (punctiliar adverbs)

1.3 Past (S/Patient) Contingencies

Band 2: Background

2.1 Past Progressive (S/Agent) background activities

2.2 Past (S/Experience) Cognitive states (durative adverbs)

Band 3: Flashback

3.1 Pluperfects (Events, activities, which are out of sequence)

3.2 Pluperfects (Cognitive events/states that are out of sequence)

Band 4: Setting (expository)

4.1 Stative verbs/adjectival predicates/verbs with inanimate subjects (descriptive)

4.2 "Be" verbs/verbless clauses (equational)

4.3 "Be"/"Have" (existential, relational)

Band 5: Irrealis (other possible worlds)

5.1 Negatives

5.2 Modals/futures

Band 6: evaluation (author intrusion)

6.1 Past tense (compare setting)

6.2 Gnomic present

Band 7: Cohesive band (verbs in preposed/postposed Adverbial clauses)

7.1 Script determined
7.2 Repetitive
7.3 Back Reference

This approach has been applied to many languages, particularly of Africa and Asia (Longacre 1990b; Longacre and Shaler 1990). The point is that discourse-type recognition is essential for identifying the meaning of a particular verb form in use. The discourse types are defined by a combination of presumably universal features, *Agent-orientation* and *Contingent succession.* Narratives have the feature combination [+Agent-orientation; +Contingent succession], Procedural Discourse [−Agent-orientation; +Contingent succession], Behavioural Discourse [+Agent-orientation; −Contingent succession] and Expository Discourse [−Agent-orientation; −Contingent succession].[6] In addition, there may be language-specific discourse types: for example, Longacre (1989a, 1992) postulates a discourse type of predictive discourse for Biblical Hebrew, for which there is no analogy in his analysis of English (1989b).

However, these strong claims about the dependence of the verb system on discourse type are weakened by the fact that the various grounding levels and their marking in different text types are often not that different. Consider the following grounding levels and their marking for (Biblical) Hebrew (Longacre 1992).

(14) a. *Rank scheme for Biblical Hebrew narrative (Longacre 1992:180)*

Band 1: Storyline
1.1 Preterite: primary
1.2 Perfect: secondary
1.3 Noun + perfect: secondary (with noun in focus)
Band 2: Backgrounded Activities
2.1 Noun + imperfect: implicitly durative/repetitive
2.2 *Hinnēh* ['behold'] + participle
2.3 Participle (explicitly durative)
2.4 Noun + participle

Band 3: Setting

3.1 Preterite of *hāyâ* 'be'

3.2 Perfect of *hāyâ* 'be'

3.3 Nominal clause (verbless)

3.4 Existential clause with *yēš* ['to exist']

Band 4: Irrealis

4.1 Negation of verb (in any band)

*Band 5: Cohesion (back-referential) (*wayehî *[preterite of* hāyâ*] + temporal phrase/clause)*

5.1 General reference

5.2 Script-predictable

5.3 Repetitive

b. *Rank scheme for Biblical Hebrew Predictive Discourse (Longacre 1992:181)*

Band 1: Storyline (Predictive)

1.1 *Wāw* ['and']-consecutive + perfect (primary)

1.2 Imperfect: secondary

1.3 Noun + imperfect: secondary (with noun in focus)

Band 2: Backgrounded Activities

2.1 *Hinnēh* + participle

2.2 Participle

2.3 Noun + participle

Band 3: Setting

3.1 *Wāw*-consecutive perfect of *hāyâ* 'be'

3.2 Imperfect of *hāyâ* 'be'

3.3 Nominal clause (verbless)

3.4 Existential clause with *yēš*

Band 4: Irrealis

4.1 Negation of verb (in any band)

*Band 5: Cohesion (*wayehî *+ temporal phrase/clause)*

5.1 General reference

5.2 Script-predictable

5.3 Repetitive

In these two discourse types, only the storyline band (band 1) is crucially different. In Band 2, narrative discourse has a rank (2.1 Noun + imperfect: implicitly durative/repetitive) which is not found in predictive discourse. In Band 3, the two ranks involving forms of the auxiliary 'to be' are encoded with different forms. From rank 3.3 (in both discourse types) downwards, the scheme is identical. There is thus a large overlap in the forms and constructions occupying the rank schemes of these respective discourse types. Furthermore, Longacre (1994) claims that *waw*-consecutive + perfect forms (more commonly called *weqatal* forms) constitute the backbone (that is, foreground) rank in no less than three discourse types: procedural, predictive (quoted above) and instructional. These observations suggest that the use of verb forms and verbal constructions is not very different in the various discourse types. It seems that important generalisations are missed in this system.

Niccacci (1994) has noticed this state of affairs and rejects Longacre's analysis of the Hebrew verb on the basis that too many discourse types are postulated. However, he still accepts the claim that the verb system in Hebrew as well as in other languages (he cites the Romance languages French, Spanish and Italian) is sensitive to a certain discourse-type distinction, namely that between narration and quotation. Niccacci discusses only prose texts, so there is yet another superordinate discourse type influencing linguistic marking.

To sum up, the approaches to grounding reviewed in this subsection agree that consideration of discourse type is essential in the pragmatic interpretation of verb forms. From the discourse comprehension point of view, this raises the question of how the addressee can recognise discourse types in a psychologically adequate way. This problem is compounded by the admission that discourse types may be embedded. The computational problem with embedded discourse types has been discussed in Chapter 2, and it was concluded that there will be no psychologically plausible process of discourse type recognition if discourse type is claimed to be crucial for comprehension and discourse-type embedding is allowed. This, together with the observation that existing claims about the influence of discourse type on the use of particular verb forms or constructions often miss generalisations, suggests that the claims about a linguistic function of genre are not convincing.

4.3.2 Discourse type and the comment value of topic-constituting questions

While Longacre (1989a,b, 1990a,b) was by and large not concerned with explaining how an explicit theory of discourse type recognition could be integrated with his account, van Kuppevelt has shown how this might be done in his system. Van Kuppevelt (1995b:813) points out that substructures belonging to the main structure 'provide the final comment value to the (discourse) topic defined by the main question.' In Footnote 9 he further suggests that this final comment value also defines the text type. The idea behind this is that when the final item of information providing a satisfactory answer to the main question is an event, then the text is a narrative; when it is a description, the text is expository; and so on. Although these remarks do not amount to a theory of discourse typology and its role in comprehension (which van Kuppevelt 1995b was not designed to provide), it is easy to see that an account along these lines might be developed into a (semantic) identification procedure for discourse types. Unfortunately, on this approach, the discourse type won't be recognised by the hearer until towards the end of the text. It follows that discourse type recognition cannot be an essential part of discourse comprehension, and can therefore have neither a cognitive nor a linguistic function.

4.4 Conclusion

In this Chapter I have reviewed various approaches which use notions of information-staging or grounding in discourse to deal with issues related to global coherence. I have argued that no adequate definition of the foreground-background distinction has been found. However, research in this area has produced a wealth of interesting cross-linguistic data which have not yet received a theoretically adequate explanation. From the point of view of this book, the most important data are those concerning the use of verb forms as indicators of grounding: it is claimed that such indications are typically sensitive to discourse-type distinctions. If existing accounts of these phenomena fall short of explanatory adequacy, there remains the question of how they are to be explained. I will take up this challenge in a later chapter, where I hope to show that relevance theory can indeed provide a better explanation for a wide range of these data. Before embarking on this project, it is necessary to lay the theoretical foundations. In the next chapter, I will therefore discuss aspects of relevance theory which might provide the basis for an alternative account of global connectivity and grounding in discourse.

Conclusion

Part 2

EXPECTATIONS OF RELEVANCE AND GENRE

5 Expectations of relevance

5.1 Introduction

The previous chapters of this book were designed to assess the nature and implications of existing approaches to genre based on the theory of global coherence. I want now to present an alternative, relevance-based account by developing some of the ideas sketched in previous chapters. In Chapter 2, I examined the view that a notion of global coherence might form the basis for a theory of genre. I argued that there is no need for a notion of global coherence in a relevance-based account, since its work can be done by direct appeal to the notion of relevance. In this chapter I will take up this suggestion and develop it into an explicit theory.

5.2 Expectations of relevance and complex stimuli

Any act of ostensive communication communicates a presumption of its own optimal relevance. This is the essence of the communicative principle of relevance, and follows from the assumptions underlying the cognitive principle of relevance. In other words, assumption (1) is one of the set of assumptions **I** communicated by any utterance:

(1) The ostensive stimulus is at least relevant enough to be worth the addressee's processing effort, and is also the most relevant one the communicator was willing and able to produce.

Of course, the hearer does not have to believe every assumption communicated by an utterance. Whether he does will depend on how much he trusts the speaker. In some circumstances, the hearer may trust the speaker enough to expect actual optimal relevance, whereas in other circumstances the expectation may be revised to one of attempted optimal relevance or even (in deceptive cases) of purported optimal relevance. Each of these revised expectations requires a further degree of sophistication in the hearer, the development of which can be traced in some of the literature on acquisition of pragmatics (see Sperber 1994; Wilson 2000). In what follows, I will illustrate this complication briefly, but ignore it where possible.

What is more important for my purposes is that the expectations of relevance created by particular utterances may be more or less specific. In the first place, the degree of relevance expected may vary from occasion to occasion; in the second place, there may be more specific expectations about how the stimulus will achieve relevance, that is, about the kind of cognitive effects it will achieve. For example, someone who asks a question makes it manifest[1] that there is certain information which he would regard as relevant enough to be worth processing if true. An utterance which immediately follows a question and is addressed to the questioner will probably create an expectation that it is intended to answer the question: in other words, that it is intended to supply the information which the questioner has indicated is relevant enough to be worth processing. This explains how indirect (implicated) answers are understood (Sperber and Wilson 1995:194). If the information is not explicitly expressed, it must be implicated.

How do questions create these expectations? A question is used to represent a relevant answer, that is, information which the questioner would regard as relevant if true (Sperber and Wilson 1995:252). In this situation, the easiest way for the addressee to achieve relevance in turn is by producing an utterance which expresses or implies an answer to the question. It is thus rational for the addressee to produce such an utterance so long as she is willing and able to do so (compare clause (b) of the definition of optimal relevance). She may be unable to do so through ignorance (in which case a partial answer may be accepted as relevant enough); she may be unwilling to do so because it is not in her interests to provide the required information (or because some more urgent information must be given first). All this provides a relatively strong constraint on the expectations with which the questioner may approach the following utterance.

On this account, a question gives evidence about the cognitive environment of the questioner, his preferences: it becomes mutually manifest[2] that certain information would be relevant to him. Since estimates of what the audience regards as relevant play a crucial role in communication, a rational speaker will try to take this evidence into account.

Consider now example (2):

(2) A: What do you think are the merits and defects of X's new book?

Here, A's question expresses not a proposition but a propositional schema whose completion might yield many answers that A would regard relevant if true. It should be manifest to both participants that B is unlikely to be able to provide an optimally relevant answer by uttering just one complex sentence (the processing effort required would be too high). It is therefore reasonable for A to expect B to produce a series of utterances intended to be jointly relevant (or to achieve relevance 'as a unit'). Thus, the expectation of relevance created by an utterance may concern not only the type of cognitive effects to be achieved or the level of relevance to be assumed, but also the way in which the cognitive effects are presented, which should itself be geared to achieving optimal relevance, that is, to yielding a complex (possibly ordered) set of cognitive effects on the path of least effort. Rational addressees should therefore not expect each utterance to achieve a constant level of relevance; for example, early utterances in a discourse may have limited relevance on their own, but they may contribute to increasing the effects and reducing the processing effort required for later utterances, thus optimising relevance over the discourse as a whole.

It follows that in cases like (2) a presumption of relevance of the form in (3) is communicated:

(3) The communicator will produce a complex stimulus (consisting of a sequence of utterances) which is relevant enough to be worth processing, and is also the most relevant

stimulus compatible with the communicator's abilities and preferences.

This presumption is about the complexity of ostensive stimuli. The ostensive stimulus in Chapter 1, example (2) was a simple one, consisting of a single gesture. In cases such as Chapter 1, example (8), the stimulus is a single utterance, consisting of one sentence. However, ostensive behaviour may be more complex than that: a piano teacher might explain to her student how to play a certain phrase, saying 'Here *legato*, and now *staccato*' as she is demonstrating it on the piano at the same time; a master may explain to his apprentice how to exchange the shock absorbers of a car, doing the action as he speaks. These are all examples of complex stimuli (compare Blakemore 1992:99 for a similar example). Notice that the complexity of these stimuli is not only in their consisting of gestures and speech simultaneously; it is also in their consisting of several actions in sequence, which will not be complete until the end is reached. Take the case of the master showing and explaining to his apprentice how to exchange the shock absorbers of a car: it is obvious from the beginning that this task will require a sequence of actions, and a sequence of utterances to explain them. The whole task is seen as a unit of behaviour, a complex stimulus. It should not be surprising that texts can be regarded as complex stimuli in this sense, the complexity being mainly that they typically consist of a sequence of utterances. Texts or discourses are hence seen as units of ostensive behaviour, not as linguistic units made up of smaller linguistic constituents such as speech acts, utterances or sentences. Thus, the view that text or discourse can be analysed as a complex stimulus does not commit one to the view that discourse is hierarchically structured, or even linguistically structured in any way. In fact, I have argued in Chapter 3, and more extensively in Unger (1996), that there is no evidence that discourse is hierarchically structured and that discourse organisation is best explained pragmatically as a by-product of processing texts following the relevance-theoretic comprehension procedure. I will return to this point below in this chapter and in the following one.

The presumption of optimal relevance of a complex stimulus in (3) is communicated once for the whole complex stimulus. In addition, each individual utterance may create its own expectations of relevance, which may be constrained and calibrated by the expectation of relevance created for the sequence as a whole. In this way, early utterances in the sequence may raise relatively low individual expectations of relevance and yet be worth the addressee's attention for the contribution they are expected to make to the discourse as a whole, while for others, the individual expectations might be higher and more determinate.

Thus, the expectations of relevance created by an utterance may affect the interpretation of later utterances. In situations where it is mutually manifest that the speaker will produce a sequence of utterances and intends to optimise relevance over this complex stimulus, the presumption of relevance which is communicated may induce various expectations about the joint contribution of the present and later utterances to the overall relevance of the discourse. Similar arguments should apply not only to (2) but to written communications such as books and newspaper articles, and to some varieties of oral communication such as (scheduled) radio programmes, story-telling sessions, lectures, sermons etc. In these cases it is mutually manifest from the beginning that the communicator intended to produce a complex stimulus: the size of the book or article, the allotted time for radio programs, and the nature of stories (that they can't be told in just one utterance) is known in advance.

However, expectations of relevance of complex stimuli in this sense may also be raised in a different way. Consider the case of a conversation where one participant expands her turn into a monologue, although this is not required by the mutual cognitive environment at the beginning of the discourse:

(4) A: It's a nuisance with computers these days.

B: Oh yes, that's true! They get outdated almost as soon as you buy them. But if you don't keep up with the most recent models, you'll pay a fortune for repairs. Look: a friend of mine thought he was being smart in buying a used laptop, and that, with a little investment, just by buying more RAM, he could make this computer workable for him. But when he ordered a RAM expansion he found that this particular model was so special that the chips were difficult to get, and horrendously expensive. Finally he got it to work, but he paid almost as much as if he had bought a new computer.

B's initial utterance probably does not raise great expectations of relevance; however, it is at least presented as relevant. Here the presumption of relevance communicated is the familiar one in (1). This presumption will be confirmed if the interpretation process leads to a set of assumptions which (a) do not falsify the expectation that the utterance is the most relevant one which the speaker was willing and able to produce and (b) are sufficient to confirm the expectation that the utterance is relevant enough to be worth the addressee's processing effort (Sperber and Wilson 1995:163–6). Here, the utterance would achieve the minimal level of relevance by providing some confirmation that B had understood and accepted A's remark. However, B may be able to achieve more relevance than this, by providing further evidence for A's remark and revealing what it meant to her. This initial utterance thus creates an expectation that if she is willing and able to produce such evidence, she will do so. The subsequent utterances may be straightforwardly interpreted along these lines, with relevance being optimised over the resulting complex stimulus, and the presumption of relevance for this complex stimulus confirmed.

There are thus several ways in which expectations of relevance of complex stimuli may be raised. First, it may be mutually manifest at the start of the discourse that the speaker is likely to produce a complex stimulus and optimise relevance over it. Second, it may become mutually manifest in the course of the discourse that relevance can be increased by producing a more complex and elaborate stimulus, and that the speaker may be willing and able to do this. Third, an initial utterance may not achieve a sufficient level of relevance in itself, and to achieve optimal relevance the stimulus must therefore be more complex. An example of this case is (5):

(5) Sally: Remember that we talked about John yesterday? Today we got a letter from him...

The first utterance brings to mind a state of affairs. As such, it does not give the addressee much cognitive effects. However, such utterances do raise the expectation that the speaker will expand on that which this utterance brought to the mind of the addressee, by producing a complex stimulus.

Regardless of how expectations of relevance of complex stimuli are raised, they have an interesting effect on comprehension. When the addressee encounters an utterance which does not immediately confirm the presumption of relevance, he should not abandon the interpretation process, but retain the utterance in memory with the expectation that the effort spent on it will be rewarded at a later stage in the discourse. In other words, when an expectation has been raised that several utterances will jointly contribute to the relevance of a complex stimulus, a minimally relevant or irrelevant utterance may in turn create more specific expectations about the relevance of later utterances.

The present proposal can be seen as an elaboration of the account of foreground and background in Sperber and Wilson (1995:202–17). They were mostly concerned with the analysis of what they called foreground and background implications of single utterances: some implications of an utterance contribute only indirectly to relevance, by giving access to contextual assumptions (background implications), while others contribute directly to cognitive effects by carrying information which is relevant in its own right (foreground implications). Sperber and Wilson also suggest that this distinction carries over to the level of whole texts, with some utterances contributing indirectly to relevance by providing access to contextual information necessary for the interpretation of later utterances, while others achieve relevance in their own right (Sperber and Wilson 1995:217):

> In our framework, background information is information that contributes only indirectly to relevance, by reducing the processing effort required; it need be neither given nor presupposed. Foreground information is information that is relevant in its own right by having contextual effects; it need not be new.

The present account extends this proposal by making it more explicit. It also modifies Sperber and Wilson's remarks somewhat by showing that one way in which background information may contribute indirectly to relevance is by creating more specific expectations about how later utterances will be relevant. Reducing processing effort for later utterances by making some contextual assumptions easier to access is just one way of achieving this goal. Another is to create more concrete expectations about the kind of cognitive effects to be achieved in later utterance(s). I will discuss examples for background information functioning in such an effect-based way in section 5.5 below.

5.3 Expectations of relevance and parallel processing

Having discussed the various expectations of relevance raised by utterances either in isolation or in combination, I will now turn to questions about how these expectations are created.

According to Sperber and Wilson, every act of ostensive communication communicates a presumption of its own optimal relevance. This follows from the definition of ostensive-inferential communication (Sperber and Wilson 1995:155–6). The argument goes — roughly — as follows: ostensive behaviour claims the addressee's attention. It is mutually manifest that only those stimuli which appear to be relevant are likely to receive adequate attention. Thus, it is mutually manifest that the communicator expects her stimulus to appear at least relevant enough to be worth the addressee's attention. It is also mutually manifest that the more relevant a stimulus appears to be, the more likely it is that the addressee will pay it adequate attention. It is thus to the communicator's advantage if the stimulus appears to be more than minimally relevant. However, it is manifest to rational communicators that speakers are constrained by their abilities and preferences in producing (relevant) stimuli, so the expectation of relevance will never be higher than these (obvious) limiting factors allow. In other words: in every act of ostensive communication, it is mutually manifest to communicator and audience that the communicator intends it to be manifest to the audience that his stimulus is optimally relevant to the audience. By the definition of ostensive-inferential communication, this means that a presumption of optimal relevance is communicated.

The presumption of relevance is an obvious source of expectations of relevance. However, more can be said about the role of expectations of relevance in the on-line interpretive process, which involves the mutual adjustment of explicit content, context and cognitive effects in an effort to satisfy these expectations (Sperber and Wilson 1998; Wilson 1999; Wilson and Sperber 2002).

The basic idea is illustrated in (6):

(6) A: The Euro has again lost against the Dollar since yesterday.
B: How do you know that?
A: I have checked the internet.

(7) a. If A has checked the internet today, he may have looked up today's exchange rates.
b. If A has looked up today's exchange rates, he can make true statements about the rate of the Euro against the Dollar.
c. A has checked the internet today.

A's last utterance in (6) can be interpreted along the lines in (7), thus implicating that A can make true statements about the Euro exchange rate and satisfying B's expectations of relevance. However, this implicature can be derived only if the explicit content of A's utterance is taken to be something like (7c), that is, if *have checked* is interpreted as meaning *have checked today* (Wilson and Sperber 1998). Thus, the recovery of implicatures and the recovery of the explicit content is achieved in parallel, by mutual adjustment of content, context and cognitive effects.

It is important to note that the more specific expectations about how relevance will be achieved are part of this process. Sperber and Wilson (1998:194) put it in this way: 'expectations of relevance warrant the derivation of specific implicatures, for which the explicit content must be adequately enriched.' This claim is best explained by working through some examples of utterances where more specific expectations of relevance are raised. First, consider (8):

(8) A: Did you have a good trip?

B: We were caught in a traffic jam near Mainz.

B's utterance is an indirect answer to A's question. Indirect answers typically raise quite specific expectations of relevance which can be satisfied through the recovery of a small number of strongly communicated implicatures (Sperber and Wilson 1995:194–5). A relevance-theoretic analysis of A's interpretation of B's utterance can be presented in the following list of paraphrases of the mental representations entertained by A in the course of the interpretation process. The source of these representations is indicated in parentheses:

(9) (a) B has said "We were caught in a traffic jam near Mainz." (*Decoding of B's utterance.*)

(b) Information about whether B had a good trip would be relevant to A. (*Assumption made mutually manifest by A's utterance.*)

(c) B's utterance will be optimally relevant to A. (*Presumption of optimal relevance, communicated on the basis of the communicative principle of relevance.*)

(d) B's utterance will be optimally relevant to A by providing information as to whether B had a good trip. (*Expectation of relevance created by A's adopting the presumption of optimal relevance and enriching it in the light of the mutual cognitive environment.*)

(e) B and his passengers were caught in a traffic jam near Mainz on the occasion of the trip in question. (*Development of the logical form of B's utterance. Accepted as the explicature of this utterance.*)

(f) Being caught in a traffic jam is an unpleasant experience. (*Encyclopaedic information. Accepted as an implicated premise.*)

(g) If one had an unpleasant experience on the road, one did not have a good trip. (*Encyclopaedic information. Accepted as an implicated premise.*)

(h) B had an unpleasant experience on the road. (*Follows from the explicature of B's utterance and (f). Implicated conclusion.*)

(i) B did not have a good trip. (*Conclusion from (g) and (h) which satisfies the expectation of relevance (d) raised by B's utterance. Accepted as an implicated conclusion.*)

Notice that there is a highly accessible contextual assumption (9b) detailing the kind of information which A would find relevant if true. A can easily combine the presumption of relevance communicated by the utterance with this contextual information to form the belief in (9d), which amounts to a specific expectation of relevance. Assumptions (9e-i) confirm this expectation, and hence validate the presumption of relevance.

The next example illustrates the role of specific expectations of the joint contribution of several utterances to the overall relevance of a complex stimulus. The example is the first sentence of Wilson and Sperber (2002).

(10) Here are a couple of apparent platitudes.

(11) (a) Wilson and Sperber wrote "Here are a couple of apparent platitudes." (*Decoding of the utterance.*)

(b) The utterance is (the first) part of a complex stimulus, that is, a sequence of utterances. (*Contextual assumption made mutually manifest by the print medium.*)

(c) Wilson and Sperber will produce a complex stimulus which is relevant enough to be worth processing, and is also the most relevant one compatible with their abilities and preferences. (*Presumption of relevance communicated by the utterance given (b). Adopted as general expectation of relevance raised by the discourse.*)

(d) The next utterances are statements of apparent platitudes. (*Development of the logical form the uterance. Accepted as explicature.*)

(e) The next utterances are regarded by some people as platitudes. (*Expectation (derived from (d)) about the content of the following utterances.*)

(f) The next utterances are only apparently platitudes. (*Expectation (derived from (d)) about how subsequent utterances will achieve relevance.*)

In this example, the presumption of relevance is communicated by a complex stimulus since it is mutually manifest from the start that the authors are engaged in producing a complex stimulus. This presumption is accepted by the hearer and creates expectations of relevance for the discourse as a whole. On the basis of this expectation, the audience will not expect a high level of cognitive effects from this utterance, as long as the processing effort needed to interpret it is rewarded later. In this case, there is an easily accessible enrichment of the logical form which, if accepted as the explicature of the utterance, has the potential to raise more specific expectations about the content and relevance of later utterances. These expectations may alter the accessibility of contextual assumptions (see also Wilson and Matsui 1998), by providing easy access to encyclopaedic assumptions about platitudes, and may also alert the reader to look out for reasons why the 'platitudes' to be presented might be only apparent. Furthermore, since some expectations about the relevance of later utterances are already raised at this point, the mutual adjustment of content, context and cognitive effects is made easier. All this warrants the expectation that the effort invested in processing this utterance will be rewarded later.

Specific expectations of relevance have a further property which is worth exploring. They represent the outline of the contents of the expected cognitive effects, that is, they are assumption schemas. Cognitive effects are by definition assumptions which are communicated, that is, assumptions which are represented as the objects of the communicative and informative intention of the speaker. Thus, a more detailed description of the expectation of relevance raised in (10) would be:

(12) Wilson and Sperber intend
the reader to believe
that Wilson and Sperber intend
the reader to believe
that the following text will contain statements which some people treat as platitudes and which Wilson and Sperber believe are not in fact platitudes.

In other words, specific expectations of relevance are metarepresentational schemas the completion of which would validate the presumption of relevance, thus terminating the comprehension procedure. The presence of such a metarepresentational schema might be seen as triggering a search for cognitive effects which would make it complete. According to Sperber and Wilson (1995:266–72) this is an effect-based strategy (driven by a search for specific effects), as opposed to cases where comprehension is largely effort-based (following a path of least effort, with no particular expectations about the type of effects that will result).

It has been argued in the recent relevance-theoretic literature that comprehension is in fact the work of an inferential comprehension module (Sperber 2000b, 1996; Carston 1998c; Nuti 1998; Wilson 2000), which takes ostensive stimuli as input and is presumably a subpart of the theory of mind module, since it must handle quite complex metarepresentations (Nuti 1998; Sperber 2000b; Wilson 2000). The observations made in this section might be seen as providing further speculations about how this module works. First, I noted that comprehension involves the search for an interpretation which confirms the presumption of relevance. The question arises why the presumption triggers a search for validating evidence. The hypothesis that utterance interpretation is the work of a comprehension module may shed some light on this question. The comprehension module takes ostensive stimuli as its input domain; ostensive stimuli communicate a presumption of relevance. The fact that a presumption of relevance is communicated yields a very specific metarepresentation indeed:

(13) S intends
A to know
that S intends
A to believe
that the stimulus is optimally relevant.

I suggest that saying that the comprehension module takes ostensive stimuli as its domain amounts to saying that the relevance-theoretic comprehension procedure is triggered by the detection of communicated presumptions of relevance.

The relevance-theoretic comprehension procedure involves the mutual adjustment of explicit content, context and cognitive effects, guided by more or less specific expectations of relevance. Where the expectations are less specific, the comprehension procedure is largely effort-based: the most easily accessible cognitive effects which yield the expected level of relevance will be accepted as the intended ones. Where the expectations are more specific, the strategy is more effect-based: these expectations are not just about levels of relevance, but about the content of the cognitive effects which might satisfy these expectations. Hence, specific expectations of relevance direct the attention towards contextual assumptions which might yield the expected effects, thus altering the accessibility of contextual assumptions (Wilson and Matsui 1998). In effect, then, these expectations are metarepresentations which restrict the set of assumptions available to the (effort-sensitive) comprehension procedure. I suggest that the comprehension module not only checks for ostensive stimuli and communicated presumptions of relevance, but also for metarepresentations derived in the course of comprehension, which constitute more specific expectations of relevance. The presence of these enables the module to narrow the search for contextual assumptions to be used in the comprehension procedure.

5.4 Expectations of relevance and attention

I suggested in Chapter 2 that global coherence can be accounted for using this notion of expectations of relevance. Now that we have a more elaborated account of how expectations of relevance arise and what their role is, we can return to a discussion of the examples given in that chapter.

I pointed out that the main function of global coherence was to account for the oddity (or unacceptability) of coherent nonsense-texts such as (14) (example (2) in Chapter 2). I also noted that the same text can be made acceptable without any change to its internal relations on either local or global levels, as in example (15) (example (7) in Chapter 2):

(14) Samet and Schank (1984:63), their example (11).

The heads of the city's uniformed services polished their contingency plans for a strike. Queen Wilhelmina finalized her own plans for the evening. In a nearby Danish town, two fishmongers exchanged blows. Anders, by far the stronger, had a cousin in prison. Many criminals are in prison; one might say that a good number of those individuals who have violated the penal code are incarcerated...

(15) The heads of the city's uniformed services polished their contingency plans for a strike. Queen Wilhelmina finalized her own plans for the evening. In a nearby Danish town, two fishmongers exchanged blows. Anders, by far the stronger, had a cousin in prison. Many criminals are in prison; one might say that a good number of those individuals who have violated the penal code are incarcerated...

That was what John Fox remembered from his dreams when he woke up from a healthy sleep. The last two days had been filled with unusual events and strange news. He tried to understand what was going on and wondered what would happen next.

The explanation I gave earlier left the following question open: if addressees tolerate blatant irrelevance for some time, why do they stop processing at some times and not at others?

For the reasons discussed above, an addressee, when presented with an utterance (or other stimulus) which is manifestly low in relevance at the time it is uttered, will presume that the communicator is engaged in producing a complex stimulus, and is currently setting up a context which will facilitate the comprehension of later utterances. This follows from the communicative principle of relevance together with an assumption of the rationality of communicator and addressee. However, for this presumption of relevance of the complex stimulus to be fulfilled, the assumptions used in the interpretation of individual utterances must remain easily accessible, being retained, perhaps, in a kind of memory buffer; see also Sperber and Wilson (1995:138–9). For this to happen, assumptions have to be used in the interpretation process; otherwise they will drop out of the memory buffer. In the case where the following utterances are only partially related and drift off, as in example (14), the assumptions are not re-used, and may be dropped from the memory buffer; as a result, no complex set of assumptions can be inferred which would satisfy expectations of overall relevance of the complex stimulus. However, if a later utterance can achieve relevance by using some of the earlier (mildly) relevant assumptions as context, they will be retrieved and used. It may be argued that when the reader gets to the first sentence of the second paragraph in example (15), the utterances of the first paragraph are re-interpreted as the author's representation of the dreams of John Fox in a state of mind where connectedness of thought is unexpected. Thus, the expectations of overall relevance of the complex stimulus can be met.

5.5 On inferring expectations of relevance

Let us look more closely at the question of how expectations of relevance are inferred. This is best done by considering a complex example, Isaiah 5:1–7 in the Hebrew Bible. This example has been chosen because in the long history of its interpretation it hasn't given rise to major controversies apart from questions concerning its genre (see Wildberger 1972 for a detailed survey). It is therefore uniquely suited to test accounts of genre and global coherence.

(16) (1a) I will sing to my friend/lover a song of my friend to his vineyard. (1b) My friend had a vineyard on a fruitful hilltop (2a) and he dug it up and removed its stones and planted the best species of grapes in it (2b) and he built a tower in its midst, and also a winevat he dug into it. (2c) And he waited for the vineyard to yield good grapes, but it yielded wild (bitter) ones. (3) And now, inhabitants of Jerusalem and people of Judah, judge between me and my vineyard. (4a) What else was there to do for my vineyard which I haven't done, (4b) why did I expect good grapes and it brought forth sour ones? (5a) And now I will let you know what I will do to my vineyard. (5b) I will remove its hedge and it will become firewood. (5c) I will tear down its walls and it will become a trampled land. (6a) I will bring about its peril, it will not be pruned and not be dug, and in it shall grow thorns and thornbushes. (6b) And I will command the clouds to not let rain fall on it (or: ...the clouds to refrain from letting it rain over it) (7) For the house Israel is the vineyard of the Lord of hosts, and the people of Judah are the planting of his delight, and he waited for justice, but there was only injustice (or bloodshed), for righteousness, but there were only cries. (Translation CU; The Hebrew text with morpheme glosses is presented below as the analysis of this text unfolds.)

The task of interpreting an utterance involves the recognition of its explicatures and implicatures. Among the inferential sub-tasks of interpreting the initial utterance (V. 1a) are the following: reference must be assigned to the implicit first person singular pronominal reference in *I will sing...;* furthermore, the ambiguous word *dôd* needs to be disambiguated: this word can mean 'beloved' or 'father's brother.'[3]

V. 1a[4]

ʾā-šîr-â	*nâ*	*lî-dîd-î*	*šîr-aṯ*	*dôd-î*
I-will-sing	HT	to-friend-my	song-of	friend-my

lĕ-ḵarm-ô
to-vineyard-his.

'I will sing to my friend/lover a song of my friend to his vineyard.'

Consider the disambiguation of the word *dôd:* It is manifest to the Hebrew addressees that *dôd* in its meaning 'beloved' is used as a specialised one for the beloved one of a woman in a male-female relationship (in contrast to *dîd* 'friend,' which can be used either to denote a friend in a male-female relationship or to denote a friend in a general sense; its use is not specialised). Hence, the easiest accessible interpretation is that the speaker intended *dôd* to mean 'beloved.' It is further manifest that terms connected to vineyards or orchards are conventionally used as metaphors in talking about a male-female love relationship, comparing the female to the vineyard (or orchard, or fruit, and so on). This contextual assumption is made accessible by the mention of a vineyard in this utterance. Furthermore, this assumption fits in nicely with the concept of male-female relationship, which has been accessed already by the initial assumption that *dôd* means 'beloved.' Hence the provisional interpretation that the speaker intended to convey the meaning 'beloved' by using the word *dôd* is strengthened.

This means that the speaker must be a female partner in a love-relationship. That is, the referent of the implicit pronominal reference to first person singular must be a female speaker, and not the prophet Isaiah (as it appears at first sight).[5] However, since there is no female referent accessible at this point of discourse, the hearer is prompted to construct the concept of a fictitious female referent as the subject of the sentence expressed in the utterance. This concept is then available for reference assignment:

(17) Isaiah is quoting a fictitious female speaker F who says U.
U: [fictitious speaker] will sing to the speaker's friend a song about her beloved and his vineyard.

More formally, the audience will recover a higher-level explicature of U in this way:

(18) Isaiah says
 that F says
 that F will sing for her friend a song about her friend and his vineyard.

Recall that contextual assumptions about use of vocabulary, together with assumptions about the conventional usage of the vineyard-metaphor, made it necessary to recognise that Isaiah was, as it were, quoting a fictitious speaker. This makes manifest that he is speaking indirectly, that the love-song which is being quoted is probably not a real one, that the hearer must engage in a symbolic interpretation, and so on. Thus, concrete expectations of relevance are created. The symbolic interpretation is helped by the further contextual assumption *What is true of the vineyard is true of the beloved,* which is also part of the encyclopaedic entry of the concept LOVE SONG. On the basis of this assumption, the addressee can recognise analogies between vineyards and the beloved of the speaker which satisfy expectations of relevance.

Turning to the question of what is implicitly communicated by this utterance, we must first note that the text occurs after several chapters which focus on proclaiming judgement on God's people. It is manifest that Isaiah has so far mostly engaged in pronouncing God's judgement on Judah. Thus this assumption is highly salient at the time of the utterance:

(19) Isaiah is pronouncing God's judgement on Judah.

It is not obvious how the explicatures of Isaiah 5:1 make it optimally relevant in a context containing this assumption. Hence more inferencing is called for. The concept JUDAH contains an encyclopaedic assumption that Judah is (part of) the elect people of God. This in turn entails that Judah has a special relationship to God. Now, it is also manifest that lovers have a special relationship, this assumption being made accessible by the concept SPECIAL RELATIONSHIP in the above mentioned assumption:

(20) Judah is (part of) the elect people of God.

(21) Judah has a special relationship to God.

(22) Lovers have a special relationship.

A context is therefore accessible in which aspects of a love-relationship expressed in a love song might be expected to also apply to God's relationship with Judah. At this point in the interpretation, two effects are achieved: first, the expectation of relevance which exists at this point in the book of Isaiah (Isaiah pronounces God's judgement on Judah) can be seen to be satisfied in this utterance — which introduces a love-song — by providing a possible context in which a love-song might have implications for the issue of God's relationship with Judah in the light of his intending to bring judgement on it. Second, expectations about the interpretation of the following love-song are raised: correlations between the love-relationship alluded to in the song and God's relationship with Judah in the light of his judgement should be sought. Whereas in the course of inferring the intended explicatures, expectations of relevance were created which led the hearer to seek symbolic interpretations of what follows, these implications create more specific expectations about the direction in which this symbolic interpretation is to be sought. These effects are worth the hearer's attention, and are not too costly to process. Hence this interpretation confirms the presumption of relevance.

Let us return to the question of how expectations of relevance are created. The general presumption of relevance is communicated by every act of ostensive communication, as argued above. The more specific expectations are inferential developments of this general expectation. This process is part of the mutual adjustment of content, context and cognitive effects carried out by the relevance-theoretic comprehension procedure. The more accessible a contextual assumption is, the more likely it is to play a role in constructing specific expectations of relevance. In our example, one easily accessible assumption was derived from cultural knowledge of love-songs and love-imagery. This is not surprising: what makes an assumption cultural is precisely the fact that it has been attractive and fruitful enough to spread through a population (Sperber 1996). Thus, cultural knowledge is by definition frequently used, hence easily accessible, and should have a considerable influence in creating specific expectations of relevance. Insofar as genres are an aspect of culture and are culturally defined, it should not be surprising that genre knowledge can affect expectations of relevance, as the genre love-song proved to affect the understanding of Isaiah 5:1–7.

However, cultural assumptions are not always involved in creating specific expectations of relevance. Notice that assumption (19) was just a relevant summary of the preceding discourse. This assumption played a role over and above the role of genre in establishing expectations about how the following utterances would be relevant.

5.6 Expectations of relevance and connectivity in discourse

Having spelled out in some detail the role of expectations of relevance and how specific expectations of relevance are created by developing the general presumption of relevance, I will now try to illustrate how this notion of expectations of relevance can explain global and local connectivity in discourse more successfully than notions of global coherence. The example is again Isaiah 5:1–7 of the Hebrew Bible, thus extending the analysis proposed in the last section.

Recall that the main concern of accounts of global coherence is to explain the intuition that good texts do not 'drift off,' that there is some kind of coherence over the whole text, and not only between its component clauses or sentences. In previous chapters, several conceptions of global coherence have been discussed: some see it as resulting from an overarching global coherence relation operating on a higher level than local coherence relations (Samet and Schank 1984; Caenepeel 1995), and others see it as resulting from topic relevance. Even a cursory look at Isaiah 5:1–7, example (16) above, makes it clear that accounts of global coherence in terms of an overarching global coherence relation face serious problems: It is unclear what content-based coherence relation could be responsible for the global connectivity of love songs. The approach to global coherence in terms of topic relevance is also problematic: on the face of it, the text shifts from being a lyric song about a vineyard (V. 1 and 2) to what appears to be a direct accusation (V. 7). So what is the topic that links these two? If there are several topics in several units, what are the units, and what binds the topics together? If there is indeed a shift of topic, why does the text intuitively seem coherent as compared with blatantly 'drifting' texts like the one in (14)? Before discussing these problems further, I will now present a relevance-theoretic analysis of this text.

V. 1b

kerem *hāyâ* *lî-dîd-î* *bə-qeren*
vineyard there was to-friend-my in-hilltop
bĕn-šāmen
son-of fat
'my friend had a vineyard on a fruitful hilltop'

V. 2a

wa-yĕ-ˁazzĕqē-hû *wa-yĕ-saqqĕlēhû*
and-he-dug up-it and-he-destoned-it
way-yiṭṭaˁē-hû *sorēq*
and-he planted-it red ones
'and he dug it up and removed its stones and planted soreq-grapes in it'

V. 2b

Way-yiḇen *migdal* *bĕ-ṯôḵ-ô*
and-he-built a-tower in-midst of-it
wĕ-gam=yeqeḇ *ḥaṣēv* *b-ô*
and-also=winevat he dug in-it
'And he built a tower in its midst, and also a winevat he dug into it.'

V. 1b, 2a, 2b all serve to strengthen the assumption that the friend was justified in expecting a good harvest: the vineyard was situated on good soil on a hilltop where the grapes can get enough sunshine, so that they could grow and ripen. The friend invested a lot of work preparing the best ground for the best kind of grapes ('red ones;' these were regarded the best grapes in the Middle East, see Delitzsch 1984). One would expend such effort only if one could expect a good harvest of big ripe grapes. Also, it is likely that winevats are dug with special effort only in good vineyards.

V. 2c

wa-yĕqaw	*la-ˤăśôṯ*	*ˤănāḇîm*
and-he waited	for-to yield	good grapes
way-yaˤas	*bĕʔušîm.*	
and-it yielded	wild grapes	

'and he waited for the vineyard to yield good grapes, but it yielded wild (bitter) ones.'

The first half of this utterance (*wa-yĕqaw la-ˤăśôṯ ˤănāḇîm* — 'and he waited for the vineyard to bring good grapes') satisfies an earlier expectation of relevance by confirming the strongly implicated assumption *The friend is justified in expecting a good crop from the vineyard.* This assumption is contradicted and eliminated by the second part of this utterance. In other words: the second half of this utterance — on the most easily accessible interpretation — has the cognitive effect of contradicting and eliminating an earlier assumption. Does this contribute to satisfying the expectations of relevance created by the utterance? It does not seem to do so if taken as nothing more than narrating what happened to the speaker's friend when he planted his vineyard.[6] However, the expectation of relevance was on several 'levels': first, that the song is a love-song exploiting the imagery of the vineyard for the female part and the love-relationship, and second, that the application of this song to a love-relationship should reveal something about the relationship between God and Judah in the light of the judgement which God is — according to Isaiah, Chapters 1–4 — about to inflict on Judah. It is at these levels that the cognitive effects of this utterance multiply.

In a context containing the assumption *What is true of the vineyard is true of the beloved,* both the assumptions *The friend took great care with the vineyard* and *A good lover takes great care for his beloved and their relationship* can therefore be seen as related.

Thus, by conveying assumptions about the friend taking great care of his vineyard, the speaker can indirectly communicate assumptions about a lover taking great care of his friend and therefore justifiably expecting a rewarding relationship.

The explicature of the second half of this utterance contradicts this assumption. But so would the corresponding assumption based on the analogy between the vineyard and the beloved contradict the others: that is, the expectation of a rewarding relationship is not fulfilled. Assumptions about the human love relationship have (intuitively) a wider 'personal relevance' than assumptions about vineyards: further assumptions about emotional states and life management are activated. All these assumptions are accessible with minimal processing effort, as expectations of relevance created by the utterance of V. 1 guided the search for effects along this path. It is mutually manifest to speaker and hearer that these assumptions increase the relevance of the utterance; hence they are implicatures of this utterance.

Among the assumptions about emotional states and life management made manifest (or more manifest) by this utterance may be the following:

(23) If the friend has done everything for the maintenance of the relationship and his lover behaves as if she were not cared for, then the friend will be outraged.

If the friend is outraged, then he may want to divorce his lover.

The friend may want to divorce his lover.

Divorce includes a court proceeding and a judgement by the elders in the city gate. (Encyclopaedic entry of DIVORCE)

A love song conveys rich assumptions about the beauty of a great relationship.

X's love song conveys assumptions about failure of a relationship and divorce.

The speaker of this song is switching into something like a 'divorce-song,' something for which there is no precedent.[7]

These assumptions are weakly communicated. Notice in particular that they give access to the concept DIVORCE, and more precisely, to certain encyclopaedic assumptions which are likely to constrain further expectations about how the next utterances will be relevant (is the friend seeking divorce? How does this song continue as the curious case of a 'divorce song?').

Notice that the expectations of relevance created in V. 1 lead the hearer to expect the love relationship portrayed in this song to reveal something about God's relationship to Judah. This assumption leads the reader/hearer to look for relevance by exploring further possible analogies:

(24) The fictional speaker of the love song intends to make manifest that X took the best possible care of the vineyard.
What is true of the vineyard is true of the beloved.

A good lover takes the best possible care of his beloved and their relationship.
What is true of good lovers is true of God.

God cares to his very best for Judah and their relationship.

If a lover takes the very best care of his beloved and their relationship, he is justified in expecting a rewarding relationship.
What is true of the lover is true of the vineyard.

The lover is justified in expecting a rewarding relationship.

> If a gardener takes the best possible care of his vineyard, he is justified in expecting a rewarding crop.
>
> What is true of the gardener is true of God.
>
> If God takes the best possible care of Judah and their relationship, he is justified in expecting a rewarding relationship.
>
> A rewarding relationship between God and men is indicated by godly behaviour of men.
>
> ---
>
> God is justified in expecting godly behaviour from Judah.

Again, this assumption is contradicted by the second part of this utterance. Contrary to justified expectations, Judah did not show godly behaviour. This in turn is likely to trigger many more assumptions about the significance of men not pleasing God and the consequences thereof.

Furthermore, the assumption that God takes the best possible care of Judah and their relationship is likely to significantly modify the cognitive environment of the addressees of Isaiah's performance of this song, as they apparently did not entertain or believe it, or even rejected it as false:

V. 3

wĕ-ˁattâ *yôšēḇ* *yĕrûšālayim* *wĕ-ˀîš*
and-now inhabitants of Jerusalem and-man of
yĕhûdâ, *šip̱ṭû=nâ* *bên-î* *û-ḇen*
Judah, judge=HT between-me and-between
karm-î.
vineyard-mine.

'And now, inhabitants of Jerusalem and people of Judah, judge between me and my vineyard.'

The addressees will have encyclopaedic knowledge about making judgements: a judgement is a part of a court proceeding, which takes place in the city gate and which involves the elders of the city as well as bystanders. In the preceding utterance, the concept DIVORCE was already made accessible. This concept will have among its encyclopaedic entries some specifying that a divorce procedure includes a court proceeding and a judgement by the elders in the city gate, that the divorce proceedings include the initiating party bringing forth his charges before the elders of the city in the city gate, and that the proceedings of the elders in the city gate are watched by many citizens of the city.

These assumptions provide bridges for reference assignment: the speaker is the friend, the party who brings forth his charges, and the addressees are the elders and bystanders of the court proceeding.

Note that this example poses problems for the theory of bridging of Asher and Lascarides (1998a). These authors maintain that bridging inferences are made in the process of establishing a discourse representation, on the basis of coherence relations. Isaiah 5:3, however, is intuitively rather unconnected to V. 2 if the bridging assumptions listed above are not recognised. This is evidenced for example by the fact that Delitzsch (1984:75) maintains that the song of the vineyard ends with V. 2. While maintaining that the vineyard song continues after V. 2, Motyer (1993:68–9) groups V. 3–4 together as one unit, distinct from V. 1b-2. This, too, illustrates the perception of a certain unconnectedness between V. 3 and the preceding verse.

Even having established the connection with the previous utterances, it seems quite unclear how this relation could be labelled in terms of formal coherence relations. Maybe one candidate that comes to mind is the relation RESULT: the speech-act of V. 3 (that is, bringing divorce charges in court) is the result of the state described in V. 2 (the unexpected disappointment). It is obvious that recognition of this relation is parasitic on a whole range of inferences (including the ones outlined above), and indeed on an elaborate understanding of the utterances concerned.

In other words: this relation is inferable only upon a 'full integration' of the utterance into world knowledge. According to Asher and Lascarides (1998a), bridging inferences fall outside the stage in discourse interpretation which deals with the integration of the discourse into world-knowledge. This example suggests that this cannot be the case. Thus, it is indirect evidence for the account of bridging in relevance theory (Wilson 1992; Matsui 1995; Wilson and Matsui 1998).

The text continues as follows:

V. 4a

mah=la-ˤăsôṯ *ˤôd* *lĕ-ḵarm-î* *wĕ-loˀ*
what=for-to do more to-vineyard-mine and-not
ˤāsî-ṯî *b-ô,*
have done-I for-it,
'What else was there to do for my vineyard which I haven't done?'

The persistent analogical interpretation of the vineyard as representing the beloved will allow the hearer to understand the speaker as implicating assumptions about his innocence, and conveying the further implication that as the innocent party in the failure of the relationship, he is justified in bringing divorce charges. This in turn is expected from the one bringing charges in a divorce case. That is, expectations of relevance are confirmed in this interpretation (which is accessible at minimal cost).

Let's turn to the next utterance:

V. 4b

maddûaˤ *qiwwē-ṯî* *la-ˤăsôṯ* *ˤănāḇîm*
why have waited-I to-bring good grapes
way-yaˤas *bĕˀušîm?*
and-it brought sour grapes?
' Why did I expect good grapes and it brought forth sour ones?'

The explicature of this utterance can be represented as follows, taking into account the relevance-theoretic semantics of questions as metarepresentations of relevant answers (Sperber and Wilson 1995:252):

> It is relevant to the speaker to know and the responsibility of the hearer to provide a reason why the friend expected good grapes but the vineyard produced bad ones.

The relevance of such an answer would lie in contradicting and eliminating the speaker's belief (communicated by that last utterance) that there is no reason why the vineyard should produce bad fruit. Because he has indicated that he holds this belief quite strongly (he has produced evidence for this), at the same time it becomes manifest to the audience that the speaker intends them to hold this belief, too.

Again, the word 'vineyard' is understood by way of analogy. On this interpretation the utterance achieves relevance by strengthening assumptions about the innocence of the speaker, the guilt of the lover, and the justification of the divorce demand, and so on. Notice that this requires other analogies to be made: producing good grapes as enjoying a rewarding relationship, and producing sour grapes as breach of a good relationship. This analogy-based interpretation is probably facilitated by knowledge of the use of vineyard-imagery in love-songs (that is, genre knowledge).

Consider now V. 5a:

V. 5a

wĕ-ˁattâ	*ˀôdîˁâ=nâ*	*ˀeṯ-ḵem*	*ˀēṯ*
and-now	I let know=HT	ACC-you	ACC

ˀăšer=ˀănî	*ˁoseh*	*lĕ-ḵarm-î*
what=I	do.PCP	to-vineyard-mine

'And now I will let you know what I will do to my vineyard.'

This sounds like the announcement of a verdict. It is inconsistent with the divorce procedure setting that the accuser presents his own verdict. However, in the beginning the expectation was created, that the utterances that follow will also have implications about God's relationship to Judah, his chosen people. The intended reader's general encyclopaedic knowledge includes the information that God has repeatedly presented himself as one who loves his people and has invoked the human love relationship comparison. This general encyclopaedic knowledge also includes the information that God can rightfully judge people and that he is also the one who can make true accusations. Thus, this utterance and the following ones can be expected to receive a consistent interpretation on this level of relevance expectations. Notice, though, that this interpretation demands a second-order analogical interpretation of the word 'vineyard:' the 'lover' is to be understood as 'the people of Judah.' This latest turn in the interpretation of the word 'vineyard' also gives the hearer easy access to assumptions about the use of 'vineyard' imagery as relating to the people of Judah as a nation-state, a figure of speech used for example in Isaiah 3:14–15:

> The Lord enters into judgment against the elders and leaders of his people: "It is you who have ruined my vineyard; the plunder from the poor is in your houses. What do you mean by crushing my people and grinding the faces of the poor?" declares the Lord, the LORD Almighty. (New International Version)

In other words: the expectation is created that the utterances which follow may achieve relevance by implicating assumptions about God's relation to the people of Judah as a nation or state. This sets the stage for V. 5b:

V. 5b[8]

ʔāśîr	*mĕśûkāṯ-ô*	*wĕ-hāyāh*
I will remove	hedge-its	and-it will become

lĕ-ḇāʕēr
to-firewood
'I will remove its hedge and it will become firewood'

In the previous utterance, expectations of relevance led in the direction of interpreting the vineyard metaphor in a wider sense as being symbolic of Israel-Judah as a nation-state. An easily accessible analogy can be seen to hold between the outer fence of a vineyard and the outer border area of a state. This, together with the encyclopaedic knowledge that setting fire to houses and fields is a method of warfare, yields inferences to the effect that God (resembling the owner of the vineyard) will let the outer border region of Judah be captured by foreign forces (who can be expected to use their normal methods of warfare).

This brings us to V. 5c:

V. 5c

pāroṣ	*gĕḏēr-ô*	*wĕ-hāyā*
I tear down	wall-its	and-it will become

lĕ-mirmāś
to-trampled land

'I will tear down its walls and it will become a trampled land'

By a similar line of interpretation to the one taken in the previous utterance, the wall of the vineyard may be seen as intended to resemble the inner border area of the nation-state of Judah. Then, by inferences parallel to those used in interpreting the last utterance, the utterance will yield implications to the effect that Isaiah is predicting that God will also let the inner border areas of Judah (that is, the individual fortress towns) be captured by foreign forces.

To survey the overall on-line interpretation of V. 6a, it is helpful to break it down into two parts, V. 6aa and V. 6ab respectively:

V. 6aa

wa-ʾăšîṯē-hû	*ḇāṯāh*	*loʾ*	*yiz-zāmēr*
and-bring-for him	peril	not	it-will be pruned

wĕ-lô	*yeʿāḏēr*
and-not	it-will be dug

'I will bring about its peril, it will not be pruned and not be dug,'

This utterance unit will easily give rise to the following implications:

(25) If a vineyard is not cared for, the plants will grow wild.
The friend does not care for the vineyard any more.

The plants will grow wild.

If the plants grow wild, then no fruit can be expected any more.

The plants will grow wild (contextual effect of previous inference).

No-one can expect any fruit from the vineyard any more.

If a vineyard is not cared for, then wild bushes will grow and take over.

The friend does not care for the vineyard any more.

Wild bushes will grow and take over.

The explicature of the second part of this utterance (V. 6ab) strengthens the last implicature of the previous part of this utterance:

V. 6ab

wĕ-ˁāl-āh šāmîr wā-šāyiṯ
and-on-it thorns and-thornbushes,
'and in it shall grow thorns and thornbushes.'

This process of anticipating the consequence of an action by implication and then explicitly confirming it has the effect of highlighting the fact that this time natural expectations are confirmed, by contrast with the situation described earlier where justified expectations blatantly failed to come true.

The expectations of relevance created so far prompt the reader to look for symbolic interpretations making use of the vineyard imagery on two levels: that of the love relationship and that of the nation-state relation of Judah to God. On both levels, relevant cognitive effects multiply. Not being cared for by God effectively means that Judah is no longer in a special relationship with God, and that *thorns will take over* can be interpreted as implying that the people of Judah will cease to live in the land and other people will come to inhabit this land. Thus it could be seen as a (veiled) prediction of the Babylonian exile. This is consistent with the symbolic interpretation of the previous verse as implying that the outer and inner borders of the country will be destroyed. It is also consistent with a recurring theme in the book of Isaiah, even in the Chapters 1–4.

Now consider V. 6b:

V. 6b

wĕ-ˤal he-ˤāḇîm ˀă-ṣawweh mē-hamṭîr ˤālāy-w
and-to the-clouds I-command from-raining on-it
māṭār.
rain.

'And I will command the clouds not to let rain fall on it.' (Or: '. . . the clouds to refrain from letting it rain over it.')

The original hearer presumably had easy access to the encyclopaedic information that only God controls the rain. In a context containing this assumption, the fact that the friend is quoted as saying *I will command the clouds not to let rain fall on it* will yield the implication that the 'friend' must be God. This identification of the 'friend' is no longer easily compatible with the scenarios of a lover singing about her friend. Thus, the relevance of this utterance is expected to rest only in the symbolic implications. These suggest that God is threatening to bring about complete destruction.

Finally, Isaiah talks explicitly about the intended meaning of the text:

V. 7

kî kerem YHWH ṣĕḇāˀoṯ bēyṯ yisrāˀēl
For vineyard of God of hosts house Israel
wĕ-ˀîš yĕhûḏāh nĕṭaˤ šaˤăšûˤāy-w
and-man of Judah planting of delight-his,
wa-yĕ-qaw lə-mišpāṭ wĕ-hinneh mispāḥ,
and-he-waited for-justice and-behold injustice,
li-ṣdāqāh wĕ-hinnēh ṣĕˤāqāh.
for-righteousness and-behold cries.

> 'For the house of Israel is the vineyard of the Lord of hosts, and the people of Judah are the planting of his delight, and he waited for justice, but there was only injustice (or *bloodshed*; the meaning of this word in Hebrew is uncertain), for righteousness, but there were only cries.'

The prediction, made in the last utterance, that God is threatening to bring about complete destruction of Judah calls for justification. It is in strong contradiction to the expectations of the originally intended audience — the people of Judah — who presumably thought themselves in a special covenant relation with God. The particle *kî* indicates that the author intended this verse (utterance) to be relevant as a justification of this provocative statement (see Follingstad 2001 for a detailed analysis of this particle). The wording of this utterance is such that it leads the hearer to relive the interpretive stages of the preceding symbolic literary piece: The vineyard is indeed a metaphor for the house of Judah, the house of Judah and Israel was indeed God's beloved, whom he cared for and from whom he could have truly expected a reciprocal relationship, which would be seen in godly behaviour. This godly behaviour would include conforming to the terms of the covenant, that is, behaving righteously. But the people of Judah and Israel are lacking this virtue; now what would be done with a vineyard which doesn't bear good fruit? What would a lover do with his friend who for no apparent reason doesn't respond to his love? The hearer is pointed back to the interpretation process he went through before.

We are now in a position to compare this relevance-theoretic explanation of the connectivity of this text with a topic-based global coherence account. Notice that the specific expectations of relevance created by the introductory part of V. 1 (discussed in the last section) were enough to guide the comprehension procedures for all parts of this text in a way that leads to many cognitive effects with little processing effort, that is, radical context shifts are avoided. Specifically, this interpretation strategy allows for a rich interpretation of crucial analogies on several levels of symbolic interpretation. These expectations had to be only minimally adjusted to realise a certain shift in the use of the vineyard metaphor within this passage. Notice that many interpreters (for example Delitzsch 1984) tend to allow only one consistent interpretation of the vineyard metaphor within a passage. However, if the vineyard metaphor in the first part of this text (V. 1–4) were to be understood as symbolising Judah as a nation, as seems to be required in V. 6, then many of the points made in the first part of this text could not be appreciated; indeed, the above analysis would suggest that the connection between V. 2 and V. 3 would be totally lost. Conversely, if the vineyard metaphor were understood only as symbolising the lover and alluding to a love relationship, then V. 6 would sound strange. Moreover, V. 7 seems to combine both interpretations of the metaphor: the 'vineyard' is 'the planting of God's delight' and this is the people of Judah and Israel — both the special relationship of this people to God, which is characterised by affection on God's part, and the nationhood of Judah are alluded to. Thus, one must not only **allow** the vineyard metaphor to receive slightly different interpretations within this text, but also allow both interpretations to **occur together**. This is achieved in the relevance-theoretic account by taking expectations of overall relevance of complex stimuli to guide the interpretation of the utterances in sequence.

One of the most striking consequences of this analysis is the explanation of the connectivity between V. 2 and V. 3. Expectations of relevance regarding the symbolic interpretation of the text led to the provision of bridging assumptions for the interpretation of V. 3, in this case assumptions about divorce proceedings. I argued above that these inferences could not have been recognised on the basis of coherence relations. Also, knowledge about the conventional use of the vineyard imagery in love-songs was essential in making these inferences accessible. This is arguably an influence of genre knowledge. Notice that this influence of genre on the interpretation of texts could not have been mediated through notions of coherence, local or global.

It can be concluded, then, that the connectivity of this text can only be successfully explained as a result of inference processes guided by specific expectations of relevance which were created in V. 1 and further elaborated in the course of the text.

5.7 Summary and conclusion

In this chapter, I have developed the relevance-theoretic claim that more or less specific expectations of relevance guide the inferential comprehension procedure. Sperber and Wilson (1995) argued that every act of ostensive communication communicates a presumption of its own optimal relevance. This means that the general presumption of optimal relevance is one of the assumptions which the communicator intends to make manifest (or more manifest) by means of his utterance. I argued that specific expectations of relevance may not only concern the relevance of single utterances, but also the joint contribution of several utterances to the overall relevance of a complex ostensive stimulus. Such expectations arise when it is manifest to the audience that the communicator is producing a complex ostensive stimulus (where a discourse is seen as a special case of a complex ostensive stimulus). Specific expectations of relevance arise as developments of the general presumption of relevance communicated by every act of ostensive communication. I argued that this conception of expectations of relevance can better explain intuitions of global connectivity of texts than existing accounts of global coherence. It was also argued that genre information, being highly accessible cultural information, can contribute to the formation of specific expectations of relevance. In the next chapter I want to apply this explanation of the working of expectations of relevance to issues surrounding the theory of genre.

6 Expectations of relevance, implicit questioning in discourse, and genre

6.1 Introduction

In the last chapter, I looked at the notion of expectations of relevance and their role in the interpretation of discourse. In this chapter, I want to extend my account to a number of issues related to genre. I will argue that issues relating to the role of implicit questions in discourse and the origin of narrative structure should be re-examined in this light. To the extent that genre can be seen as influencing and constraining the kind of implicit questions which arise in a discourse, I will argue that expectations of relevance should play a central role in the analysis of genre. I also hope to show that experimental data usually taken to provide psycholinguistic evidence for a cognitive role of genre can be re-analysed using the notion of expectations of relevance.

6.2 Implicit questioning in discourse and expectations of relevance

At various points in this book I have alluded to the role of implicit questioning in discourse, and discussed theories which take as a guiding principle to account for discourse structure the intuition that implicit questions are answered in discourse (Klein and von Stutterheim 1987; van Kuppevelt 1995a,b, 1996). These researchers also suggest that genre information can be seen as placing constraints on which implicit questions will arise. In the relevance theory literature, this intuition has also been mentioned as one of the recurrent intuitions about discourse structure which most analysts share. In this section I want to examine these intuitions on a deeper level, showing that they can be explained in terms of the way expectations of relevance are raised and managed in on-line utterance interpretation. If this is true, it follows that all the effects of genre which might be attributed to the role of implicit questions in discourse comprehension can instead be explained by appeal to expectations of relevance.

6.2.1 Conjunction, juxtaposition and implicit questioning

Carston (1993) investigates some pragmatic properties of conjoined and juxtaposed sentences such as those in (1) and (2):

(1) a. Susan worked hard on her thesis today and she is exhausted.

b. Susan worked hard on her thesis today; she is exhausted.

(2) a. Susan is exhausted; she worked hard on her thesis today.

b. Susan is exhausted and she worked hard on her thesis today.

In (1a), it would generally be understood that a causal relation holds between the clauses: the first clause is presented as causing the eventuality described in the second one. This causal relation must be pragmatically inferred: it is not due to the semantics of *and*, as is shown by (1b), where the same relation holds between juxtaposed clauses. Whatever the pragmatic explanation for the causal readings in (1), it must also allow for the data in (2), where the order of the clauses is reversed. Here, conjunction and juxtaposition differ in the pragmatic readings they allow: (2a) suggests a causal relation analogous to that in (1): *She worked hard on her thesis today* (here the second clause) describes the reason why Susan is exhausted (here the first clause). However, this causal reading is not possible in the conjunction (2b).

Carston (1993) proposes an explanation of this pragmatic phenomenon which makes crucial use of the intuition that implicit questions are raised during discourse comprehension. The explanation runs roughly as follows: conjoined sentences are seen as constituting a single utterance, that is, as creating a single presumption of optimal relevance. Not so for juxtaposition: here the clauses are treated as separate utterances, with separate presumptions of relevance. It follows that in a juxtaposed utterance, the first clause may (implicitly) raise a question, and it may be relevant to interpret the second clause as answering this question. The question is often a *why*-question, whose answer may provide an explanation either in analytical or causal terms. In the relevance-theoretic framework, it is plausible to assume that our cognitive systems are geared to look for explanations, which contribute substantially to relevance.

Carston (1993:42) further points out that this analysis carries over to cases such as (3) where the questions raised are not strictly linked to explanation:

(3)
a. I ate somewhere nice last week; I ate at MacDonalds.
b. I ate somewhere nice last week and I ate at MacDonalds.
c. I met a great actress at the party; I met Vanessa Redgrave.
d. I met a great actress at the party and I met Vanessa Redgrave.
(Carston 1993:42; examples suggested by Deirdre Wilson)

So the main point is: in juxtaposed sentences, there are separate units of processing (utterances) which create individual presumptions of relevance. In this situation, the first utterance may be designed to raise a question which the following utterance is designed to answer. This is not possible in conjoined utterances, which are designed to be processed as a unit. *Why*-questions are more likely to come to mind, because the cognitive system is geared to look for explanations; but as (3) shows, other questions can also be raised.

How are these implicit questions raised? In Carston's examples in (3), it looks as if some element in the propositional form of the utterance was ostensively underdetermined: 'somewhere' in (3a), 'a great actress' in (3c). It is manifest that these utterances could be made more relevant by supplying the missing information: where did the speaker eat in (3a), and who was the great actress the speaker met in (3c). A speaker aiming at optimal relevance should provide this information as long as she is willing and able to do so. Thus an expectation of relevance is created for the following utterance. This expectation concerns the types of cognitive effects to be achieved. Thus the interpretation strategy is largely effect-based.

There are cases where there is no blatant underdeterminacy of the type created by 'somewhere' or 'a great actress' in (3):

(4) a. Jim has a new girlfriend. He goes to New York every weekend. (Carston 1993:43)

b. Peter went hiking last Sunday. He walked all the way from Imsbach to Steinbach.

I suggest that in these examples no question need be implicitly raised by the interpretation of the first utterance. Rather, in interpreting the second utterance, the hearer is constrained by the relevance-theoretic comprehension procedure to seek relevance with as little context change as possible. If adequate cognitive effects are found in a context made easily accessible by the interpretation of the previous utterance, the hearer is justified in accepting it as the intended one.[1] This interpretation will achieve a relevance relation to the previous utterance - by justifying or providing evidence for it, for example. Here the interpretation strategy is mostly effort-based.

Notice that in this last case, the interpretation is not necessarily driven by an implicit question raised by the first utterance, though it may be described in this way after the interpretation has taken place and may suggest that such a question would have been appropriate. In the examples in (4), the hearer's aim is to establish the relevance of the second utterance in a context created by the first one. In the examples in (3), the hearer's goal is to find additional effects which the first utterance has led him to expect.

In other words, we can distinguish cases where it is plausible that an 'implicit question' is actually raised in the process of utterance comprehension and cases where the comprehension process itself does not include this but could be described as if there had been an implicit question raised (such cases are sometimes described in the literature as involving 'accommodation'). In the first type of case, the comprehension process is mostly effect-driven, and in the second, it is mostly effort-driven. It is conceivable that there could be intermediate cases. In any case, it appears that the expression 'an implicit question is raised' is a pre-theoretical description which plays no theoretical role; it is expectations of cognitive effects which account for the intuition that 'an implicit question is raised.'

6.2.2 Implicit questioning, topic and focus

In the relevance-theoretic framework, implicit questioning has also been described as occurring in the on-line interpretation of a single utterance. Sperber and Wilson (1995:202–17), in their account of topic and focus, appeal to the intuition that implicit questions are raised in discourse in the context of developing a relevance-theoretic account of the on-line processing of utterances.[2] Thus, in interpreting the utterance *Jennifer admitted stealing*, the hearer comes across the first constituent *Jennifer*, which is a noun phrase. The syntactic anticipatory hypothesis can then be formed that the noun phrase will be followed by a verb phrase (based on facts about the grammar of English). By substitution of logical variables for syntactic labels, the hearer can form the corresponding logical hypothesis that the proposition expressed will convey the information that someone called Jennifer did something. Here an appropriate referent has to be assigned to the noun phrase *Jennifer.* Suppose that the hearer has a context easily accessible in which the assumption that *Jennifer O'Hara did something* is relevant. By the relevance-theoretic comprehension procedure, the hearer is entitled to take the speaker as intending to refer to Jennifer O'Hara, since this is the first accessible hypothesis that looks likely to yield adequate cognitive effects.

Consider now an alternative scenario: at the stage where the hearer has formed the hypothesis that someone called Jennifer did something, there is no obvious assignment of reference (to Jennifer O'Hara, Jennifer Smith, or other candidate referents) on which this assumption would be relevant to the hearer. In this case it may be manifest to the hearer that a completion of the assumption schema *Jennifer O'Hara did X* or *Jennifer Smith did X* would be relevant to him.[3] In this case, he is again entitled to assign reference accordingly and expect the rest of the utterance to satisfy this more specific expectation of relevance. Sperber and Wilson (1995:207) put it this way: the utterance, on this assignment of reference, raises at this stage of processing the relevant question *What did Jennifer O'Hara do?* This question is relevant in the sense that an answer to it is likely to be relevant to the hearer.

Notice that the intuition that a relevant question has been raised can be further analysed in theoretical terms: the assumption schema creates a specific expectation of relevance, but is not determinate enough to yield enough cognitive effects to satisfy this expectation. This triggers an effect-driven processing strategy designed to satisfy the expectation of relevance.

Comparing the processing accounts of juxtaposition (Carston) and focus (Sperber and Wilson 1995), an apparent inconsistency arises. Carston's account of juxtaposition and conjunction rests on the assumption that the 'unit of processing' is the sentence. 'Implicit questions' are raised by an utterance which as a unit creates an expectation of optimal relevance. Sperber and Wilson's account of focus considers on-line processing within the utterance, and assumes that implicit questions can be raised by syntactic constituents of the sentence uttered. It is certainly true that, intuitively, implicit questions may be raised both during the interpretation of a single utterance, and as a result of interpreting an utterance. But if this is so, there is a problem for Carston's account: the question arises why in our original problematic example (2b), no implicit *why*-question is raised as part of the on-line interpretation of the utterance. Carston's account, of course, relies on the fact that no such question does arise.

I would like to suggest that this tension can be resolved by analysing the intuition that implicit questions are raised both in utterance and discourse interpretation by appeal to expectations of relevance. Consider the sources of the presumption of optimal relevance communicated by an act of ostensive verbal communication. A linguistic stimulus is automatically analysed by the linguistic input module, which automatically expends the required processing effort. As a result, an expectation of relevance is created (Sperber and Wilson 1995:177–8). Such expectations of cognitive effect are created throughout the processing of a linguistic stimulus. Thus, even if the hearer of the utterance *Jennifer admitted stealing* has a context available in which the assumption *Jennifer O'Hara did something* is relevant, he will continue processing until he retrieves the propositional form of the utterance, which could be informally represented as *Jennifer O'Hara confessed to stealing something at* $t_{[past]}$. On the other hand, when no further linguistic processing is required, the search for higher-level explicatures and implicatures will continue only until the expectations of relevance already created by the utterance are satisfied. In this way one can distinguish on a principled basis between on-line processing within a sentential utterance, and on-line processing of utterances in sequence, while maintaining a unified view of the driving forces behind the respective phenomena: the search for an interpretation which will satisfy the expectations of relevance created by the act of communication concerned.

6.2.3 Implicit questioning in bridging reference

Wilson and Matsui (1998) show how the relevance-theoretic comprehension procedure can account for bridging reference by analysing a straightforward example:

(5) (their example 22b)
Sara left Australia for England. She hates the sandy beaches.

In an experiment carried out by Matsui (1995), 100% of subjects agreed that the sandy beaches refers to the beaches in Australia rather than England. This can be explained by noting that Australia is the most easily accessible antecedent for bridging reference here, for several reasons. Furthermore, on this assignment of reference the second sentence can be seen as answering a question which is implicitly raised by the first sentence (*Why did Sara leave Australia for England?*) At this point, Wilson and Matsui note that what they mean by saying that the first part of the utterance raises an implicit question is nothing more than saying that it provides easy access to a context in which an answer to such a question would be adequately relevant to the hearer. In other words: the intuition that an implicit question is raised finds a deeper explanation in the way this sequence of utterances is processed for relevance. It seems that this example can be most easily explained as involving an effort-driven strategy for establishing the relevance of the second utterance in the context created by the first one. However, since the human cognitive system is disposed to search for causal connections,[4] one might argue that after processing the first utterance, the hearer may be expecting some sort of causal explanation (albeit weakly so).

In discussing another clear-cut case of bridging reference assignment, Wilson and Matsui (1998) point out that the 'implicit questions' raised in discourse need not be specific. For example, the first part of the utterance in (6) may give rise to a certain range of questions, which can be indicated as in (6 a.-c.). If *The traffic* is understood as referring to the traffic in town — a referent which is easily accessible and does not incur much processing effort — the second part of (6) can be seen as achieving relevance by providing answers to some such questions:

(6) I prefer the town to the country. The traffic doesn't bother me. (Wilson and Matsui's 1998 example 33)

a. Isn't the town too noisy?

b. Wouldn't she rather have the quiet of the country?

c. Isn't there anything she dislikes about the town?

(a.-c. are Wilson and Matsui's 1998 example 34)

Another way of presenting this analysis might run as follows: an easily accessible context for interpreting the utterance *I prefer the town to the country* is one which contains the assumption people normally prefer the country to town and lists several stereotypical reasons for this preference, including — among others — the assumption *The traffic in towns usually bothers people.* A speaker uttering *I prefer the town to the country* must therefore implicitly reject some of these assumptions, that is, imply that she doesn't herself share them. It is with this expectation about kinds of effects that the hearer will embark on interpreting the second part of the utterance, *The traffic doesn't bother me.* On the easily accessible assumption that the traffic refers to the traffic in the town, this part of the utterance will confirm the expectation: the speaker is herself rejecting one of the stereotypical reservations people have about towns. Thus it seems that the intuition that implicit questions are raised can be explained in a deeper sense by appealing to the way expectations of relevance are raised by (parts of) utterances. These expectations may be more or less specific in content, prompting largely effect-based or largely effort-based strategies of comprehension.

6.2.4 Question-based accounts of discourse structure

The question-based accounts of discourse structure proposed by Klein and von Stutterheim (1987) and van Kuppevelt (1991, 1995a,b, 1996) were discussed in detail in Chapters 3 and 4. I found them wanting for various reasons. However, I also pointed out that they are based on an important intuition: that the organisation of discourse is intricately linked to intuitions of 'aboutness,' that is, to intuitions of what the discourse segments and the discourse as a whole are about. In this section, I want to argue that this 'aboutness' of discourse is a natural consequence of the cognitive and communicative principles of relevance.

Consider the definition of relevance: information is relevant to an individual to the extent that it achieves positive cognitive effects in some context available to the individual, and to the extent that the processing effort needed to achieve these is low. Positive cognitive effects are contextual effects which are actually true, thus genuinely enhancing the individual's representation of the world. To achieve positive cognitive effects, it is necessary for this new information to combine with contextual assumptions. Information is relevant only if it achieves such effects. This could be paraphrased in another way: information is relevant only if it is related to some other information available to the individual. Consider now the ordinary language use of 'about.' This word is standardly used in exchanges like the one in (7):

(7) Peter: What was John's talk about?
Mary: His talk was about the syntax of prepositional phrases.

If Peter is a syntactician and has access to assumptions about syntactic theory, then he will get some idea of what John's talk was about. If not, he may well continue to say 'I have no idea what this is.' This indicates that at least some intuitions of what some utterance (or discourse) is about are connected to the availability of contextual assumptions which can be expected to bear on the understanding of it (in this case of John's talk). In other words: 'aboutness' seems to be intricately linked to relevance, and intuitions of what an utterance or discourse is about can be at least partially explained by the relevance-theoretic definition of relevance (compare Sperber and Wilson 1995:246 footnote 5).

Indeed, Sperber and Wilson's (1995) account of topic and focus, foreground and background can be seen as an explication of the pre-theoretic notion of 'aboutness' in terms of relevance. In essence, the topic provides access to contextual information which allows the addressee to compute the intended cognitive effects of the focus, that is, realise what the focus is 'about.' I have also shown that the intuition that (implicit) questions are raised in discourse could be re-analysed in terms of the way expectations of relevance are raised in comprehension. Therefore the intuitions of (implicit) questioning in discourse, 'aboutness' and topicality which van Kuppevelt (1995a) seeks to capture, are accounted for in relevance theory by the very definition of relevance and the notion of expectations of relevance.

Van Kuppevelt (1995a) also seeks to account for discourse organisation: he claims that his notion of topic can account for the hierarchical structure of discourse. I have argued in Chapter 3 that his arguments do not go through.

In Unger (1996) I have argued (following suggestions by Blass 1990) for a dynamic rather than hierarchical account of discourse organisation following from the communicative principle of relevance. According to this principle, considerations of processing effort normally require communicators to construct their discourses (that is, sequences of utterances) in such a way that the audience does not need to access radically different contexts from utterance to utterance. Thus, normally a discourse will adhere to a 'theme,' and shifts in 'sub-themes' will be kept to a minimum. Sometimes more substantial shifts in context are unavoidable; after such shifts (that is, at paragraph boundaries), it will be relatively effort-consuming to refer back to a participant in the previous paragraph with a pronoun, or to use a single utterance in the previous paragraph, rather than the whole paragraph, as antecedent to a discourse connective. However, if expectations of effect are specific enough, the accessibility of contextual assumptions may alter, and participants in previous paragraphs may become accessible to pronominal reference, or single utterances in previous paragraphs may become accessible as antecedents for discourse connectives, yielding an interpretation which satisfies the hearer's expectations of relevance.

It appears, then, that the relevance-theoretic approach to global coherence in terms of expectations of relevance developed in the last chapter does indeed capture the points on which topic-based accounts of global coherence, discourse structure and genre were right: that intuitions of 'aboutness' underlie the notions of topic and focus, and also of discourse organisation. My account differs from these topic-based accounts in that it treats the intuitions that (implicit) questions arise in discourse, which have been invoked to explain various aspects of global coherence such as topicality, grounding, and discourse organisation (Klein and von Stutterheim 1987; von Stutterheim 1997; van Kuppevelt 1995a), as following from the cognitive notion of relevance and the communicative principle of relevance. It avoids the problems which arise out of van Kuppevelt's (1995b) claim that discourse is hierarchically structured.[5] It can also, unlike van Kuppevelt's approach (1995a; 1995b; 1996), account for both the unacceptability of (2) in Chapter 2 and the acceptability of (7) in Chapter 2, as argued in the last chapter. Moreover, the communicative principle of relevance applies to every instance of ostensive communication, and hence to verbal communication. It is therefore possible to account for intuitive restrictions even on free, discontinuous discourse (in the sense of van Kuppevelt 1995a; see Chapter 3): even in such a discourse the sequence of utterances is constrained by the accessibility of contexts. However, the accessibility of contexts is not determined solely by choice of topic. Thus it is possible to analyse discourse in more subtle ways than the notion of topic would allow. It follows that a discourse typology such as the one discussed in Chapter 3 (van Kuppevelt 1995a) is not necessary and can be dropped from the theory of discourse.

Turning more specifically to genre, the *quaestio* theory of Klein and von Stutterheim (1987) and von Stutterheim (1997) and the topic-based theory of van Kuppevelt (1995a,b, 1996) share an interesting insight: the type of question which the text (or discourse) appears to answer can account for the genre-specific structure of the text. Thus, a narrative of a personal experience answers the question *What happened to you at* $t_1 \ldots t_n$*?* As a result, the mainline utterances in the text describe punctiliar, sequential events and the predicates involved tend to follow the familiar restrictions (Hopper 1979; Hopper and Thompson 1980; see Chapter 4). A description of one's living-room, however, answers a different question (*What does your living room look like?* Or: *Where is what item in your living room?*), and the utterances in such a discourse are subject to different constraints (Klein and von Stutterheim 1987:165–6). However, to develop an adequate theory of genre along these lines, one would have to provide an account of how (implicit) questions are raised in discourse, and how the audience recognises which (implicit) question underlies a given utterance or discourse (segment). While Klein and von Stutterheim (1987) do not address this issue, van Kuppevelt (1995b) proposes a formal theory of it: the final comment value indicates the type of discourse (see Chapter 4 for details). In other words, according to van Kuppevelt's account, recognition of discourse type is possible only at the end of the discourse. In the relevance-theoretic account based on expectations of relevance, this difficulty can be overcome: the intuition that an implicit question is raised and answered in the discourse can be analysed as resulting from the recognition that a specific expectation of relevance has been raised, which is partly satisfied by the utterance (on an interpretation arrived at following a path of least effort). Thus, discourses are classified into genres depending on the specific expectations of relevance (that is, the specific expectations of cognitive effects) they raise. These expectations of relevance play a role in the mutual adjustment of context, content and cognitive effect; thus, hypotheses about the specific expectations of relevance raised in discourse can be arrived at as soon as enough contextual indications are available, and can be stabilised or changed as the discourse proceeds. In the same way, the genre of a discourse can be recognised during on-line processing. A formal account of genre along the lines suggested by van Kuppevelt (1995b), together with the problems it entails, can thus be avoided, and a theory of genre based on the intuitions of (implicit) questioning in discourse can be made more explanatory than Klein and von Stutterheim's (1987) treatment suggests.

It appears, then, that the notion of expectations of relevance differs from notions of global coherence in just the right way to yield an explanatory account of genre, building on the intuition that genre relates to the type of (implicit) question answered by a particular text or discourse. In the next section I want to show that the notion of expectations of relevance can shed new light on psycholinguistic evidence about the role of genre in communication and comprehension. This will strengthen the claim that expectations of relevance are central to an adequate account of the cognitive role of genre.

6.3 Expectations of relevance and the cognitive role of genre

In this section, I will argue that the notion of expectations of relevance developed in the last chapter can be used to re-interpret some psychological experiments which have been seen as providing evidence for the psychological reality of genre.

I will begin with Thomson and Adnan Zawaydeh (1996). These authors ran an experiment to test the morphological hypothesis that inflected forms of verbs are stored in the lexicon. If this were true, one would expect there to be priming effects on unrelated words: for example, *jumped* would have a priming effect on *poked* because they share the same affix. To test this hypothesis, Thomson and Adnan Zawaydeh presented subjects aurally with sentences containing priming words as they reacted to visually presented target words on a computer screen. The priming sentences were of two types: one had three verbs with regular past tense morphology, as in (8), while the second had a verb in the past progressive, as in (9):

(8) The doctor delivered the baby, paddled its behind and listened to it holler.

(9) Just before dawn, the soldiers were nervously guarding the entrance to the palace.

This was to check whether any priming effect was due to the *-ed* morphology in (8) or to the general past tense context in (9) (that is, semantic rather than morphological priming). The target words were derived from one-syllable words and inflected with *-ed* (regular past tense suffix), *-s* (third person singular agreement), or uninflected. The experiment did not support the hypothesis, since the predicted priming effects did not show up. In all types of priming, subjects' responses to uninflected target words were considerably faster than to inflected targets. However, there was a difference in responses to different types of inflected target words: when the priming sentence was in the regular past tense, inflected target words took longer to respond to than when the priming sentence was in the past progressive. The question is how this difference should be explained.

Thomson and Adnan Zawaydeh offer an explanation based on a proposal by Morrow (1986), that the function of inflectional morphemes is to trigger the integration of sentences into the discourse. Sentences containing *-ed* inflected verbs tend to describe sequences of events, while sentences with verbs in the past progressive typically describe information about setting. Inflected target words have to be integrated into the discourse, but this may be easier when the priming sentence contains setting information, which can be more readily expanded in various directions, than when it contains event chains, which already suggest a specific discourse representation (Thomson and Adnan Zawaydeh 1996:122). This might account for the difficulty of subjects with *-ed* inflected target words over those which were *-s* inflected.

I would like to suggest an alternative, relevance-theoretic explanation along the following lines. The inflection of the (target) verb triggers the search for a pragmatic enrichment based on the temporal and aspectual procedural constraints encoded by the affix. Pragmatic enrichment involves access to an adequate context. The past-tense priming sentence makes an adequate context more difficult to access, hence pragmatic enrichment is more difficult in this case. So far, the explanation follows similar lines as that of Thomson and Adnan Zawaydeh (1996). Differences arise at the point where discourse functions such as 'setting' are claimed to enter the picture. In relevance-theoretic terms, a 'setting' is an utterance which does not achieve adequate relevance in its own right, but merely contributes to the relevance of subsequent utterances. Such an utterance fails to satisfy the hearer's expectation of relevance, which in turn creates an expectation that the communicator is engaging in an act of communication involving a complex stimulus. Hence, more specific expectations about the relevance of following utterances are raised. Thus, if the priming sentence is one which can be interpreted as a setting in this sense, it is natural to interpret an inflected target word as one of a sequence of further expected utterances. On the other hand, if the priming sentence can be interpreted as an utterance which already achieves actual relevance by virtue of its own cognitive effects, no expectation of a continuation is necessarily raised. Thus, the utterance of a single inflected target word at this stage calls for a pragmatic enrichment, but it is harder to find one. In this way, no recourse to discourse functions such as 'setting' or 'event line' is needed - at least not if these notions are interpreted as theoretical primitives. Thus, Thomson and Adnan Zawaydeh's experiment does not show that discourse type affects lexical access for inflected verbs, contrary to what they claim.

Another paper which argues for a cognitive function of notions specific to discourse type is Copman and Griffith (1994). These authors report an experiment which compares event and story structure recall in children with specific learning disabilities, children with language impairment, and normally achieving children. (Most studies of event and story structure recall have been carried out with normally achieving children; there are also indications that the comprehension of narratives precedes that of expository texts, see Copman and Griffith 1994:232).

Copman and Griffith presented three groups of 20 children from each of the above categories with two texts. One was a story, and the other contained the same basic content in the form of an expository text:

(10) [narrative]
Once there was a girl, who wanted to get her frightened cat down from a tree. The girl climbed halfway up the tree, and held out some cookies to get the cat to come down, but the cat did not like cookies, and it did not come down. Then the girl tried something else. The girl had a parrot. She got the parrot to fly around the cat. This upset the cat and made it run down the tree.

(11) [expository]
Here's how a girl can get her frightened cat down from a tree. The girl can climb halfway up the tree, and hold out some cookies to get the cat to come down, but if the cat does not like cookies, it will not come down. Here's another thing the girl can do. Suppose the girl has a parrot. She can get the parrot to fly around the cat. This might upset the cat and might make it run down the tree.

The subjects were all individually presented with each of these texts by an investigator; the order of texts was counterbalanced within all three groups. Then a classmate (who was not a subject) was called in and the subject was asked to retell the story to this classmate. The retellings were recorded and analysed. All groups correctly recalled more events from the narrative text than from the expository text. However, more inaccuracies were found in the recall of whichever text was presented second. Furthermore, children with language impairments had more difficulties recalling settings than the other two groups. The recall of goals was better performed by children of high verbal age group. Settings, attempts and outcomes were better recalled for the narrative text, while goals were better recalled for the expository text. Copman and Griffith (1994:243) conclude that text type has a profound impact on text recall.[6]

I have already argued that settings can be re-analysed as utterances which create further expectations of relevance, and that experimental evidence involving settings does not in itself show a cognitive role of discourse structure or genre. Here I would like to take the argument further. Copman and Griffith point to differences of settings in narrative and expository texts, noting that the form of settings in expository texts is less familiar:

> In the narrative passage, for example, the first setting, "once there was a girl," is in a form with which children are more familiar than is the first setting within the expository passage, "Here's how a girl." Children typically receive more frequent exposure to the narrative setting form in their life situations, for example, listening to bedtime stories. (1994:243).

However, there is another striking difference in these two utterances: *Here's how a girl can...*, which contains a modal, involves a higher order of metarepresentation than *Once there was a girl....* More generally, the expository text describes a situation in a possible world, whereas the narrative represents a situation as having taken place in the actual world. Modals involve an extra layer of metarepresentation: the informative intentions of speakers of the respective utterances can be roughly indicated as in (12) and (13):

(12) (Here is how a girl can X)
S intends
  B to know
    that it is possible
      that a little girl can do X

(13) (Once there was a little girl, she did X)
S intends
  B to believe
    that there was a little girl and she did X.

Thus, it is not surprising that the narrative text is easier to process and recall than the expository text.

In order to evaluate the significance of the result that settings, attempts and outcomes were better recalled for the narrative text, while the goals were better recalled for the expository text, it is necessary to have a closer look at (11). The first utterance in this text conveys an explicit statement of the goal, to get the cat down from a tree. This raises the expectation that the following utterances in this text will achieve relevance by describing ways to achieve this goal. Since such specific expectations of relevance are central to comprehension (as the search for an adequate interpretation depends on them), it is likely that hearers will store them in memory in a way which facilitates later recall. However, the expectations of relevance raised in this example are not met: the first method is explicitly described as failing, and the outcome of the second is portrayed as uncertain: 'this might upset the cat and might make it run down the tree.' The text does not reveal a method which is presented as reliable for achieving the goal. Thus, the utterances describing inadequate or implausible methods fail to be relevant in the expected way. According to the cognitive principle of relevance, they are unlikely to be stored in memory for easy access for long. In other words, the fact that Copman and Griffith's subjects had more difficulties recalling attempts and outcomes in the expository text may well have been due to the fact that the expository text is badly constructed, rather than for reasons of discourse type.

A version of the expository text in (12) which avoids these difficulties is the following:

(14) Here is how a girl can get her frightened cat down from a tree. There are several things she can try to do: if the cat likes cookies, she can climb halfway up the tree and hold out some cookies to make the cat come down. But if the cat doesn't like cookies, it won't come down. In this case the girl needs to try other food which the cat likes. But there is yet another way to get it down: if the girl has a parrot, she can make the parrot fly around the cat's head. This will most likely upset the cat so that it will come down.

In this version, just as in the original one, the first utterance explicitly conveys a goal attributed to the girl, raising specific expectations of relevance. As argued above, relevance theory predicts that these expectations will be easily recalled. However, the proposed methods for achieving the goal of getting the cat down the tree are presented in a way which suggests that the speaker regards them as likely to succeed. I would expect that the attempts and outcomes (that is, the methods suggested for achieving the goal) to be more easily recalled than in Copman and Griffith's version. However, the modal expression in the utterance describing the goal will add an extra layer of metarepresentation, and I would still expect this text to be more difficult to process and recall than the narrative, as discussed above.

If my relevance-theoretic interpretation of these experiments is right, it suggests that though goals may still be somewhat easier to recall in the expository text than in the narrative one, and that overall the expository text will be more difficult to comprehend and recall, differences in recall of attempts, outcomes and settings should not be that strong. The reason why the goal may be better recalled in the expository text is that the goal is explicitly stated in the first utterance, thereby raising specific expectations of relevance, which are crucial for the comprehension of the whole text. In other expository texts, no goal may be so clearly described. Thus, the relative ease of recall of goals, attempts, outcomes, settings and so on in narrative and expository texts should depend on a variety of factors which have more to do with properties of the individual texts, and the way expectations of relevance are created and satisfied, than with issues of genre.

Van Dijk and Kintsch (1983) develop a theory of discourse comprehension which includes a theory of genre. The basic idea is that genre constrains the macrostructure of discourses (that is, macropropositions in the sense of van Dijk 1977, 1980) by providing a schema for (sequences of) macropropositions; hence genre is also called the (schematic) superstructure of a text. According to van Dijk and Kintsch, superstructure is inferred in a strategic way (that is, by hypothesis construction using heuristics) bottom-up from clues in the text, or rather from the semantic macropropositions expressed by the sentences. These hypotheses about schematic superstructure help with the formulation of hypotheses about the discourse function of the elements in question, which are then confirmed or modified top down as the discourse proceeds, creating expectations about later utterances which facilitate comprehension by reducing processing effort (in relevance-theoretic terms). The idea is that linguistic clues (including surface features and semantic information in the macroproposition), together with contextual knowledge and action schemas, allow the reader/hearer to infer categories of semantic superstructure which indicate a higher discourse function. Thus, generic superstructure is related to, but distinct from, action schemas, and plays a distinct role in utterance comprehension.

Action schemas contain stereotypical information about the motivations, purposes, intentions and goals which are seen as underlying human action. According to van Dijk and Kintsch, discourse comprehension relies a lot on information provided by action schemas, but discourse structure cannot be reduced to this kind of information. They point out that although stories are discourses about actions, there are other discourse types, such as police reports and ethnographic descriptions, which are also about actions but are very different in character from stories. Furthermore, descriptions of actions need not recount events in the order specified in the action schema. It is also commonly accepted (following Labov and Waletzky 1967) that a story must describe an interesting event or action, otherwise it wouldn't be considered a story. However, many actions for which we arguably have scripts or schemas are not necessarily interesting. Thus it seems that the notion 'interesting point' (or something like that) must be specified in another kind of schematic structure which relates to the telling of stories, that is, a discourse schema or superstructure.

Van Dijk and Kintsch (1983) report several psycholinguistic findings from other researchers which they take to confirm the hypothesis that knowledge of superstructure (that is, genre) does influence comprehension, memory and recall, and report in detail some of their own experiments, which I will look at briefly here.

There have been two types of initial research investigating the role of schematic superstructures in discourse comprehension. One involves stories which are presented in two forms: the canonical form, that is, the original version (which conforms to the story-schema) and another one where the paragraphs of the original story are randomly reordered (Kintzsch, W. et al. 1977). Another type of experiment involves presenting subjects with stories from a quite different culture, for example presenting Apache Indian stories on the one hand, and Grimms' fairy tales on the other, to non-indigenous American college students (Kintsch and Greene 1978). This second type of experiment revealed that American college students were not good at understanding Apache stories until they had been told the story schema. The first type of experiment yielded an unexpected result: comprehension of canonically ordered and scrambled stories was equally good, as is revealed by the subjects' retellings of them. However, it took them longer to retell the scrambled versions. Also, the subjects' retellings followed the canonical order in every case, whether they were retelling the canonical (original) version or the scrambled one. Van Dijk and Kintsch (1983:252) take this as evidence that the superstructure makes the reordering of the scrambled narratives possible. The difficulty of retelling the scrambled versions is then explained by the subject's need to reorder the story mentally.

Van Dijk and Kintsch (1983:253) note that these experiments do not show whether the effects were due to non-textual schemas, such as action schemas, or to schematic superstructures *per se*. They therefore designed two new experiments to remedy this defect. The new experiments are of the first type mentioned above, that is, involving well-structured and ill-structured versions of the same text; but using descriptive rather than narrative texts. Narratives involve actions, so it is quite possible that here action schemas may be more important than textual schemas. However, this is not so in expository texts.

Before turning to these experiments, I should note in passing that there is an alternative explanation for these results, involving the relevance theory notion of expectations of relevance, with no appeal to schematic superstructures. As argued above, when an utterance makes manifest that the speaker is engaging in a complex stimulus, the hearer's expectation of relevance should include expectations as to the optimal distribution of effects and access to contextual assumptions over the whole sequence. This is achieved by ordering the story material in a natural way.[7] Should the hearer encounter difficulties in establishing the relevance of individual utterances as they occur, he has to expend more processing effort. If, in the end, his expectations of relevance are met, comprehension is nevertheless achieved. However, since memory is organised so as to tend to maximise relevance,[8] the hearer may later reorder the assumptions communicated so as to facilitate recall. All this depends on how much processing effort the hearer is willing to invest, which in turn depends on how much concession he is willing to make to the abilities and preferences of the speaker. This willingness will presumably increase as he discovers more cognitive effects which contribute to satisfying the expectation of relevance created by the act of communication concerned.

Concerning Kintsch and Greene's (1978) experiments with Grimm's fairy tales and Apache stories, it must be noted that it is not clear whether the difficulties subjects had in summarising or retelling the Apache stories as opposed to the Grimm's tales are in fact due to the story structure.[9] Kintsch and Greene argue that these difficulties are due to story structure on the basis of the fact that the subjects rated the Apache stories as more bizarre than the Grimm's fairy tales when judging the stories as a whole, but that they judged isolated sentences of the two kinds of stories as equally bizarre. However, they do not consider whether cultural knowledge such as conventional symbolism of animals in fables (for example, Westerners have the cultural knowledge that foxes in animal fables are usually sly; but they don't have cultural information as to what role coyotes may typically play in Apache stories) may influence judgements of bizarreness or cause difficulties in recall. Furthermore, it should be noted that both Grimm's fairy tales and the Apache stories (apparently an animal fable) are in fact narrative sub-genres for which cultural schemas may indeed have been stabilised; but there is no reason to suppose that one can conclude on the basis of these special cases that narratives in general are schema based. Swales (1990), for example, has argued that narrative as such is a 'pre-genre' and does not fall squarely under his concept of genre, whereas sub-genres such as fairy tales can arise as a specialised class of texts. In Chapter 10 I will provide other arguments for such a position. This means that there is reasonable doubt that one can conclude from Kintsch and Greene's experiments that all genres are based on culture-specific schemas.

Because of the limitations involved in using narrative texts (the possible interaction of story schemas and action schemas in the first type of experiments, and the influence of cultural information other than story structure in the second type) for testing the influence of generic superstructure on comprehension, van Dijk and Kintsch's own experiments (1983:253–60) based on non-narrative texts seem to be better suited for this purpose. Let me now turn to discuss these experiments. They were designed to test various rhetorical structures — such as classification, comparison and contrast, procedural description, definition — found in (scientific) essays.[10] The various experiments had the same layout except that the texts used in the first involved classification, comparison and contrast, and procedural description paragraphs, whereas the second experiment used texts containing definition paragraphs. Again, the experiments involved pairs of texts, one well-structured, the other with a distorted structure (which still preserves local coherence). Van Dijk and Kintsch (1983:256) give the following examples of texts used in the first experiment:

(15) [Van Dijk and Kintsch's] Table 7.2
An Example of a Simple Classification Text in Good Rhetorical Form

In order to obtain an understanding of how man has evolved it is often helpful to analyze him in relation to the other primates. One major way of seeing this relationship is by examining locomotor patterns.

The most developmentally constricted form of locomotion is called vertical clinging and leaping. All prosimians fall into this form. In this pattern the animal normally clings to the branch with its head above its limbs. In its predominant locomotive form the animal pushes off from the branch of the tree with its hind limbs and springs or leaps to the next.

A developmentally more advanced form is quadrupedalism. As the name suggests, all four limbs are involved in this pattern. Macaques and howler monkeys typify this form.

Next is ape locomotion, which is characterized by arm swinging and/or occasional linked branch-to-branch swinging, climbing, and knuckle walking. The gibbon, orangutan, and chimpanzee locomotive patterns are characterized by this form.

Finally, we find bipedalism, which the characteristic locomotive form of man: Bipedalism includes standing, striding, and running. This form completes an adaptive developmental sequence which began sometime in the deep past with vertical clinging and leaping.

(16) [Van Dijk and Kintsch's] Table 7.3
An Example of a Simple Classification Text in Poor Rhetorical Form

A developmentally rather advanced form is quadrupedalism. As the name suggests, all four limbs are involved in this pattern. Macaques and howler monkeys typify this form.

It should be noted that bipedalism is the characteristic locomotive form of man: Bipedalism includes standing, striding, and running. This form completes an adaptive developmental sequence which began sometime in the deep past with vertical clinging and leaping.

In order to obtain an understanding of how man has evolved it is often helpful to analyze him in relation to the other primates. One major way of seeing this relationship is by examining locomotor patterns.

The most developmentally constricted form of locomotion is called vertical clinging and leaping. All prosimians fall into this form. In this pattern the animal normally clings to the branch with its head above its limbs. In its predominant locomotive form the animal pushes off from the branch or tree with its hind limbs and springs or leaps to the next.

Ape locomotion is usually characterized by arm swinging and/or occasional linked branch-to-branch swinging, climbing, and knuckle walking. The gibbon, orangutan, and chimpanzee locomotive patterns are characterized by this form.

Furthermore, some texts involved simple structures and others more complex ones, as one of the hypotheses was that schematic superstructures might be more effective in interpreting complex structured texts than simple ones. Another hypothesis was that understanding on the 'microlevel' (that is, comprehension of individual propositions and local coherence relations) is not influenced by schematic superstructure, as the superstructure is inferred on the basis of the macropropositions of the text. The main hypothesis, of course, was the one mentioned above: that texts in 'good rhetorical form' are easier to comprehend than their counterparts in 'bad rhetorical form.' In the experiments, subjects were presented with the texts and then asked questions about the macrostructure, for example *What is this text about?* or *What are the main ideas the author wanted to get across?* (van Dijk and Kintsch 1983:254–5). To assess microstructure comprehension, a so-called cloze test was performed: for example every fifth word in a paragraph was removed and the subjects had to guess what it was. The inference processes involved in this task, it is assumed, involve understanding on a very local level and should not be influenced by global text structure.

The results of both the experiments confirm this last hypothesis: global text structure had no influence on performance in the cloze test. The main hypothesis was also confirmed: the well-structured texts were more easily comprehended. However, the second hypothesis was not confirmed: there was no correspondence between the rhetorical complexity of the texts (or paragraphs) and the influence of schematic superstructures on comprehension. Van Dijk and Kintsch (1983:257) comment: 'Rhetorical structure was just as helpful with the simple texts as with the complex ones.'

Again, these findings can be interpreted in relevance theory terms along the lines suggested above for the experiments using stories. The difficulty with ill-ordered texts results not necessarily from nonconformity to known superstructures, but could be due to the fact that relevance is not optimised over a sequence of utterances. The relevance theory analysis has the advantage of explaining the 'interesting finding' that 'no sign of an interaction between complexity and the presence or absence of rhetorical structure' (van Dijk and Kintsch 1983:257) was found: if the difficulties subjects had with the ill-ordered text are not due to an influence of schematic superstructures (genre knowledge), then these superstructures may not play a role in comprehension, and if they don't, there can be no interaction between complexity and rhetorical structure. It is interesting that van Dijk and Kintsch (1983) do not comment further on this finding apart from the remarks quoted: there is no mention of it in the discussion section on these experiments.

It must be concluded that the experimental evidence put forward in van Dijk and Kintsch (1983) does not univocally support the claim that schematic superstructures (genre schemas) are involved in utterance comprehension. The results can be interpreted as well or — in the case of van Dijk and Kintsch's own experiments — even better in relevance theory terms without recourse to such structures. To support the claim that schematic superstructures are involved in utterance interpretation, it would have to be shown that the expectations of overall relevance which guide the comprehension process can only arise by accessing information about schematic superstructure. It seems doubtful that this case can be argued for scientific essays; though these texts may have a more or less rigid common structure (depending on the scientific discipline: essays on psycholinguistic experiments seem to be more rigidly structured than essays in the philosophy of language, for example), newcomers to the discipline (be they students, or researchers from related disciplines who consult the literature occasionally) do not have to have a systematic introduction to the textual conventions in order to understand them. In Chapter 5 I argued that expectations of relevance in the case of the vineyard song (Isaiah 5:1–7) do in fact depend on genre information; however, the kind of genre information involved did not relate to the schematic layout of the text. It is plausible that in highly conventionalised institutional discourses, expectations of overall relevance of a discourse may be linked to information about the schematic layout of such texts. But there are genres which are not obviously defined in terms of schematic superstructure. In short: van Dijk and Kintsch (1983) have not made a convincing case for the cognitive role of genre for the type of texts considered. There are cases where expectations of the relevance of complex stimuli (discourses) are plausibly constrained on the basis of genre information, but this information is not always confined to schematic information.

It might be argued that genre has a cognitive role not so much in comprehension as in memory and recall. In this case, my arguments against van Dijk and Kintsch's interpretation of their experiments merely show that genre does not generally appear to have a role in comprehension. It is a virtue of van Dijk and Kintsch (1983:236) that they distinguish between 'comprehension, storage, and retrieval of discourse.' However, van Dijk and Kintsch assume that the better structured the mental representations, the easier is their retrieval and recall.[11] On the further assumption — which van Dijk and Kintsch (1983) do not make explicit — that the structure of the mental representation of a discourse is directly derivable from the discourse itself, it follows that schematic superstructures should play the same role in comprehension, memory and retrieval. As van Dijk and Kintsch (1983:237) claim:

> ...the highly complex task of understanding, storing, and retrieving discourse necessarily requires that the language user assign an optimal structure to the discourse, and that such structures be strategically organized in known categories.

That is, discourse understanding involves the audience assigning an optimal structure to the discourse, and this one structure plays the same role in comprehension, memory and recall. However, there is no *a priori* reason to assume that there are no post-comprehension mental processes responsible for manipulating the representations derived from utterance comprehension into a form more suitable for memory organisation.

In fact, van Dijk and Kintsch (1983:53) themselves hint at the possible existence of such post-comprehension processes in quoting a study by Schnotz et al. (1981). These authors report an experiment where subjects were asked to give a summary of the text immediately after reading it once, and at another, later time. The subjects' first summaries contained a considerable amount of elaboration and restructuring. The second summaries were less than half the length of the original ones. For van Dijk and Kintsch, this is evidence that the reductive inferences involved in forming the macrostructure of the text apply at a late stage in discourse processing (comprehension). However, these findings can also be interpreted as supporting the view that the discourse representation in memory may be the result of post-comprehension mental processes: guided by the cognitive principle of relevance, these processes may apply so that the representation of a discourse which gets stored in memory is different from the representations which the audience entertains as a result of the comprehension process. In any case, Schnotz et al.'s experiments call into question the unspoken assumption that the structure of the mental representation of a discourse is directly derivable from the discourse itself.

If the assumption that the discourse representation in memory differs from the representations which the audience entertains as a result of the comprehension process is on the right lines, the question can be raised whether the cognitive role of genre may lie outside the realm of communication *per se*, influencing instead memory and retrieval of texts. The basic idea would be that those parts of a story (or a text of any discourse type) which conform closely enough to information stored in the genre concept, will not be stored in the representation of this story; rather, the representation of the story will contain 'pointers' to the information in the genre concept. Assume for example that an individual has schematic information about a genre — for example an animal fable — represented in memory. Assume further that this individual is (part of) the audience of a communicator telling an animal fable. The discourse will surely convey some information which closely resembles that stored in the representation of the genre 'animal fable.' This information conveyed in the discourse is thus unlikely to give rise to many cognitive effects which cannot be derived from the information stored already in memory in the representation of the genre. The cognitive principle of relevance predicts that this individual's mental representations of the newly told fable should not contain information which closely resembles information stored in the genre concept (it would include a pointer, a 'cross-reference,' to this information, though). In this way memory can be used most efficiently to facilitate the maximisation of relevance in cognition.

All these considerations are fairly speculative at present. Clearly, more experimental research needs to be done, and this lies beyond the scope of this book. However, this discussion has made several points: first, the notion of expectations of relevance developed in the last chapter can not only explain existing psycholinguistic evidence in a new way, but also raises new research questions. Second, if the assumption that the cognitive role of genre lies primarily in memory organisation is true, then this would be consistent both with my argument that van Dijk and Kintsch's (1983) experiments do not show an influence of genre on comprehension and with van Dijk and Kintsch's claim that good discourse organisation facilitates memory and recall. Third, the claim that the cognitive principle of relevance guides the processes transforming the result of comprehension into the discourse representation for memory storage can potentially provide a more flexible account of mental structure for memory than schema theories allow. Van Dijk and Kintsch (1983:48) describe the problems involved in schema-based theories in these words:

> The problem is how to get a knowledge base to deliver nicely prepackaged schemata, while at the same time retaining its flexibility and context sensitivity. It is simply not the case that every time we need the 'bus' schema, we want the same package. Rather, in each new context, it is a subtly different complex of information that becomes relevant.

Indications that fixed structures may not be the kind of organisation which facilitates processing for relevance can be found in Matsui (1998), who shows that schema-based theories fail to account for the context-selection processes involved in assigning bridging reference. The cognitive principle of relevance may well constrain mental processes which reorganise memory in order to facilitate processing of information for relevance, forming something like *ad-hoc* schemas as opposed to operating with fixed schemas only. Similarly, Barsalou (1987) argues, on the basis of experimental evidence that the graded structure of categories is unstable, varying widely across contexts, individuals, and within individuals over time, that categories are not represented by fixed structures such as prototypes, but that concepts are constructed in working memory from various sources of information in long-term memory. Moreover, he argues that the representation of schemas should be approached in a similar way, as *ad-hoc* constructs in working memory. According to experimental evidence in Barsalou et al. (1985), the variables in a schema representation are not all active across contexts: 'a schema does not appear to have an invariant set of variables relevant to every context.' (Barsalou 1987:125; see also the quote from van Dijk and Kintsch 1983:48 above).

However, for the purposes of this book there is no need to expand on these speculations further. I have argued that while van Dijk and Kintsch (1983) do not succeed in showing that genre knowledge crucially enters into comprehension for the discourse types they investigate, there is reason to believe that genre may nevertheless be important in comprehension, albeit in a different way than van Dijk and Kintsch (1983) envision: genre knowledge can not be reduced to text schemas, and the cases where it *is* so reduced are maybe confined to highly constrained institutional discourse. Thus, the picture which is emerging is that while the cognitive role of genre may extend beyond the realm of communication and comprehension *per se*, genre sometimes has a role in comprehension (and communication), and this needs to be explained. My claim is that the notion of expectations of relevance is the proper locus of a cognitive pragmatic account of genre. In the remainder of this book I will focus on this issue.

6.4 Conclusion

The argument of this chapter has been that a great many of the intuitions usually attributed to the role of genre in discourse comprehension may have their source in other phenomena more directly related to the role of expectations of relevance in the course of on-line utterance interpretation in discourse. There is also some indication that this alternative explanation is superior to the one involving genre knowledge, for example in explaining the experimental results of van Dijk and Kintsch (1983).

I have suggested that the role of genre may be quite different for comprehension than for memory organisation and retrieval. Since comprehension is guided by the communicative principle of relevance, whereas the organisation of memory, as well as cognitive processes operating on it, are (arguably) guided by the cognitive principle of relevance, it can be expected that the study of genre can shed more light on how these principles interact, and therefore on the relation between cognition and communication.

7 Empirical issues in global coherence and text typology

7.1 Introduction

In the previous chapters I have argued that the notion of global coherence cannot be made precise, and that it had better be abandoned. I also developed an alternative account of the intuitions which the notion of global coherence was designed to explain, based on the creation and maintenance of expectations of relevance in ostensive communication, and argued that this alternative account is empirically adequate for some cognitive aspects of the theory of genre. It remains to be shown that this relevance-theoretic account can also account for a number of linguistic data which have been (or might be) claimed to show the influence of genre on the semantics of certain linguistic markers or constructions. This is the burden of the present chapter. My central concern is with whether discourse type considerations directly affect the semantics of verb forms. The relevant data were introduced in Chapter 4; in Section 7.2 I suggest a relevance-theoretic account. Section 7.3 discusses the use of (Koine) Greek *participium coniunctum* in various discourse types, Section 7.4 anaphora in different discourse types.

7.2 The interpretation and use of verb forms

I suggested in the last two chapters that grounding can be explained in terms of relevance: the most foregrounded utterances are those whose main contribution to satisfying expectations of relevance is via the cognitive effects they achieve. The most backgrounded utterances are those whose main contribution to satisfying the (global) expectation of relevance is to create or fine-tune expectations about the relevance of later utterances.

This places 'groundedness' on a fully continuous scale. No utterance is exclusively foreground or background. It also treats groundedness as something which is not encoded in language. How grounding effects are achieved, moreover, is thoroughly context-dependent.

However, the linguistic properties of utterances can affect the online search for relevance in subtle ways. Sperber and Wilson (1995) have argued that contrastive stress should be approached in this way: stressing different syntactic constituents of an utterance encourages the audience to treat different propositional schemas or entailments of the proposition expressed by the utterance as background assumptions (Sperber and Wilson 1995:202–17). Here, the use of stress is no more than a pointer to the intended interpretation; it is the task of the interpretation process to follow this indication through in the direction desired.

In similar ways, the speaker can use linguistic pointers to ensure that the audience interprets her utterances along the intended lines, by creating expectations of relevance linked to the degree of foregroundedness (or backgroundedness) of the communicated information. What linguistic pointers may there be?

Let us assume that it is mutually manifest to communicator and audience that the communicator is recounting something which happened to her in the past. In this case, the audience's expectations of relevance should include the expectation that she will be describing events (they may, of course, be more specific, but for our purposes this is the aspect which we need to focus on). So an utterance which manifestly describes a past state (as opposed to an event) will not be taken to contribute directly to the relevance of the discourse. Rather, the audience should expect it to contribute indirectly to the relevance of other utterances which do describe events.

However, not all the communicator's descriptions of past events can be expected to be highly foregrounded. How could she indicate to the audience that the event she is describing is intended to be a background event? An obvious method is to use aspectual forms which make the event seem more like a state. In languages where aspect is standardly encoded, this can be achieved by using an imperfective aspect marking on the verb. Other languages may use word order to indicate differences in predicate type: in (Biblical) Hebrew, Arabic (and arguably in other Semitic languages), for example, verb-first clauses are usually associated with the predicate types event and activity, while other word orders are usually associated with the predicate types state or process (Gesenius 1985:§140f; Niccacci 1994; Bailey and Levinsohn 1992; Niccacci 1994; Longacre 1989b).

I will briefly illustrate some of these strategies to indicate foreground and background with examples from Biblical Hebrew. It has long been recognised that the so-called imperfect consecutive form of the verb is predominantly used in clauses which continue the narrative. Joüon and Muraoka (1996:390, §118c) give the following example:

(1) Genesis 14:5ff: "And in the 14th year Chedorlaomer came (*bâ*) [perfect]... and they beat (*wayyakkû*) [impf. cons.] the Rephaim..., (7) and they returned (*wayyāšūḇû*) [impf. cons.]... etc."

However, the imperfect consecutive form is also used in speech introductory clauses, as in the following example:

(2) Genesis 3:1–4
(1) Now the serpent was more crafty than any of the wild animals the Lord God had made. He said (*wayyomer*) [impf. cons.] to the woman, "Did God really say (*āmar*) [perfect], 'you must not eat from any tree in the garden'?" (2) The woman said (*wattomer*) [impf. cons.] to the serpent, "We may

> eat fruit from the trees in the garden, (3) but God did say, 'You must not eat fruit from the tree that is in the middle of the garden, and you must not touch it, or you will die."' (4) And the serpent said (*wayyomer*) [impf. cons.] to the woman:...

It is not clear in which sense speech introductory clauses can be argued to convey foreground information. Murray Salisbury (personal communication) suggested to me that the speech introductory clauses introduce the speech turns in their temporal sequence, and could therefore be regarded as foreground-like. However, one would not get a good summary of this story by just extracting the sentences containing imperfect consecutive forms. So, by the criterion of salience of information, the speech introductory clauses should not be considered foreground.

In the pragmatic account of information grounding suggested above, these examples are interpreted in a different way: grounding is a purely pragmatic phenomenon, and grounding level is not encoded by any linguistic form. However, narratives suggest that the relevance of the text lies mainly in the successive events described in it. This suggests that forms associated with event-like predicate types are preferred. In Biblical Hebrew, the imperfect consecutive form is such a form, and this accounts for its being the main verb form in foreground sentences of narrative (example 1). However, it is clear from the content of speech introduction clauses that the audience is not likely to interpret them as foregrounded. Therefore the communicator does not need to indicate grounding in a special way, and is free to use the imperfect consecutive form for its semantic value alone (indicating temporal sequence)[1] in example (2). The point is that whether a linguistic form is used to indicate grounding in a given instance depends on factors of context, content and relevance expectations, and is not part of what is linguistically encoded. Therefore a form which is generally well suited to indicate foreground in narrative does not inevitably do so in every instance, as illustrated in example (2).

Imagine now that it is mutually manifest that the communicator is explaining relevance theory to the audience. In this case, the predicate types of the eventualities described yield no obvious predictions about whether a particular utterance is likely to be relevant in its own right or not. Rather, the 'groundedness' of the various utterances depends solely on the meanings of the utterances themselves. However, since the audience can not be expected to grasp the relative importance of some of these utterances on the basis of their meaning alone (if the audience doesn't know relevance theory, then it doesn't know where the complexities are, which aspects of the theory are crucial, which auxiliary, and so on), it would be desirable for the communicator to indicate the intended level of grounding. One way of doing this is to use linguistic pointers such as parentheticals (as in 'X — and this is important — Y'). However, non-linguistic pointers such as page layout, paragraphing, underlining (in written communication), use of blackboard schemas, gesture (in a lecture), and so on may be more important in this case.[2]

Different discourse types, then, may require the use of different linguistic (or non-linguistic) indicators to point the audience towards the intended interpretation. Strictly speaking, it is manifest expectations as to how the discourse as a whole will achieve relevance that affect which linguistic or non-linguistic devices may be used to point the audience to the intended level of grounding. Only to the extent that discourse types can be characterised as associated with stereotypical expectations of relevance do they (indirectly) play a role in this account. However, neither grounding nor discourse type is encoded in these linguistic indicators. On the contrary, what they encode is something quite different (aspect, predicate type, and so on). Whether or not a certain linguistic form — for example imperfective aspect — is used as a linguistic indicator of grounding in discourse is not even partially encoded in the semantics of the particular device — it is only recoverable as a by-product of interpreting the particular utterance in the intended context, taking the linguistic form of the utterance as a crucial guide to the intended interpretation.

Notice that this account of grounding does not face the problem of discourse type recognition in a system where embedding of discourse types is allowed. It is the expectations of the overall relevance of the discourse that are active at the time of utterance interpretation which influence how grounding levels can — if necessary — be linguistically indicated. These expectations may shift within a single discourse belonging to a single genre, as shown in Chapter 5.

This thoroughly pragmatic analysis of grounding can help to explain why the claim that discourse type directly affects the interpretation of linguistic form is mostly developed with respect to verbal forms involving tense and aspect. Code-based analyses such as those examined in Chapter 4 offer no answer to this question. On the inferential approach, there is an answer: the expectations of global relevance created by narratives typically have to do with the description of events. It follows that linguistic markers which affect the aspectual interpretation of utterances are well suited for use as pointers to grounding levels. Aspectual information is typically marked on the verb, or through the syntactic position of the verb in a sentence. Other discourse types, which create other types of expectations of 'global' relevance, require different indicators of grounding. Thus, the use of the verb will appear to be different in narrative texts than in texts from other genres (though, again, this is not because the verb forms have a different meaning, but because the effects on pragmatic inference may be different). However, this still leaves open the possibility that linguistic indicators of grounding other than verbal inflection or word order may also be used in narrative.

7.3 Greek participial clauses

7.3.1 The interpretation of participial clauses in Koine Greek

A related point can be made with Koine Greek participial clauses. Participial clauses are subordinate clauses, which can have different relations to the main clause: temporal subordination, causal subordination, and so on, as is well known. One way of accounting for the differences in interpretation would be to say that the only relation the participle signals is that of subordination. In narrative, the script associated with the genre would be organised around temporal order, so temporal subordination would be a default interpretation of participial clauses in narrative texts. In argumentative texts, the script is organised around reason and result, so the default interpretation in argumentative texts would involve causal or consequential subordination.

Traditional grammars call the use of the participle we are interested in the *participium coniunctum* (Blass et al. 1984:§418). Five types of usage are standardly considered:[3]

1. Corresponding to a causal clause.

(3) Matthew 1,19:

Josêf	*de*	*ho*	*anêr*	*autês*	*dikaios*
Joseph	but	the	husband	of her	righteous

ôn	*kai*	*mê*	*thelôn*	*autên*
being (PCP)	and	not	wanting (PCP)	her

deigmatisai	*eboulêthê*	*lathra*	*apolysai*	*autên.*
to expose	wanted	secretly	to forsake	her.

'But Joseph, her husband, was a righteous man and did not want to expose her (publicly), and therefore wanted to leave her secretly.'

Other examples: Mark 2,4; Luke 2,45; Acts 4,21; Titus 2,8.

2. Corresponding to a conditional clause.

(4) Luke 9,25

ti	*gar*	*ôfeleite*	*anthrôpos*	*kerdêsas*	*ton*
what	for	benefits	man	gaining (PCP)	the

kosmon	*holon*	*heauton*	*de*	*apolesas*	*ê*
world	all	himself	but	destroy (PCP)	or

zêmiôtheis?
comes to ruin (PCP)?

'For what does it benefit if one gains the whole world but dies or comes to ruin?'

Other examples: Acts 15,29; (Romans 1,20); Philippians 2,28; 1 Timothy 4,4.

3. Corresponding to a concessive clause.

(5) Matthew. 7,11

ei	*oun*	*hymeis*	*ponêroi*	*ontes*	*oidate*
if	so	you	evil	being (PCP)	know

domata	*agatha*	*didonai*	*tois*	*teknois*	*hymôn,*
gifts	good	to give	the	children	of yours,

posô	*mallon*	*ho*	*patêr*	*hymôn*	*ho*	*en*	*tois*
how much	more	the	father	of yours	the	in	the

ouranois	*dôsei*	*agatha*	*tois*	*aitousin*
heavens	will give	good things	those	asking

auton.
him.

'So if, though you are evil, you know how to give good gifts to your children, how much more will your father in heaven give good things to those who ask him?'

Other examples: Luke 11,13; Acts 13,28; 1. Corinthians. 9,19; 1. Thessalonians 2,7.

4. Corresponding to a final clause

(6) Luke 7,6

...epempsen	*filous*	*o*	*hekantontarchos*
...he sent	friends	the	hekantontarch

legôn	*autô...*
saying (PCP)	him...

'...the hekatontarch sent his friends that they say to him...'

Matthew 27,55; Luke 23,49; John 21,19; 1. Corinthians 4,14; In another construction: Matthew 11,2; 1. Corinthians 4,17.

5. Corresponding to a circumstantial clause, either modal or temporal. This is the most common usage.

(7) (a) modal: Mark 1,5

ebaptizonto	*exomologoumenôn*
he baptised	testifying (PCP)

'he baptised testifying...'
Alternatively: 'he baptised and testified...' (temporal)

Acts 27,38

ekoufizon	*to*	*ploion*	*ekballomenoi*	*ton*
they-lightened	the	ship	throwing (PCP)	the

siton	*eis*	*tên*	*thalassan.*
wheat	into	the	sea.

'They lightened the ship by throwing the wheat into the sea.'

Hebrews 11,27 (non-narrative text)

Pistei	*katelipen*	*Aigypton*	*mê*
through-faith	left	Egypt	not

fobêtheis	*ton*	*thymon*	*tou*	*basileôs.*
fearing (PCP)	the	anger	of the	king.

'Through faith he left Egypt, not fearing the anger of the king.'

(b) temporal: Matthew 2,10:

idontes	*de*	*ton*	*astera*	*echarêsen*
seeing (PCP)	but	the	star	they rejoiced

'But when they saw the star, they rejoiced...'

Other examples: Matthew 4,18; Mark 1,16; John 20,20

It is interesting that while, for all the non-temporal uses, there are examples listed from both narrative and non-narrative texts, only examples from narrative texts are listed for the temporal usage of the participle. In fact, there are exceptions. Consider the opening verses of the epistle to the Hebrews, for example:

(8) Hebrews 1:1–2a

(1) *polymerôs kai polytropôs palai ho theos*
(1) many times and manyfold in the past the God
lalêsas tois patrasin en tois profêtais
spoke (PCP) to the fathers through the prophets
'After God spoke at many times and in many ways to our fathers through the prophets,'

(2) *ep eschatou tôn hêmerôn toutôn elalêsen*
(2) on last of the days these he spoke
hêmin en hyô, ...
to us through son, ...
'in these last days he has spoken to us through the Son...'

Whatever the text type of Hebrews is, it is not narrative, but the participles in the first three verses can really only be interpreted as encouraging a temporal interpretation. Similarly with Colossians 1, 3–4:

(9) Colossians 1,3–4

(3) *Eucharistoumen tô theô patri tou kyriou*
(3) We give thanks to the God father of the Lord
hêmôn Iêsou Christou pantote peri hymôn
our Jesus Christ always for you
proseuchomenoi
praying (PCP)
'(3) We give thanks to God, the father of our Lord Jesus Christ always when we pray for you,

(4) *akousantes tên pistin humôn en Christô*
(4) having heard (PCP) the belief yours in Christ
Iêsou...
Jesus...
'since we have heard of your belief in Christ Jesus...'

The second *participium coniunctum, akousantes* in verse (3), must be interpreted in a temporal sense.

The participles in the Christ hymn in Philippians 2,6–11, especially Philippians 2,8 may be seen as 'temporal,' although they are probably merely coordinating. At least, it is difficult to classify them into any of the above usages. Nevertheless they are instances of *participium coniunctum.*

(10) Philippians 2,6–8 (free translation from New International Version)

(6) 'he who was in very nature God, did not consider equality with God something to be grasped,'

(7) *alla*	*heauton*	*ekenôsen*	*morfên*	*doulou*
(7) but	himself	he emptied	form	of servant

labôn	*en*	*homoiômati*	*anthrôpôn*
taking (PCP)	in	likeness	of men

genomenos.	*kai*	*schêmati*	*heuretheis*	*hôs*
becoming (PCP).	And	appearance	be found	like

anthrôpos
man

'but made himself nothing, taking the very nature of a servant, being made in human likeness. And being found in appearance as a man,

(8) *etapeinôsen*	*heauton*	*genomenos*	*hupêkoos*
(8) he humbled	himself	becoming (PCP)	obedient

mechri	*thanatou,*	*thanatou*	*de*	*staurou.*
until	death	death	even	of cross.

'he humbled himself and became (genomenos) obedient to death — even death on a cross.'

Thus, all possible interpretations of *participium coniunctum* are in fact realized within narrative texts. Conversely, all types of *participium coniunctum* are realized in non-narrative texts. Nevertheless, there is a tendency for the temporal interpretation of *participium coniunctum* to be found mostly in narrative texts, and less frequently in other text types.

A possible explanation for this in the coherence based framework might go as follows: the temporal interpretation of *participium coniunctum* is the one which fits the generic expectations for a narrative text (a narrative time-line has to be constructed), and is thus the default or unmarked interpretation. Variation from the guidelines of the genre is always possible, but is more costly to process, so other interpretations may occur, but less frequently.

7.3.2 On the pragmatics of participial clauses in Koine Greek

I have noted that there is a statistical tendency in narrative texts to interpret participial clauses (of the type *participium coniunctum*) as temporally related to their subordinate clauses. A possible explanation suggested above was that the temporal relation corresponds to the main (global) relation linked to the narrative genre. However, this explanation runs into problems as is shown by the fact that there often seem to be ambiguities between a temporal and a causal reading of the participial clause in narratives, as in example (11):

(11) John 20:20b

echarisan	*oun*	*hoi*	*mathetai*	*idontes*	*ton*
they rejoiced	so	the	disciples	seeing (PCP)	the

kyrion.
Lord.

a. So the disciples rejoiced when they saw the Lord.
b. So the disciples rejoiced because they saw the Lord.

A similar problem arises with the interpretation of discourse connectives, as in example (12):

(12) John 19:12

ek toutou	*ho*	*Pilatos*	*ezêtei*	*apolysai*	*auton.*
from this	the	Pilate	sought	to free	him.

a. From this time Pilate sought to let him free.

b. Therefore Pilate sought to let him free.

If the narrative genre causes a strong preference to assume temporal relations between events, such ambiguities should not arise since the temporal (or narrative) relation would be the preferred interpretation. However, interpreters and translators have often resolved the ambiguities in different ways, and the texts do not seem to be incoherent (or less coherent) if the causal interpretation is chosen. Thus, it seems that the genre-specific preference on the interpretation of successive discourse segments can be easily overridden. But if this is so, then the role of genre-specific default preferences for coherence relations is called into question (unless the factors which override these default values could be made explicit).[4]

There is thus reason to look for a different account of the interpretation of Greek participial clauses. In this subsection I want to outline a relevance-theoretic account. At the heart of this account is the observation that *participium coniunctum* clauses are syntactically subordinate constituents of a sentence and thus achieve relevance as one unit together with the superordinate clause(s), in a way similar to conjoined utterances (Carston 1988, 1993, 2002). According to Carston, conjoined propositions are supposed to satisfy the expectation of optimal relevance as a whole, rather than each conjunct individually. To this end, the semantics of the conjoined propositions has to be enriched in a certain way. Hypotheses about possible pragmatic enrichments are ordered in terms of accessibility: those based on scripts made available by concepts expressed by the utterance, or other contextual assumptions derivable from these, are easily accessible, and hence the first to be considered under the relevance-theoretic comprehension procedure. If the resulting interpretation satisfies the hearer's expectation of relevance, he is therefore entitled to accept it.

This pragmatic account, developed for sentence conjunction carries over to *participium coniunctum.* This analysis is motivated by data of the kind represented in examples (13) to (15):

(13) Acts 16:6

diêlthon	*de*	*tên*	*Phrygian*	*kai*	*Galatikên*
we went through	but	the	Phrygian	and	Galatian

chôran	*kôlythentes*	*hypo*	*tou*	*hagiou*	*pneumatos*
region	hindered (PCP)	from	the	Holy	Spirit

'we went through the regions of Phrygia and Galatia but were hindered by the Holy Spirit...'

(14) Acts 16:7

elthontes	*de*	*kata*	*tên*	*Mysian*	*epeirazon*	*eis*
coming (PCP)	but	through	the	Mysia	they tried	to

tên	*Bithynian*	*poreuthênai,*	*kai*	*ouk*	*eiasen*	*autous*
the	Bithynia	to go,	and	not	allowed	them

to	*pneuma*	*Iêsou.*
the	spirit	of Jesus.

'But when they came through Mysia, they tried to go through Bithynia, but the spirit of Jesus didn't allow them.'

(15) John 8:7[5]

a. Textual version chosen in the Nestle-Aland 27th edition:

hôs	*de*	*epemenon*	*erôtôntes*	*auton*
as	but	they remained	questioning	him

anekypsen	*kai*	*eipen*	*autois:...*
he.straightened.up	and	said	to them:...

'As they kept on asking him, he straightened up and said to them:'

b. Variant reading of some manuscripts:

hôs	*de*	*epemenon*	*erôtôntes*	*auton*
as	but	they remained	questioning	him

anakypsas	*eipen*	*autois:...*
straightening up (PCP)	he said	to them:...

'As they kept on asking him, he straightened up and said to them:'

Notice that in example (13) (Acts 16:6) the participle *kôlythentes* is pragmatically enriched to a counter-to-expectation reading (indicated in the translation with 'but'). The conjunction *kai* 'and' in example (14) (Acts 16:7) undergoes the same pragmatic interpretation. In example (15) (John 8:7), it is interesting to see that there are actually two variant readings in the textual tradition, which can be understood to convey the same meaning, but differ in that the variant (15b) uses a *participium coniunctum* instead of indicative in both verbs connected with *kai* 'and.'

Having motivated the claim that the pragmatic analysis of conjunction in general carries over to *participium coniunctum,* I will try to show how examples (3) to (7) above can be accounted for along these lines.

Consider first (3). At the point where the reader/hearer is about to process the third clause, s/he will have the following assumptions easily accessible:

a. A righteous man must sever his ties with his fiancée if she is found to be with child, since this presupposes immorality. (Encyclopaedic knowledge: cultural assumption)

b. If a woman is publicly abandoned by her fiancée on charges of immorality, it is a big disgrace for her and her family. (Encyclopaedic knowledge: cultural assumption)

c. A righteous man seeks to avoid public disgrace for others. (Encyclopaedic knowledge: cultural assumption)

d. Joseph was a righteous man.

e. Joseph wanted to avoid bringing Mary into public disgrace.

The third clause will then provide access to the following assumption:

> Leaving the fiancée secretly may be a way of avoiding public disgrace.

This assumption in turn is relevant to the reader/hearer to the extent that it may suggest a plan for achieving the goal implied by the previous conjunct, that Joseph must have wanted to avoid bringing Mary into public disgrace. Thus, the predicate conjunction is pragmatically interpreted as conveying a causal meaning.

Next, let us consider a conditional reading of the *participium coniunctum,* in example (4).

The most natural way to interpret the sequence of participial clauses is that they picture a sequence: person X gains the whole world and subsequently dies or comes to ruin (after all, gaining the whole world is an activity of living persons, hence the temporal sequence). Since it is manifest that the speaker had no specific referent for person X in mind, the two participial clauses express a condition which, if fulfilled, render the rhetorical question asked in this utterance relevant.

The use of the *participium coniunctum* corresponding to a concession clause can likewise be analysed along these lines. Consider example (5):

A proposition involving the predicate expressed by the participial clause, such as *Men are by nature evil people,* gives rise to the following implicatures:

(16) a. Evil persons don't know how to give good things to people.
b. Men don't know how to give good things to people.

The relevance of a proposition involving the superordinate predicate must be established against this background, perhaps along the following lines. It is true that evil people do give good things to their children (information derived from the superordinate predicate and previous utterances) and it is also true as a general principle that evil people do not give good things to people (implicature involving the first predicate and encyclopedic entries of the concept EVIL PEOPLE; these claims can be reconciled by a concessive interpretation: Though in general evil people do not give good things to people, they do it for their children. This interpretation is consistent with the hearer's expectation of relevance. Hence it can be assumed to be the one intended by the speaker.

The various instances of *participium coniunctum* corresponding to a circumstantial clause (Number 5 in Blass et al. 1984:§418) can be analysed on the same pattern. Let us work through an example of a temporal-circumstantial interpretation:

(7b) Matthew 2,10:

idontes	*de*	*ton*	*astera*	*echarêsen...*
seeing (PCP)	but	the	star	they rejoiced...

'But when they saw the star, they rejoiced...'

An assumption made easily available by the previous utterances of the story is *The wise men believe that if they see the star right above them they will know that they have found the place where the King of the Jews is born.* From a proposition involving the predicate expressed in the participial clause together with this assumption, it is possible to infer *The wise men believe that they have found the place where the King of the Jews is born.* From the previous part of the story, the hearer will also have available the assumption *The wise men rejoice when they find the place where the King of the Jews is born.* The proposition involving the second predicate conjunct will strengthen this assumption, thereby establishing the relevance of this utterance.

Example (6) can be explained pragmatically along the following lines. A natural implicature involving the predicate expressed in the main clause would be that the hekantontarch sent his friends with a purpose. To the extent that the predicate expressed in the participial clause can be relevant as providing a purpose for the sending of the friends of the hekantontarch the utterance is consistent with the expectation of relevance.[6] To the extent that this pragmatic analysis carries over to other examples of this type, it ought to be preferred over the syntactic one, since it simplifies the syntactic analysis without introducing explanatory machinery which is not independently needed.

Note that genre-specific information is not involved in the explanation of the interpretation of *participium coniunctum.* Every instance of this construction can be explained by general principles needed for utterance interpretation across different discourse types. This does not shed light on any statistical tendency (if there is one) to prefer a temporal interpretation of participium coniunctum in narrative texts. Indeed, it is not clear if there is anything left to explain here: if the hearer is able, using general principles of utterance interpretation, to infer the intended interpretation of the utterance without having to access special genre information, then it does not matter whether in the particular text there is a preference for one subcase of *participium coniunctum* or another. Perhaps it could be argued that if, over time, it becomes manifest to an addressee that in a certain type of text, the temporal interpretation of *participium coniunctum* is the most likely, then s/he may adopt a strategy of first attempting a temporal interpretation. It is not clear, though, how on such an account the phenomenon of ambiguity between temporal and other interpretations (witness example (7a) and see the discussion at the beginning of this subsection) could be explained. I conclude, then, that data from Koine Greek *participium coniunctum* does not provide evidence for a linguistic function of genre.

7.4 Anaphora

7.4.1 Anaphora in different genres

Fox (1987) claims that the use of anaphora is also dependent on genre. She aims to demonstrate this by studying (discourse) anaphora in spoken and written expository texts in English. Starting from the premise that anaphora is closely interrelated with discourse structure, and that this structure is hierarchical in nature, she chooses different tools to analyse texts in the different modes: conversational analysis (Sacks et al. 1974) for spoken texts, and Rhetorical Structure Theory (Mann and Thompson 1986, 1988) for written expository texts. Her claim is that since the different discourse types are made up of basic units of different kinds, the methods used to analyse the texts must reflect this difference.

Since the basic units in the respective text types are of different kinds (turn-taking pairs in conversation and discourse segments joined by coherence relations in written texts), Fox (1987:140) argues that the patterns of anaphora are necessarily different. A major consequence is that while long-distance anaphora in conversation seems to be largely unconstrained, long-distance anaphora is severely restricted in written expository texts Fox (1987:140).

In essence, the analysis can be summarised as follows: in written expository texts, pronominalisation is possible only in clauses which are in a coherence relation to a (previous) clause containing the referent, as in example (17). This relation may be a transitive one, that is, other clauses may intervene so long as they are also linked by a coherence relation to the clause containing the referent, as in example (18):

(17) Paul travelled to Giessen. It was his first visit to Germany.

(18) Paul travelled to Giessen. It was all very exciting: it was his first visit to Germany.

In (17), the second clause *It was his first visit to Germany* is in a background relation to the first clause, so a pronoun can be used to refer back to Paul. In (18), the second and third clauses are linked by the relation of elaboration, and form a single discourse segment which stands in the background relation to the first clause. So a pronoun can be used in the third clause to refer back to Paul.

In conversation, pronouns can be used to refer back to some referent as long as the current structure has not been — in an intuitive sense — 'closed down' (Fox 1987:18). Fox (1987:20–40) lists a variety of cases were a structure in a conversation is not 'closed down,' such as in between turns in an adjacency pair, in expanded turns or across (topically) related adjacency pairs. However, she does not define what it means that a structure is 'closed down.'

Long-distance anaphora are made possible by a structural configuration which Fox calls 'return-pop.' Return-pops are different in the two discourse types investigated: in written expository texts, return-pops occur when a clause stands in a coherence relation not with the clause preceding it, but with a previous clause, as illustrated in (19):

(19) Paul travelled to Giessen. It was his first visit to Germany.
He was truly excited.

The third clause is arguably not related to the immediately preceding clause, but stands in a background relation to the first one, just as the second clause is related by the background relation to the first clause. Fox (1987) argues that in return-pops in expository texts, a pronoun can be used to refer to a participant in a previous clause as long as the intervening material either itself contains a reference to the participant referred to in the return-pop, or is structurally simple, that is, does not involve a complex network of propositions linked by coherence relations.

Return-pops in conversation are made by returning to a focal adjacency pair and continuing the sequence which this initiated. The adjacency pair returned to may be far back. Thus, while return-pops in expository written texts are narrowly constrained, return-pops in conversation are largely unconstrained.

Essentially, in Fox's view, the difference between the patterns of anaphora in the two discourse types depends on whether the text is organised mainly in terms of coherence relations (written expository text) or not (conversation). In this sense, her study can be seen as claiming a connection between coherence and genre. Fox also distinguishes between the influence of the communicative possibilities and purposes of spoken and written texts and the further influence of social conventions particular to a text type, commenting that 'the patterns exhibited by written narratives, for example, more closely resemble the patterns of the conversational texts than those of the expository texts' (Fox 1987:143). However, she does not provide further details of how genre (understood as social conventions on a particular text type) can influence anaphora.

7.4.2 Anaphora, genre, and relevance

Fox's claims about the relation between anaphora and discourse structure depend mainly on two premises: that discourse is hierarchically structured, and that conversation necessarily calls for the use of descriptive devices other than those used for written expository texts. Both these assumptions have been challenged. Toole (1996) points out that the use of different discourse models in fact precludes a comparison across genres: 'to validly compare across genres it is necessary to have standard terms and concepts' (Toole 1996:265). Moreover, Moeschler (1993) argues that conversation falls squarely within the scope of relevance theory, which deals with all varieties of ostensive communication. Unger (1996) takes issue with the view that discourse is hierarchically structured, on the ground that the assumption of hierarchical discourse structure does not do justice to effects observed in the interaction between scope effects of discourse connectives with paragraphing. Chafe (1979) also argues for a 'flow model' (or process model) of discourse as opposed to a hierarchical one (see also Chafe 1987). Rejecting Fox's two premises, it remains to be shown that a theory of ostensive communication can indeed throw light on the observations about anaphora made in Fox (1987).

Relevance theory claims that reference assignment is intimately affected by the accessibility of referents. The referent of a pronoun, in particular, must be very highly accessible (Ariel 1985, 1988, 1990, 1994, 1996; Gundel 1996; Gundel et al. 1988, 1989, 1990; Gundel, J. K. et al. 1993). Fox's (1987) argument amounts to the claim that it is not only psychological accessibility which is involved, but also linguistic structure with respect to discourse organisation in the sense of a network of coherence relations.

Toole (1996) tested the predictions of Accessibility Theory (Ariel 1985, 1988, 1990, 1994, 1996) in a sample of texts from four different genres (science fiction novels, academic book reviews, informal conversations, current affairs interviews). Accessibility was found to account for referential choice in all four genres, thus providing evidence against Fox's claim.

Against the view that discourse is organised into units by a network of coherence relations, it has been argued extensively in the relevance theory literature that connectivity in texts results not from coherence relations but from underlying relevance relations between text and context (Blass 1986, 1990; Blakemore 1988; Unger 1996; also Part 1 of this book). In other words, coherence relations — where they are identifiable — may be seen as resulting from the pragmatic interpretation of a sequence of utterances. Suppose the hearer has reached a point where he is interpreting an utterance containing a pronoun. At this point, he has certain assumptions easily accessible — those assumptions which were used in interpreting the previous utterance. This initial set of contextual assumptions can be extended in the way described in more detail in Sperber and Wilson (1995). Note that this process follows the path of least effort dictated by the relevance-theoretic comprehension procedure. Now the most easily accessible assumptions apart from those used in interpreting the last utterance are those used in interpreting the second to last utterance, and so on. Should one of these assumptions provide a suitable referent for the anaphor in the current utterance, and should the resulting interpretation satisfy the hearer's expectation of relevance, this referent should be taken as the intended one. If a referent for the anaphor cannot be found by following a path of least effort through this 'network' of assumptions contributing to the (complex) relevance relations in the text, more processing effort will be required, perhaps so much that no interpretation which satisfies the hearer's expectation of relevance can be found; in this case an anaphor should not have been used. Hence intuitions about the interaction of anaphor use and the presence of (superficial) coherence relations can be explained in a principled way.

Since the relevance-theoretic account of anaphora just outlined does not rely on structural relations (semantic or otherwise), the same account can be run on the conversational data. In this way, the otherwise unmotivated similarities between the explanation of anaphora in these two genres in Fox's analysis — such as the notions of return-pop and closed-down units — can be motivated.

However, Fox's (1987) account and the relevance-theoretic account of anaphora are not just the same analysis expressed in different terms; they do make different predictions. One obvious point is that the relevance-theoretic account considers connectivity between utterances in a text to be a matter of degree (Unger 1996:426 and 430). In an account based on hierarchical discourse structure — such as Fox's — this is not so. As a consequence, on the relevance-theoretic account one would expect to find degrees of acceptability of anaphora across unit boundaries. That this expectation is really borne out in natural language data is illustrated in (20):

(20) Then there was a pause, and after it many swift scenes followed that Frodo in some way knew to be parts of a great history in which he had become involved. The mist cleared and he saw a sight which he had never seen before but knew

> at once: the Sea. Darkness fell. The sea rose and raged in a great storm. Then he saw against the Sun, sinking blood-red into a wrack of clouds, the black outline of a tall ship with torn sails riding up out of the West. Then a wide river flowing through a populous city. Then a white fortress with seven towers. And then again a ship with black sails, but now it was morning again, and the water rippled with light, and a banner bearing the emblem of a white tree shone in the sun. A smoke as of fire and battle arose, and again the sun went down in a burning red that faded into a grey mist; and into the mist a small ship passed away, twinkling with lights. It vanished, and Frodo sighed and prepared to draw away.
>
> But suddenly the Mirror went altogether dark, as dark as if a hole had opened in the world of sight, and Frodo looked into emptiness. In the black abyss there appeared a single Eye that slowly grew, until it filled nearly all the Mirror. So terrible was it that Frodo stood rooted, unable to cry out or to withdraw his gaze. The Eye was rimmed with fire, but was itself glazed, yellow as a cat's, watchful and intent, and the black slit of its pupil opened on a pit, a window into nothing. (J. R. R. Tolkien *The Lord of the Rings*. London: HarperCollins Publishers, 2001:354–5)

Although all conditions of Fox's theory are thus that *Frodo* could be referred to by a pronoun in the last sentence of the first paragraph, the referring expression is used instead. Furthermore, since *Frodo* is the focal participant in this section of the narrative, it should be possible to refer to him with pronouns throughout the second paragraph, but the author chose otherwise. Indeed, if pronouns were used in all these cases instead, the reader would have no difficulty identifying the intended referent, although one would still agree that the author's choice makes for a better style. Notice furthermore that the use of a pronoun instead of *Frodo* in the last sentence of the first paragraph would raise the acceptability of the same throughout the second paragraph. Thus there are degrees of the acceptability of pronominal reference both within and across paragraph boundaries.[7]

There is therefore reason to believe that there are both theoretical and empirical grounds for preferring a relevance-theoretic account of anaphora to one based on hierarchical discourse structure. As the relevance-theoretic account does not appeal to genre considerations, it follows that anaphora does not demand an explanation in terms of genre.

7.5 Conclusion

In this chapter, I have examined four types of linguistic data which have been, or may be, taken to support the thesis that genre — understood as directly or indirectly related to coherence — may influence the semantics of certain linguistic markers or constructions, that is, have a linguistic function. In each case it turned out that an alternative analysis along relevance-theoretic lines is available which does not appeal to genre information. I also argued that these relevance-theoretic accounts are empirically better evidenced than accounts based on genre information. Thus, a considerable range of alleged counterexamples to the claim of the previous chapters — that genre can not be expected to serve a linguistic function via some notion of (global) coherence - have been shown to be invalid. This not only strengthens the conclusions of Part 1 of this book with regard to genre in general, but also points the way towards interesting new approaches to a whole range of linguistic data.

Part 3

GENRE IN INFERENTIAL THEORIES OF COMMUNICATION

8 Genre in code-based theories of communication

8.1 Introduction

Whereas in the previous chapters I was mainly concerned with approaches to genre which claim a linguistic function (that is, which claim that genre affects the semantics of linguistic forms), I will now, in the third part of this book, discuss approaches to genre which claim a hermeneutical function (that is, which claim that genre information facilitates comprehension). One approach of this kind is articulated within the framework of systemic-functional linguistics (Halliday 1978, 1985; Halliday and Hasan 1976, 1980, 1985), under the name of register and genre theory. In recent years there has been a growing interest in systemic-functional register and genre theory. In this chapter I want to discuss this theory, asking in particular what it has to say about the functions of genre and their causes.

8.2 Register and context

The starting point of systemic-functional register and genre theory is the observation that texts with the same subject matter may nevertheless be quite different. Eggins and Martin (1997) open their introduction to register and genre theory with two texts on the same theme, the concept 'postmodernism,' and show that there are interesting differences with respect to the use of linguistic features such as nominalisation, expanded or elementary noun phrases, emotive vocabulary, and so on. The conclusion is that since these texts were produced in different settings (one was taken from a textbook, the other from an oral lecture), the social context influences the make-up of the text. According to Eggins and Martin, it is the linguist's task to isolate those aspects of the social context which systematically correlate with the linguistic realisation of a text.

Register theory, as introduced by Halliday (see Downing 1996:13–14 for a survey and bibliographical references; also Eggins and Martin 1997), claims to have isolated three areas in which social context is systematically correlated to the linguistic realisation of texts: *mode, field,* and *tenor.* The *mode* parameter has to do with the details of the communication situation: whether it is a face-to-face interaction, a conversation over the phone, a lecture, a textbook, and so on. These situations affect in particular the degree of interaction of the communicators and the feedback they can give each other (Eggins and Martin 1997:232). The *field* parameter relates to the subject matter of the communication event, and how much the communicators know of it: how much technical vocabulary is assumed, the level of intertextuality (that is, the knowledge of which other texts the hearer is assumed to have), and so on (Eggins and Martin 1997:233). Finally, the *tenor* parameter relates the social roles of the communicators to the text they produce (Eggins and Martin 1997:233).

Crucial to understanding this notion of register (and the notion of genre based on it) is an understanding of the notion of context used in systemic-functional linguistics. Whereas most pragmatic theories in the Gricean tradition treat context as a set of assumptions (propositions) used in the interpretation of a given utterance (Sperber and Wilson 1995:15–16; Gazdar 1979; Lascarides and Asher 1993; but see Levinson 1983:22–3 for discussion), the notion of context in systemic-functional linguistics is a pre-Gricean one, and refers to the setting in which a text is produced and received, or rather to those features of the setting which systematically affect the linguistic realisation of a text (Orta 1996:31–3). The social context in register and genre theory has therefore little to do with the content of the utterance or preceding utterances, and is a separate notion from co-text. Context in this sense is given in advance of the interpretation process (see Duranti and Goodwin 1992b for a similar, but more flexible conception of context).

The central claim of register theory is that register, via its three parameters, narrows the linguistic choices a speaker can make. In this sense, register can explain linguistic variation, understood not in a rigid, deterministic sense, but in a weaker one: register opens up a certain range of linguistic options while demoting others from the total set of options available in the language at large (Eggins and Martin 1997:234). This is a probabilistic approach to language variation.

Register thus provides a link between social setting and linguistic form. In my terms, this means that register is claimed to have a linguistic function, here in the sense of systematically limiting or directing means of expression. As meaning in systemic-functional linguistics is seen as primarily due to paradigmatic choice (Orta 1996:30–1; 29 footnote 1), register is also said to influence the meaning-potential of texts.

8.3 Register and text typology

The notion of register can certainly be used as the basis for text typology: one could, for example, group together texts with the same value for the *field* parameter; and texts could similarly be sorted according to the values of the other two parameters. Thus one might distinguish detective stories from historical novels (*field*), sermons from pamphlets (*mode*), (*tenor*). As Orta (1996) and Downing (1996) point out, text typology in the early days of systemic-functional linguistics was indeed based on register. However, in recent years the notion of genre has been added. In the remainder of this section I want to look at the reasons for this shift; in the following section, I will look more closely at the resulting concept of genre.

A first indication of the need for a distinction between register and genre can be drawn from informal language use. Downing (1996:12) observes:

> Speakers in informal settings, nevertheless, intuitively make a distinction [between register and genre]. When someone says of Sir Randolph Quirk that he can handle all the registers, it clearly means that he can talk to different kinds of people on different things in different situations, not that he is equally successful as a writer

> of grammars, sonnets, sermons and newspaper articles. Conversely, on the occasion of one writer being introduced to another writer a question might conceivably be "What's your genre?" but never "What's your register?"

Another indication that register on its own may not be sufficient for a fully-fledged, linguistically-relevant text typology comes from ethnographic studies. Ethnographers have analysed typical communication situations such as service encounters, buying in the marketplace, and so on as staged activities with obligatory and optional elements in a certain order (see summaries in Downing 1996:19–22; Eggins and Martin 1997:239–41). This staging seems to be part of the cultural setting. It is thus on a different level of 'context' than the social setting.[1] Furthermore, in the notion of register there seems to be no natural place to incorporate generic structure.

A similar point can be made from a linguistic perspective. According to Eggins and Martin (1997:235), the coherence of texts rests only partially on textual cohesion. Generic structure also contributes to the coherence of texts, and is claimed to be another facet of textual coherence.

8.4 Genre

The notion of genre was thus introduced into systemic-functional register and genre theory as a means of handling the generic (schematic) structure of texts. This is the main feature which distinguishes genre from register. What the two notions have in common is that both relate sociocultural context to the linguistic realisation of texts. However, the kinds of context involved are seen as lying on different levels. The culture defines different types of social interaction, with associated generic organisations. It is within these types of social interaction that register parameters become operative. Thus, the context of culture is seen as wider than the context of social setting. Register is then constrained by genre: the genre determines which register variables are operative in a given text. It is in this sense that register is said to be the realisation of genre (Downing 1996:22–5; Orta 1996:36).

Another approach to genre starts from the recognition that genre is linked to the (main) purpose or goal of a group of texts (Downing 1996:17), their intention or discourse function. Each culture is seen as defining its own set of communicative purposes and ways of achieving them. This is how the function of genre (purpose, goal, intention) is connected with the schematic structure of a genre: the culture defines staged ways of achieving typical purposes or goals. Orta (1996:35–6) puts it this way:

> Within each culture there have evolved ways of getting things done, or ways of going about achieving common goals or purposes in life. Examples of genres include service encounters, ordering meals in restaurants, recounting the day's events, telling stories, writing stories, arguing a point of view. Each involves, in one way or another, the use of language and each results in a different text type, or genre. Each genre is distinguished by a distinctive schematic structure, that is, a distinctive sequence of beginning, middle and end stages that enable the overall purpose of a genre to be realized. Each culture has evolved its own ways of going about doing things, and thus there may be considerable variation of genres from one culture to another.

8.5 Evaluation and research questions

Systemic-functional register and genre theory is essentially a code theory of language use: 'In this chapter we have explained how R> [register and genre theory] views text, and therefore the lexical, grammatical and semantic choices which constitute it, as both encoding and construing the different layers of context in which the text was enacted' (Eggins and Martin 1997:251). The central concern is to establish systematic relations between certain dimensions of (social) context which restrict choices of linguistic items and structure, and thereby the meaning of texts. As noted above, Eggins and Martin (1997:234–6) emphasise that this systematic correlation is probabilistic: while certain contextual factors may make certain choices more likely than others, untypical choices may nevertheless occur and are not to be ruled out. However, this emphasis on probabilistic determination of textual properties by contextual factors turns systemic-functional register and genre theory into a rather weak code theory. The question arises how texts exhibiting choices which were less likely in their context are nevertheless understood.

Another factor which turns systemic-functional register and genre theory into a weak code theory is the claim that there might be other layers of context — such as ideology — which play a role and which have not yet been investigated or even discovered (Eggins and Martin 1997:237). This affects both register and genre, but the open-endedness of the theory is particularly obvious with respect to the notion of genre. Genre, in the sense of generic structure of texts, is described as '*a* further significant device which enables each text to function as a semantic unit' (Eggins and Martin 1997:emphasis mine). Coherence (which supposedly establishes semantic units) is thus a product of cohesion, genre, and possibly other unnamed factors. Furthermore, the effects of genre are due to more than generic structure: 'We can see these differences of purpose reflected both in the way the texts achieve coherence and in the way each text unfolds dynamically' (Eggins and Martin 1997:236). However, in the next paragraph Eggins and Martin focus on generic structure: 'Thus, the major linguistic reflex of differences in purpose is the staging structure by which a text unfolds' (1997:236). As a result, the discussion of genre is narrowed down to the 'major' linguistic effects of the relevant contextual factor (purpose, in this case). Thus, neither the notion of genre nor its functions are clearly delimited. This leaves the theory incomplete, which is especially unsatisfactory for a code theory, as little of the explanatory power of a code remains.

A further problem with systemic-functional register and genre theory is that it appears to underestimate the problems involved in explaining how understanding is achieved. This is probably best illustrated by looking at the sample analysis of two texts in Eggins and Martin (1997:244–51).[2] The analysis starts with the observation that:

> both texts seek to persuade readers to comply with a directive, and yet they do so in very different ways. Technically, the texts are from the same genre (directive), but exhibit variation in register (field, tenor, mode). We will now briefly explain the linguistic features which realize these contextual dimensions, and suggest reasons for the differences between the texts. (Eggins and Martin 1997:245)

The hearer's understanding of the main purpose (intention) — persuasion in this case — is taken to be unproblematic and treated as the starting point of the analysis. A cognitively realistic explanatory theory, however, must say something about how the hearer recognises the intentions of speakers. Since systemic-functional register and genre theory doesn't explain understanding, it is not clear whether any of the descriptive statements made are relevant for the process of utterance interpretation. Furthermore, the explanation that is offered is a purely sociological one: sociological functions are the basis for language use. Thus, Halliday (1978, 1985) sees language as a social semiotic, and Eggins and Martin (1997:251) say that texts are 'semiotic constructions of socially constructed meanings.' No cognitive role or function of genre or register is, strictly speaking, claimed to exist. Moreover, Thibault (1999) argues explicitly that verbal understanding should not be explained in cognitive terms but in socio-semiotic terms, contrasting the systemic-functional approach directly with relevance theory:

> Rather than looking for the basis of meaning in an ontologically distinct domain of thought, meaning-making is located in the interactions between participants and between these and the world. The lexicogrammatical and phonological and graphological resources of language constitute the smaller-scale choices out of which larger-scale social activity is dynamically assembled in the real-time of interaction. This always occurs with reference to the genre and intertextual conventions of a given community. (Thibault 1999:557)

In other words, it is claimed that the lack of cognitive orientation and interest in cognitive processes of utterance comprehension is a virtue rather than a defect, and that social interaction rather than mental processing accounts for understanding. The interesting point to note here is that genre is seen as a *sine qua non:* the assembly of meaning 'always occurs with reference to the genre.' This means that genre is understood to have a very strong hermeneutical function: without the recognition of genre, text comprehension has not been achieved. From this perspective, systemic-functional linguistics seems to claim that genre does not have a cognitive role, but a strong hermeneutical function. Clearly this claim needs to be investigated, and I will turn to a discussion of it in the next section.

8.6 Genre in a non-cognitive account of communication

Thibault (1999) explains utterance interpretation in his theory with the following example:

(1) A: Peter is bald. (p. 566)

The first aspect of the sign-system used in interpreting this utterance is the linguistic code. Thibault claims that adjectives in clauses of the type in (1), which is part of the sign system (2), 'name a general class of quality.' This quality-class classifies the noun of which the predicate is an attribute. The referent of the noun is then taken as instantiating the quality-class named in the attributive adjective.

(2) a. Peter is bald.
b. John is handsome.
c. Mary is beautiful.

This semantics which Thibault assigns to the (linguistic form of) the utterance (1) crucially avoids saying that it refers to a state of affairs in the world where the proposition *Peter is bald* is true. It is decidedly not a truth-conditional or referential semantics, which would apply as well to propositions or thoughts. Rather, Thibault (1999:568) stresses that the linguistic choice of the speaker 'construes or interprets some real world state of affairs through the categories of the language system.' In the case of (1), the construal is one of simply stating something, without any (explicit) modal claim. It thus represents a choice in the sign system (3):

(3) a. Peter is bald.
 b. Mary declared Peter bald.
 c. Mary thought Peter bald.
 d. Mary wished Peter bald.
 e. Mary saw Peter bald. (p. 569)

The utterance of (1) is linguistically construed as being situated not only in the sign systems (2) and (3), but also in a system of registers:

(4) a. Peter is bald.
 b. Peter is hairless.
 c. Peter is napless.
 d. Peter is tonsured. (p. 573–4)

As noted above, registers are claimed to be further embedded in a system of genre, which might be further embedded in a system of ideologies. In looking at this example, I have only discussed so-called 'ideational' meanings, that is, semantic patterns. However, any utterance realises discourse functions such as giving a reason, providing a motivation, getting the hearer to act, causing the hearer to trust the speaker, and so on. Some of these (for example the last two) concern the interpersonal level of meaning. Utterance interpretation includes the task of locating an utterance on this level of (interpersonal) discursive functions.

In the way outlined above, the speaker's choice of words and grammar delimits an array of potential utterance meanings. Producing an utterance and thereby delimiting such a potential array of meanings is the first step in the process of discursively negotiating the speaker's meaning, which is what utterance interpretation is all about. Other steps include the hearer's responding to the speaker's utterance according to a (more or less arbitrarily chosen) meaning and checking his understanding against the speaker's reaction to this understanding (Thibault 1999:590).

The role of genre in this account of utterance interpretation is twofold: first, the lexicogrammatical choices made in the utterance can point to a certain register (for example the choice of the word 'bald' instead of 'hairless'). The use of register is further constrained by genre (as explained above in Section 8.4), so that choice of a certain register can point to the use of a certain genre. On the other hand, the discourse functions of utterances are constrained by (schematic) genre specifications (see above, Section 8.4), so that the knowledge of the genre used can aid the recognition of the intended discourse function. However, in all these cases genre is just one sign system in the complex semiotic network of codes which is used to interpret utterances. In other words: genre is one element of the complex system of contextual and intertextual factors involved in communication.

In fact, Thibault's main point against relevance theory is that it does not pay attention to the highly complex communicative contexts in real discourse.[3] That is, he charges relevance theory with an impoverished account of context. However, this claim is made solely on the basis of two works in relevance theory: Sperber and Wilson (1995) and Franken (1997). But from Sperber and Wilson (1995), he cites as evidence only the discussion of loose talk (Sperber and Wilson 1995 Chapter 4, Section 8:231–7) without referring to the discussion of context selection (Sperber and Wilson 1995 Chapter 3, Sections 3 and 4). Moreover, Thibault's paper contains an interesting example illustrating the superiority of the relevance-theoretic account of context selection to the systemic-functional view of context as given in advance of interpretation. This example is taken from an Australian television documentary about the life of a family in Sydney.

(5) [A dialogue between a young married couple, Paul and Dion. They are in the kitchen of their Sydney home and look at the mess which Paul's pet cockatoo has made.]

Dion: (1) look at the mess Paul (2) you're going to have to clean up in here (3) it's a pigsty

Paul: (4) it is rather a pigsty

Dion: (5) yes (6) well (7) it's your animal

(Thibault 1999:584–5)

Thibault gives a detailed account of how — according to his theory — clause (5:3) *it's a pigsty* is interpreted. He comments on the interpretation of *it:* 'In this clause, *it* refers exophorically to the immediate situational context. In particular, *it* refers to the kitchen in which the conversation takes place.' (p. 585) However, in this situation, there are several possible referents for *it:* the kitchen, the kitchen table, the whole house, and the cockatoo. How does Paul understand that *it* refers to the kitchen? Thibault offers no account of this; he rather presupposes that Paul understands correctly. Relevance theory, on the other hand, has an explicit account of reference assignment on offer (Sperber and Wilson 1995 Chapter 4, Section 3, esp. pp. 187–8; Smith and Wilson 1992; Wilson and Matsui 1998; Wilson and Sperber 2002): the hearer should access the most easily available referent. If (and only if), on this interpretation, the utterance satisfies the hearer's expectations of relevance, he should accept this interpretation as the intended one. This is an instance of the general relevance-theoretic comprehension procedure. My conclusion is that Thibault's systemic-functional theory of context is not explanatorily adequate, and that relevance theory fares better in this respect.

The point is that the hearer needs to choose which context to access and use in order to understand the speaker. There are many potential contexts available, suggesting different referents for *it* (or referring expressions in general): the kitchen, the house, the kitchen floor, the cupboards, and so on. The speaker can potentially use this very same expression *it* (in *it's a pigsty*) to mean something different: the kitchen is a pigsty, the house is a pigsty, and so on The same utterance, uttered in the same set of potential contexts, can be used to express quite different thoughts. It seems that in a theory which treats context as given and the meaning of utterances as determined solely by their linguistic forms and the extra-linguistic setting cannot account for this fact. In such theories one would have to say that the resulting indeterminacy of meaning is irrelevant to communication. But notice that it makes a lot of difference to Paul whether he is expected to clean up the kitchen or the whole house. So one cannot resort to this kind of argument. My conclusion is that the empirical facts about reference assignment and context selection in communication cannot be explained without recourse to the notion of speaker's intention, which must be understood as more fine-grained than the semantics of natural language alone allows. This argues in favour of the relevance-theoretic description of communication — inspired by Grice — as a process in which the audience is to infer the communicator's (informative) intentions.[4]

I conclude that the explicitly non-cognitive approach to communication argued for in Thibault (1999) is not tenable. In particular, it fails to provide an adequate account of context and context selection, which is crucial for an analysis of genre.

However, this does not mean that the systemic-functional account of register and genre has to be completely dismissed. Thibault's strong insistence on a non-cognitive approach to communication and genre notwithstanding, the claim that the (main) distinctive feature of genre is to carry information about generic structure can be construed in a way relevant to a cognitive theory of utterance comprehension. Thus one could claim that the recognition of schematic structure facilitates comprehension by directing hearers to certain anticipatory hypotheses about the intended interpretation of the text.[5] Understood in this way, systemic-functional register and genre theory does point to a research question relevant to the topic of this book: is genre mainly characterised in terms of cognitive schematic structures of texts? This question will be taken up in the next section.

8.7 Genre and schematic structure

As we have seen, systemic-functional linguistics distinguishes between register and genre mainly by saying that genre has to do with the schematic structure of texts. The claim is that these structures have developed in a culture ('language') as staged ways of getting things done. In this section I want to examine this claim that genre is definable in terms of schematic text structure.

Notice first that there are texts where genre knowledge does intuitively play a crucial role in interpretation, but where this knowledge is not about schematic text structure. Isaiah 5:1–7 is a case in point. This text is quoted in full in Chapter 5.1 and discussed in detail there. Here I would merely like to note that the reader (or hearer) who knows that this text starts off as a love song will interpret it in a unique and rich way. The effects on interpretation range from reference assignment to the pronominal subject in the first clause (*I will sing of my friend and his vineyard;* 'I' refers to a fictitious female speaker, not to the prophet Isaiah), to disambiguations of word meaning (the word *dôd* is used in the sense of 'the beloved one,' not in the sense of 'father's brother'), and to the interpretation of figures of speech (for example 'vineyard' as a standard metaphor for 'lover') and the impact they are supposed to achieve (for example that the addressees should identify themselves with the lover who was cared for so much and yet did not bring forth 'good fruit,' that is, an appropriate response in the relationship).

Notice that all the information that the hearer would have accessible by recognising the love-song genre is information about the conventional use of metaphors such as 'vineyard' for the lover. No appeal to structural information or staging of actions has to be made. Thus there is genre information which does not reduce to schematic structure, and genre cannot be characterised solely or primarily in terms of schematic text structure information.

It is also clear that schematic text structure is not always sufficient to define a genre. The psalms of the Hebrew Bible are a case in point. While several kinds of psalms have been identified and described in the literature in terms of their schematic structure (see for example Westermann 1977), it does not seem possible to define the genre 'psalm' in general in terms of schematic structure.

Another point worth noting is that an account of genre in terms of schematic structure does not explain why texts which strictly follow the pattern may be judged dull or uninteresting (Samet and Schank 1984). Consider the following well-known parable:

(6) Listen! A farmer went out to sow his seed. As he was scattering the seed, some fell along the path, and the birds came and ate it up. Some fell on rocky places, where it did not have much soil. It sprang up quickly, because the soil was shallow. But when the sun came up, the plants were scorched, and they withered because they had no root. Other seed fell among thorns, which grew up and choked the plants, so that they did not bear grain. Still other seed fell on good soil. It came up, grew and produced a crop, multiplying thirty, sixty, or even a hundred times. (The gospel of Mark 4:3–8; New International Version)

What makes this text a parable rather than, say, a description of farming practices, seems to be that the hearer is led to attribute to the speaker the intention to communicate something more than what it says at face-value. This expectation seems to be created not by structural means, nor by cultural expectations, but by contextual information: that this parable was told by Jesus in the course of his teaching the crowd about religious matters.

On the other hand, texts which show considerable variation from the schematic norm may be judged especially artistic. For example, it has been demonstrated in detail by Kotthoff (1995) that the (oral) genre of Georgian toasts is characterised both by a strict pattern and by variation. In contests, both adherence to the abstract pattern of a toast and individual variation are taken into account in judging the performance of orators.

It follows that simple closeness-of-fit judgements of a text against the purported schematic formula of its genre cannot explain how knowledge of genre is exploited in text comprehension. Again, aspects of the speaker's intention in producing a certain text seem at least as central to an account of genre as structural considerations.

The conclusion I draw from this discussion is that an analysis of genre in terms of schematic structure alone is not adequate. A notion of genre must be found which can account both for cases where genre knowledge has an influence on interpretation but does not involve knowledge of schematic structure, and for cases where schematic structure does play a role. In this latter case, however, due attention must be paid to the role of variation and style. Attention must also be paid to the role of the speaker's intentions in communication and the hearer's recognition of these — in other words, the role of genre needs to be studied within an ostensive-inferential account of communication.

Before turning to this, some words need to be said on the notion of register. If it can be shown that the notion of genre in register and genre theory is inadequate, the question arises of whether a text typology based on the notion of register may nevertheless be more promising. It has also been claimed that an inferential theory of communication such as relevance theory needs an account of register to be fully explanatory (Goatly 1994). It is to these questions that we now turn.

8.8 On register

As mentioned above, the notion of register alone may provide a basis for text typology, that is, genre definition. In this section I want to look at one proposal to treat genre in terms of register, that of Goatly (1994). Goatly's proposal is particularly important for this book because he explicitly relates systemic-functional register theory to relevance theory.

Goatly outlines the way in which register theory can supplement relevance theory by discussing the use of metaphor in various genres Goatly (1994:159–76). The relevance-theoretic account of metaphor involves the claim that metaphorical utterances generally weakly communicate a whole range of implicatures: that is, they typically result in a slight increase in the manifestness of a wide range of assumptions, rather than making a small set of assumptions strongly manifest (to the addressee). Goatly's point is that knowledge of the field-tenor-mode parameters of genres effectively narrows down the processing effort the hearer has to expend. To support this claim, he presents an analysis of metaphors in a sample of texts from the genres *conversation, national daily news reports, popular science articles, magazine advertising,* and *modern English lyric poetry.* After analysing the field-mode-tenor parameters of these genres (Goatly

1994:160–1), he offers five hypotheses about how these settings of the register parameters influence the occurrence and use of metaphor in the different genres, together with evidence from texts to support these hypotheses (Goatly 1994:161–76):

> Hypothesis 1: The detection (disambiguation) of metaphorical meaning as opposed to literal meaning will depend on the principle of relevance in relation to field (subject matter). (p. 161)
>
> Hypothesis 2: The kinds of implicated assumptions will be determined by the principle of relevance in relation to the purposes inherent in field and tenor. (p. 166)
>
> Hypothesis 3: The computation of what is adequately relevant will be determined by the principle of relevance in relation to the purposes inherent in field and tenor. (p. 171)
>
> Hypothesis 4: The greater the processing time, an aspect of mode, the more likely we can presume that relevance is achieved by weakly implicating a large number of assumptions. (p. 174).

It is worth noting in passing that these hypotheses amount to the claim that genre has a hermeneutical function in the sense adopted in this book, that is, that genre facilitates comprehension by constraining the type and range of implicatures to be expected from the text as a whole.

Regarding hypothesis 1, it is worth mentioning that Sperber and Wilson (1995) have argued that the literal-figurative dichotomy is illusory. Utterance interpretation does not involve a step of deciding whether an utterance is intended in its literal or figurative meaning. For one thing, whether a stimulus is interpreted as strongly communicating one or two assumptions or weakly communicating an unspecified range of assumptions is a matter of degree; there is no cut-off point that coincides with a borderline between literal and metaphorical or poetic interpretation. As always, the first interpretation which satisfies the expectation of relevance created by the utterance is the one the hearer should choose. The interpretation process follows a path of least effort: the context will be constructed by accessing assumptions from an initial context containing information used in the interpretation of the last utterance (if any), information about the situation the communicators are in, and so on and extending this initial context to include other assumptions in order of cognitive accessibility. In other words, in relevance theory the 'disambiguation' (to use Goatly's term) of metaphors in an utterance is part of the regular relevance-theoretic comprehension process, drawing on any suitable assumptions, including the subject matter of the communication process. Thus, Goatly's example *I shot an eagle,* uttered by a golf player in the clubhouse to a friend after a round of golf, will find a natural explanation in relevance theory: the concept GOLF (which is highly salient in the mutual cognitive environment of speaker and addressee at the time of utterance) gives easy access to encyclopaedic information about golfing, including the information that an 'eagle' is a rare and successful achievement. If the utterance, when interpreted in this context, satisfies the hearer's expectation of relevance, other interpretations will not be considered.

Consider example (7):

(7) I had to shift gears quickly.

I may use this utterance in a conversation with colleagues about my experiences teaching two consecutive sets of students the same topics in pragmatics. Then the utterance is intended as 'metaphorical.' I could also use this same utterance in a conversation with a friend in describing a difficult situation while driving to work. In this case the utterance will (conceivably) receive a 'literal' interpretation. Yet the setting of the field parameter for the genre conversation as given by Goatly (1994:160) does not help at all in accounting for these different interpretations. What is central to an adequate explanation of these data is a workable account of context selection in utterance interpretation. Such an account is offered in Sperber and Wilson (1995).

Let's turn to Goatly's hypothesis 4. Sperber and Wilson give an extreme example of weak communication (1995:55–6):

> Mary and Peter are newly arrived at the seaside. She opens the window overlooking the sea and sniffs appreciatively and ostensively. When Peter follows suit, there is no one particular good thing that comes to his attention: the air smells fresh, fresher than it did in town, it reminds him of their previous holidays, he can smell the sea, seaweed, ozone, fish; all sorts of pleasant things come to mind, and while, because her sniff was appreciative, he is reasonably safe in assuming that she must have intended him to notice at least some of them, he is unlikely to be able to pin her intentions down any further. Is there any reason to assume that her intentions were more specific? Is there a plausible answer, in the form of an explicit linguistic paraphrase, to the question, what does she mean? Could she have achieved the same communicative effect by speaking? Clearly not.

It is interesting to note that this case of communication does not involve either a long production time or a long interpretation ('reading') time. Yet a whole range of assumptions are weakly communicated. Thus a simple equation of length of production and processing time (as specified in the mode parameter of register) with the likelihood of communication achieved by a large array of weakly communicated assumptions cannot be maintained.[6] Whether communication is achieved in this weak way is more directly connected with the intention of the speaker, and the proportion of decoding to inference, rather than with external factors such as production or reading time, or medium of communication.

Hypotheses 2 and 3 have a common purpose: they claim that register/genre information plays a role in creating the particular presumption of relevance which is communicated by a given utterance. These two of Goatly's hypotheses and his comments on them seem to fit well with Sperber and Wilson's own remarks:

> Imagine a group of people having a conversation in a café or a pub after work, just a light conversation between friends, Here a modicum of relevance should be enough: nobody will be willing to put in much processing effort,

> or expect major contextual effects. For that matter, nobody will put enormous effort into producing stimuli that would be worth extensive processing. By contrast, consider what is supposed to happen in a seminar. Here everyone is supposed to be on the alert, ready to put a considerable amount of intellectual effort into producing and processing information. In these circumstances, information relevant enough to be worth the addressee's attention is quite relevant indeed. There is little point, in one set of circumstances, in expecting a level of relevance only normally achieved in quite different circumstances, and a reasonable addressee will adjust his expectations accordingly... On various social occasions, the expected level of relevance is culturally defined. (Sperber and Wilson 1995:161)

In the Postface to the second edition of their book *Relevance,* Sperber and Wilson build much of the substance of these comments into the formulation of the communicative principle of relevance itself: in ostensive communication, the stimulus creates a presumption of optimal relevance, defined as in (8):

(8) *Presumption of optimal relevance (revised)*

  (a) The ostensive stimulus is relevant enough for it to be worth the addressee's effort to process it.

  (b) The ostensive stimulus is the most relevant one *compatible with the communicator's abilities and preferences.*

(Sperber and Wilson 1995:270. Emphasis mine.)

The suggestion that genre information — whether defined in the form of register parameters or otherwise — affects the presumption of relevance seems a plausible one, and has been made more precise in Chapter 5. What is questionable is whether the notion of register as it stands can be usefully employed as a basis for explaining the cognitive processes involved.

Goatly (1994) explains the content of hypothesis 2 with the following (made up) example:

(9) a. [Utterance made in a biology class]
The kidney is the sewer of the body.
(Goatly's example 22, p. 167)

b. A: Do you want to go on a boat trip on the river?
B: What, on that sewer?
(Goatly's example 23, p. 167)

The metaphor *sewer* is used with a different goal or point of comparison in these examples. In (9a) it has an explanatory function, while in (9b) it is used because of its emotive impact. Goatly (1994:167) comments:

> Because conversation, both in field and tenor, has a strongly interpersonal function, one dimension of which is the expression of affect, it would be reasonable to look for implicated conclusions of an affective kind in interpreting [(9b)]. Whereas in [(9a)], where the field is scientific education, and the social distance of the tenor is greater, one would expect the motive for metaphor to be explanatory rather than affective, ideational rather than interpersonal.

However, (9a) can as well be used in conversation:

(10) Child: Daddy, what's the kidney?
Father: The kidney is the sewer of the body.

Thus it appears that field or tenor specifications are not enough to explain expectations about the kind of cognitive effects to be achieved by metaphors in a given utterance.

The main impact of hypothesis 4 is to account for differences in productiveness intended in the use of metaphors in different genres. Because one expects richer effects in, say, lyric poetry than in news reports, one does not go on to try a rich interpretation on dead metaphors in news reports. In poetry, however, metaphors are usually exploited, and the hearer expects to look for relevance via a rich interpretation of metaphors (Goatly 1994:172–4). However, even in lyric poetry the richness of metaphors varies. For example, the metaphor '*ears plastered down* on its knobbed skull' (describing a rat) in the poem 'An advancement of learning' by Seamus Heaney (quoted in Goatly 1994:165; line 23) is surely not as rich as other ones in the same poem as he points out: ' the river **nosed** past,/ **pliable, oil-skinned, wearing / A transfer** of gables and sky.' (Emphasis as in original)

> Instead of regarding these metaphors as mixed in a pejorative sense we can see that the poet is making successful transitions between them, based on the sharing of grounds. Noses are pliable and are covered in skin. One reading of oil-skinned 'covered with a skin of oil' disposes us to observe that oil is less viscous than water and that the word pliable therefore applies to it more literally, The alternative reading of oil-skinned 'covered with an oilskin' suggests the clothing used by fishermen and sailors which is literally pliable and suitable for wearing. The paint used for the transfers which children use to make pictures is also, presumably, oil-based, making a further link. (Goatly 1994:172–3)

The register variables of genres are thus too crude a tool to account for the mechanisms involved in interpreting metaphors which differ in richness.

The result of this discussion is that the spirit of Goatly's hypotheses 2 and 3, which relate to how genre might be involved in the creation of concrete expectations of relevance for a given utterance, are worth considering further. This has been taken up in Chapter 5. However, the notion of register as given in systemic-functional register and genre theory doesn't help in this task: the role of context in utterance interpretation is much more flexible than a characterisation of aspects of context in terms of register variables would predict. What is needed is an account of how the hearer goes about choosing the contextual assumptions which the speaker expected or intended him to use. To deal with the contribution of genre or register knowledge, one would then have to discuss the role of this kind of information within the overall process of inferential utterance interpretation. Does this information play a special role which sets it apart from other contextual information? In Unger (1994), I suggested that there are indeed some assumptions pertaining to cultural or social information which have a high degree of accessibility and can therefore influence language use in an interesting way.[7] Cultural or social information is highly accessible because it is often communicated within a society, and hence entertained by members of the society (Sperber 1996). Given that register or genre information is cultural information of this kind, it will be highly accessible for being selected as part of the context by the relevance-theoretic comprehension procedure. On this account, register or genre information is privileged for context selection only in the sense that it is easily accessible by virtue of its cultural role.

8.9 Conclusion

In this chapter, I have summarised and evaluated the position of systemic-functional linguistics on genre. This theory is primarily a social-semiotic one, in which genre is mainly seen as a construct relating social phenomena to language use. Thus, genre is claimed to have both a sociological and a linguistic function in the sense described in Chapter 1. In some varieties of genre theory it is also claimed to have a hermeneutical function. There is an ambivalence, though, in the systemic-functional linguistics literature as to whether register and genre theory makes any claim that genre has a cognitive role. While I have argued that some of the claims in register and genre theory can be restated in a way relevant to a cognitive theory of utterance interpretation, Thibault (1999) explicitly argues against a cognitive approach to communication in general, and to genre in particular. After arguing against Thibault's anti-cognitive account of communication and genre, I turned to an evaluation of the central claims of genre theory, re-interpreted in a way relevant to a cognitive approach to communication. The central claim of genre theory was that genre is mainly characterised in terms of its schematic structure. I have argued that this claim cannot be upheld as it stands. Thus, the systemic-functional theory of genre is inadequate. Furthermore, an adequate explanation of genre and the (limited) role it assigns to schematic structure needs to address the points raised in this chapter. I have argued that attempts to analyse genre in terms of register variables are also inadequate, since register theory fails to explain how register information and other contextual assumptions are chosen and used in utterance interpretation. Still, the discussion of systemic-functional register and genre theory has indicated important directions for further investigation and confirms claims made earlier in this book: the role of schematic structure in utterance interpretation needs to be reconsidered, and the role of genre information may be to contribute to forming the expectations of relevance created by a given utterance (as argued in Chapter 5). Most importantly, the evidence provided in this chapter shows that genre (and register) are best approached within an ostensive-inferential account of communication; thus, it is necessary to move away from theories which do not acknowledge the psychological role of intention (such as systemic-functional linguistics or semiotics). These themes will be investigated in the following chapters.

9 Conversational maxims and genre

9.1 Genre in an inferential theory of communication

As has been shown in the last chapter, theories of genre are often linked to code-based approaches to conversation. It may be tempting therefore to hypothesise that theories of genre are needed only in code-based theories of communication, not in inferential ones. However, this hypothesis is premature since suggestions have been made in the literature to incorporate accounts of genre into Gricean pragmatics. These proposals fall into two broad categories: one approach — taken for example by Kitis (1999), Harris (1995), and Holdcroft (1979) — argues that the Cooperative Principle has to be abandoned because it is operative only in some discourse types. The application of other maxims in these approaches is directly regulated by genre. The second type of approach — taken by Green (1995) — retains the Gricean system of maxims and especially the Cooperative Principle, saying that genre influences what the talk-exchange requires, thus fleshing out the substance of the Cooperative Principle to suit a specific stage in a given conversation. In this chapter I want to discuss these approaches and examine whether they lead to a feasible theory of genre in an inferential account of communication.

9.2 Discourse types and the universality of pragmatic maxims

A question which has been discussed in pragmatics over the years is whether Grice's Cooperative Principle is universally applicable or whether it applies only to certain discourse types, or only in certain cultures (Kitis 1999; Harris 1995). Holdcroft (1979) was among the first to suggest that the Cooperative Principle may not be operative in highly constrained institutional discourse; Harris (1995) makes a similar point. Holdcroft was mainly concerned with cases such as cross-examination in court, where the participants have unequal 'discourse rights.' The person under cross-examination, for example, cannot of his own volition change subjects or terminate the discourse. Other similar discourse types include interrogations, interviews, examinations, and so on (Holdcroft 1979:132; Kitis 1999:645).

According to Holdcroft, even in these cases of highly constrained institutional discourse, where the participants have unequal participation rights, the Cooperative Principle is indirectly in force: insofar as the institution is accepted, the Cooperative Principle is inherent in the institution itself. This more abstract version of the Cooperative Principle amounts to the injunction that communicators should make their contribution such as is required by the accepted purpose of the (social) institution. Holdcroft's formulation of a generalised Cooperative Principle abstracts from Grice's even further:

> Make your contribution to the discourse such as is required, at the stage at which it occurs, by the purposes you have in entering into, or which you have accepted as the purposes of, or which are the generally accepted purposes of, the discourse in which you are a participant. (Holdcroft 1979:139)

He also observes that not all of the maxims are operative in all discourse types, even under this generalised version of the Cooperative Principle. In order to appreciate what this claim amounts to, it is necessary to recall that in Grice's original conception, the individual maxims (quantity, quality, manner, and relation) spell out in more detail aspects of the Cooperative Principle. In his 'Retrospective Epilogue', Grice (1989:371), comments:

> I have so far been talking as if the right ground plan is to identify a supreme Conversational Principle which could be used to generate and justify a range of more specific but still highly general conversational maxims which in turn could be induced to yield particular conversational directives applying to particular subject matters, contexts, and conversational procedures, ...

In this theoretical architecture, it could be argued that Holdcroft's point that not all the maxims are operative in all discourse types amounts to the claim that the Cooperative Principle has a different character in different discourse types, or in other words, that the content of the Cooperative Principle varies. This claim is made more explicit in Kitis (1999), who argues precisely that Grice's 'supreme Conversational Principle' takes on a different content in each discourse type. She differs from Holdcroft, though, by claiming that this supreme principle of conversation is not Cooperation but Relevance.

For Kitis, Relevance is 'a forceful social parameter determining the process of conversation.' (Kitis 1999:647) This follows from the pivotal role this maxim plays in the generation of implicatures (Kitis 1999:647; Koutoupis-Kitis 1982). Implicatures, according to Kitis, arise primarily in adjacency pairs in conversation.[1] Adjacency sequences furthermore create and constrain expectations about what the other communicator might say. 'Adjacency sequences... give rise to certain expectancies in relation to what comes next which can be thought of as part of the domain of the maxim of Relevance.' (Kitis 1999:647) Therefore, argues Kitis, Relevance needs to be defined in social terms. As adjacency sequences in discourse are embedded in social events, it is by and large the type of social event in which the conversation (or talk-exchange, to use Grice's term) occurs which governs the particular instantiation of Global Relevance. Kitis nowhere defines what she means by Relevance, but the allusion to the (typical) goals of social events in which the discourse takes place suggests that her supermaxim of Global Relevance should read: be relevant to the goal or purpose of the present social event type.

Social events themselves are represented in the mind as frames or scripts (Kitis 1999:650). In these scripts, typical goals or purposes of the event in question are inscribed. These typical goals define the discourse type appropriate for the social event. The discourse type in turn specifies which maxims are operative in it, and how they are weighted in importance: 'Global Relevance relates first the discourse type to the social event (or domain) and only then are (aspects of) other maxims made contingent.' (p. 652) Thus, discourse type has a central role to play in this theory; not only is the precise instantiation of the conversational supermaxim different in different discourse types, but different sets of maxims are also operative in each discourse type. Understanding the intentions of the speaker thus depends on a recognition of the discourse type involved. In my terms, this is a strong claim about a hermeneutical function of genre.

In both Holdcroft's and Kitis' accounts, it is claimed that different conversational maxims are operative in different discourse types, and this claim extends to the supermaxim (Relevance or the Generalised Cooperative Principle), whose content is different in different situation types. But Holdcroft (1979:141) goes even further:

> The claim that acceptance of [the Cooperative Principle] and of its generalized version can involve the acceptance of different sets of maxims in different discourse-types, and even within different discourses of the same type carried on with rather different ends in view, is plausible, but frustrating.

The source of the frustration is as follows: if different maxims can be at work even within one discourse type, then the proposed procedures for recognising the particular instantiation of the supermaxim based on situation type and corresponding discourse type do not help any further. It is then unexplained how the hearer can understand a discourse which deviates from the standard type.

Kitis (1999:658) doesn't share this frustration. She comments on this quote from Holdcroft: 'However, the frustration, I think, originates from the lack of a typology of discourse types anchored in social domains. But this need not be so in theory.' In order to arrive at such a typology, she proposes to look first at institutional discourse, because it is easier to characterise than other discourse types (Kitis 1999:655). This raises the question of whether institutional discourse can be regarded as basic enough to provide a justifiable starting point for pragmatic theory. Furthermore, Kitis (1999:659) contends that even a relatively sophisticated typology would not cover every occurring discourse. She comments:

> One... must be aware that this approach offers only an initial and rather limited navigational orientation as events are not fully, or even correctly, represented in fossilized, static, abstracted, generalized and socially normalized models, but are also dynamically adapted to individualized cognitive interfaces... (Kitis 1999:663)

However, an adequate pragmatic theory must be able to account for the bulk of communicative events, not just the idealised ones. It is therefore obvious that Kitis' proposal to work out a better discourse typology does not remedy Holdcroft's frustration. Given this, Holdcroft's and Kitis' theories do not provide an adequate account of the role of discourse type in communication.

The starting point for both Holdcroft's and Kitis' theories was concern over certain kinds of highly constrained institutional discourse, which are seen as providing counter-evidence to Grice's original formulation of the Cooperative Principle. However, these discourse types are not necessarily a reason for abandoning Grice's Cooperative Principle. Grice's purpose in constructing the scheme of maxims and the over-arching supermaxim was to describe what makes conversational conduct rational or irrational; the Cooperative Principle and maxims were thus intended to be general enough to apply to every kind of conversation (Grice 1989:369). Grice was aware of discourse types such as cross-examination and argues that these 'honour the cooperative principle at least to the extent of aping its application' (Grice 1989:369–70).

It is clear, therefore, that the approach to discourse type advocated by Holdcroft and Kitis is not the only one conceivable within a broadly Gricean pragmatic framework. I will now turn to the proposal of Green (1995), who suggests how a theory of discourse type might be incorporated into a thoroughly Gricean account, with the original maxims and Cooperative Principle still in force.

9.3 Conversation types and conversational requirements

Green (1995) deals with implicatures said to arise as a result of Grice's quantity maxims. He argues that the common re-interpretation of these maxims as maxims of volubility, requiring speakers to 'give as much information as is compatible with the current purposes of the exchange' (p. 85), is not warranted. In particular, volubility, understood in this way, does not follow from Grice's formulation of the quantity maxims. Green demonstrates this by means of theoretical argumentation (pp. 85–8) and counterexamples (pp. 95–100).

It has often been claimed in the literature (Green 1995 cites Harnish 1976; Levinson 1983; Horn 1984, 1989; Hirschberg 1985) that the volubility interpretation of Grice's quantity maxims is necessary to account for scalar implicatures. Green proposes an alternative way of calculating implicatures which takes into account what is meant by '. . . for the current purposes of the exchange.' The idea is that the current goals and plans of the interlocutors influence what inferences are licensed by the (quantity) maxims. Different types of exchanges may have different plans and goals. In some cases, of course, the quantity maxims might be interpreted as volubility maxims. This is not so in others, and in these cases scalar implicatures will not be entertained. In other words: different discourse types regulate indirectly how the conversational maxims interact to generate implicatures, by specifying the parameter in the Cooperative Principle which relativises the nature of communicative cooperation to the requirements of the current talk exchange.

While Green's purpose is limited to explaining scalar implicatures, it is obvious that this proposal could be extended to yield a theory of genre within a truly Gricean pragmatics. In such a theory, genre will be seen as occasionally influencing the derivation of implicatures. In my terms, such a genre theory would claim a weak hermeneutical function for genre: in some cases, knowledge of genre will influence the audience's comprehension of implicitly communicated information, though comprehension of explicit meaning (including temporal and aspectual interpretation) will be largely uninfluenced by genre information. Thus, genre knowledge will be seen as indispensable in understanding the finer details of discourse meaning, although not a prerequisite for understanding as such.

9.3.1 Quantity and volubility

Grice's (1989:26) formulation of the quantity maxims is as follows:

> [Quantity] 1. Make your contribution as informative as is required (for current purposes of the exchange).
>
> [Quantity] 2. Do not make your contribution more informative than is required.

Green attempts to show that Quantity 1 is not the same as what he calls the Volubility Maxim. This latter maxim says that a speaker is obliged to give as much information as he has evidence for, as he knows, as is relevant to the current purpose of the exchange. The first maxim of quantity, on the other hand, says that a speaker is obliged to give enough information to enable the current purpose of the exchange to be achieved. These statements are not equivalent. A speaker who adheres to Volubility will also satisfy Quantity 1. The reverse is not true, as the following example demonstrates:

(1) A: What are three or four primes between one and fifty?
B: Eleven, thirteen and nineteen
B′: Three, five, seven and eleven (p. 88)

Answer B′ gives as much information as is permitted (naming four primes) and doesn't add more information than is required (naming no more than four primes). Answer B, on the other hand, gives as much information as is required (naming three primes), and does not add more than is required for the current purposes of the exchange: A is satisfied with B's naming only three random primes between one and fifty. Both B and B′ satisfy Quantity 1 (and Quantity 2), but only B′ satisfies Volubility.

9.3.2 Scalar implicatures and volubility

As noted above, Green argues that standard accounts of scalar implicatures such as Horn (1984, 1989), Hirschberg (1985) and Levinson (1983) rely on a Maxim of Volubility. Volubility does account for scalar implicatures. But since Volubility is not equivalent to Quantity 1, should a theory of conversation be amended to include such a maxim?

Green argues against the inclusion of a Maxim of Volubility on three grounds. First, there are examples of conversations where a Maxim of Volubility would make the wrong predictions but a Quantity Maxim would not. Three examples of this kind are presented.

Green's first example is (1) above. If the quantity maxims entailed something like Volubility, answer B would be taken to imply that the speaker of B does not know other primes than the ones he mentions. If he knew, he could have said so without going beyond the current purposes of the exchange, while still respecting other maxims. For example, mentioning more primes might be relevant to A by showing that B knows the primes fairly well. However, hearers of (1) would not normally draw such an implicature. It follows that the quantity maxims do not entail Volubility.

Green's second example comes from Horn:

(2) Some of my friends are Buddhists. (Horn 1984:13)

Horn takes this to have the implicature *Not all of my friends are Buddhists.* Green constructs a context where this implicature does not arise, although there is no clash with other maxims: suppose that it is mutually known that although B asks A only whether some of his friends are Buddhists she would also be interested in knowing whether in fact all of his friends were Buddhists. Still, A might prefer to be more vague on this point, perhaps for fear of being seen as a Buddhist groupie. (Green 1995:96–7) In this context, the utterance *Some of my friends are Buddhists* does not convey the implicature *All of my friends are Buddhists,* although Quantity 1 (but not Quantity 2) is observed. Again, it follows that the quantity maxims do not entail Volubility.

Green's third example involves a conversation in which two communicators are debating a point and one is trying to convince the other:

(3) S: Some wars are just, don't you agree?

H: Yes, in the case of a tyrannical aggressor for example. (Green 1995:99)

He comments on this example that there is a basic intuition that in a debate one should use the weakest premises possible to convince one's opponent, and because of this S cannot reasonably be seen as pragmatically implying that it is not the case that many wars are just nor that he doesn't know that many wars are just.

Again, the conclusion seems to be that a Volubility Maxim would be too strong.

A second argument against incorporating a Maxim of Volubility into a theory of conversation is that Volubility is hard to justify as a maxim for rational communicators to follow on theoretical grounds (pp. 100–1). The argument goes — roughly — like this: rationality in conversation means that speakers are in part guided by self interest in producing their utterance. Making a stronger claim rather than a weaker one that satisfies the current purposes of the talk exchange equally well creates stronger liabilities for the speaker: '. . . with a stronger claim there are more ways for the speaker to be shown up, and therefore more ways for the speaker's credibility to be tarnished' (Green 1995:101). It is generally speaking not in the speaker's own interest to become more vulnerable to discredit. Therefore a Maxim of Volubility is hard to justify on rational grounds.

Green's third reason for rejecting Volubility is that since this maxim is stronger than Quantity 1, it yields more clashes with other maxims. Calculating implicatures with maxim clashes is more complex than in other cases. A less complex theory is to be preferred. In particular, Volubility will clash with Quantity 2 whenever there is a discrepancy between being as informative as necessary and as informative as possible:

(4) A: What are some prime numbers between one and fifty?

B: Twenty-nine and thirty-seven. (Green 1995:102)

In this example, B's response provides enough information to satisfy the requirements of this conversation, that is, to name more than one prime number between one and fifty. B can do so, satisfying Quantity 1, without infringing Quantity 2 which would require him to name not more than two primes. However, Volubility would require B to name all prime numbers between twenty-nine and thirty-seven, and hence always clash with Quantity 2. Since Volubility will clash with other maxims whenever Quantity 1 does so too, a Volubility Maxim makes for more maxim clashes than Quantity 1. Thus, a system with Quantity 1 rather than Volubility should be preferred on grounds of simplicity.

9.3.3 Conversational requirements

Green (1995) proposes that an adequate account of implicatures can be constructed by taking into account 'what a conversation and its component illocutions as such require' (p. 104). This may change from point to point in the conversation, but at any given point the requirements of the conversation interact with the quantity maxims, for example. Thus, in a debate where one person is trying to convince another of some point, it is only necessary to give as much information as is compatible with the requirements of the conversation (if it is possible to do so without infringing other maxims). In another type of conversation, however, it might be expected that the quantity maxims are to be satisfied by way of Volubility, as in the case of exchanges.

In this way a system of conversation types, or genres, can be built and incorporated into a theory of implicatures within an inferential account of communication. The genre affects comprehension by influencing the way implicatures are calculated. A question which arises at this point is whether relevance theory should take into account the effects of discourse type on implicatures in the same way as Green (1995): by claiming that discourse type will affect the audience's expectations of relevance. I turn directly to a discussion of this question, starting with an examination of relevance-theoretic accounts of scalar implicatures, the phenomenon which motivated Green's proposal in the first place.

9.4 Scalar implicatures in relevance theory

So far, the literature on scalar implicatures within relevance theory has focused mainly on whether the so-called 'implicatures' are indeed implicatures or would be better treated as explicatures (Carston 1988, 1995; but see Carston 1998a for a more comprehensive account of scalar implicature). However, the main question addressed in Green (1995) is how to explain cases where the predictions of Gricean pragmatics about when such implicatures occur are apparently not borne out. This question is largely independent of whether scalar 'implicatures' are really implicatures or explicatures; in either case, pragmatic principles must explain their presence or absence. Sperber and Wilson (1995) discuss this second question raised by what are generally known as scalar implicatures in the context of a discussion of the revised presumption of relevance (Sperber and Wilson 1995:276–8). The issues raised in this discussion are directly linked to the question of whether relevance theory should handle discourse types in a similar way to Green (1995). I will therefore discuss the issues in some detail.

Consider first an analysis of scalar implicatures using the original version of the presumption of optimal relevance, which might be formulated in essence as follows:

(5) (a) The ostensive stimulus is relevant enough on the cognitive effects side to be worth the addressee's attention;

(b) The ostensive stimulus does not put the addressee to any unjustifiable effort in processing it optimally.

It follows from this that the hearer is licensed to take the first interpretation of an utterance which is (or appears to be) relevant enough as the one intended by the speaker. This version of the presumption of relevance can explain the absence of scalar implicatures in cases like the following (example (6)):

(6) A: If you or some of your family members are allergic to household dust, you should consider buying a special vacuum-cleaner.

B: Thanks. I am not allergic, but some of our relatives who frequently visit us are.

Here the interpretation of *some* which is compatible with *all* is relevant enough. Hence a scalar implicature *Not all of our relatives are allergic to dust* is not licensed as part of the intended interpretation, correctly as it appears. However, consider example (7):

(7) A: Are all, or at least some, of your relatives allergic to dust?

B: Some of them are.

It seems that in this case the scalar implicature is not needed to establish that B's utterance is relevant enough. However, a scalar implicature interpretation seems to be called for. One way of accounting for this is to assume that an utterance like (7A) makes it manifest that nothing less than a full answer would count as relevant enough to A. In other words: in order to account for cases such as (7), a special contextual assumption needs to be made for the comprehension procedure based on the original version of the presumption of relevance in (5) to give the right result.

Recall at this point Green's (1995) proposal: whether or not scalar implicatures arise depends on the current purposes of the talk exchange. This proposal seems to be very much in the spirit of the relevance-theoretic account considered above: whether the Gricean maxims give the right result depends on special assumptions about the type of talk-exchange involved.

Sperber and Wilson (1995), however, are uneasy about a solution to the scalar implicature problem which needs the hearer to make special assumptions if the comprehension procedure is to give the right result in some cases. They call this a 'flexible' application of the relevance theory model (Sperber and Wilson 1995:277). What makes this a 'flexible' application is presumably this: in order to explain a certain type of data, one has to adjust the input conditions with more or less plausible special factors if the comprehension procedure is to give the correct result. In (7) such a special factor was the assumption that it is manifest that the speaker would regard nothing less than a full answer as adequately relevant. Only under this assumption would the comprehension procedure based on the original version of the presumption of optimal relevance give the right result (Sperber and Wilson 1995:277).

Sperber and Wilson (1995) suggest a revised presumption of optimal relevance which allows for a 'mechanical' rather than a 'flexible' account of scalar implicatures (pp. 277–8). The revised presumption of relevance is as follows:

(8) (a) The ostensive stimulus is relevant enough for it to be worth the addressee's effort to process it.

(b) The ostensive stimulus is the most relevant one compatible with the communicator's abilities and preferences. (Sperber and Wilson 1995:270)

This revised presumption allows for cases where the expected degree of relevance goes beyond what is required for merely adequate relevance. It follows that if it is mutually manifest to speaker and hearer that a certain implication would increase the relevance of the utterance, and that this implication is compatible with the speaker's abilities and preferences, then the hearer is entitled to treat this implication as an implicature (Sperber and Wilson 1995:275). The scalar implicature cases (6) and (7) would then be analysed as follows.

In (6), the implication *Some but not all of our relatives are allergic to dust* would not increase the relevance of the utterance. Here the explanation is the same as under the unrevised presumption of relevance outlined above.

In (7), however, the implication *Not all of our relatives are allergic to dust* would manifestly increase the relevance of the utterance. It is mutually manifest that the speaker has chosen a weaker answer than she could have given if she were both willing and able. It follows that the speaker is either unwilling or unable to use the stronger statement. In normal circumstances, contextual considerations would suggest that she is unable to make the stronger claim because she knows that it is not the case. It would normally also be mutually manifest that she intended this assumption to be manifest, that is, that she intended to communicate it. Hence the hearer is licensed to attribute to her the implicature *Some but not all of our relatives are allergic to dust.* (Compare Sperber and Wilson 1995:278)

According to Sperber and Wilson, this is a 'mechanical' application of relevance theory to the analysis of scalar implicatures. Under the revised version of the presumption of optimal relevance, the expected level of relevance can go beyond that of mere adequacy. Hence, no special assumptions are needed for the comprehension procedure to work correctly. The danger of providing vacuous explanations is eliminated.

Can Green's ideas about text types helping to adjust the expected level of relevance (the translation of what the conversation requires into relevance theory terms) be adopted in this revised relevance theory? If so, the account would go roughly like this: if it is mutually manifest to both speaker and hearer that the utterance belongs to a certain conversation type, say poetry, then the hearer is entitled to treat more implications as being made more mutually manifest, and hence to be treated as implicatures, than if the utterance had occurred in another conversation type, say narrative. Or if it is mutually manifest to both speaker and hearer that the utterance belongs to a certain conversation type, then the hearer is entitled to expect implications of a different type from those derivable from the same utterance occurring in another conversation type.

Before I discuss these points in more detail, it is worth looking at the differences between the three approaches just discussed.

9.5 A critical comparison of the three proposals

This critical evaluation will have three strands: first, the scope of the three proposals is considered: to how many kinds of data do they apply? Second, the consequences of a 'flexible' versus a 'mechanical' application of relevance theory in relation to a possible adaptation of Green's ideas about genre are evaluated, and tentative evidence discussed. Third, the relation between conversation types and the requirements of the conversation will be critically discussed.

9.5.1 The scope of the proposals

In the Gricean account, the conversational requirement condition is stated in the Cooperative Principle. Influence of text- or conversation-type should therefore be expected in implicatures linked to any of the maxims. A first empirical question, therefore, is whether the absence of implicatures in certain circumstances is observable only with Quantity implicatures, and whether it occurs with implicatures related to other maxims as well.

According to Grice, implicatures linked to the Quantity Maxims fall into the following sub-types:

(9) Types of Implicatures involving the Quantity Maxims

1. Particularised Conversational Implicatures
   - 1.1 Arising through a violation of the Quantity Maxims because of a clash with another maxim.
     Examples:
     A: Where does C live?
     B: Somewhere in the South of France.
   - 1.2 Arising by exploitation of the Quantity Maxims.
     - 1.2.1 First Maxim of Quantity
       Example: A professor writes: 'Dear Sir, X's command of English is excellent and his attendance at tutorials was regular.'

1.2.2 Second Maxim of Quantity
Example: Someone not only states P but gives reasons and evidence for P in a situation where stating P would have been sufficient.

2. Generalised Conversational Implicatures
Examples:
   2.1 Various implications of the use of indefinite descriptions.
   2.2 The Indirectness Condition on indicative conditionals.
   2.3 Scalar implicatures.

It seems that other (sub-) types of Quantity implicatures also occasionally fail to arise when they would be expected. Consider the following variant of Grice's example:

(10) A and B are looking at a map:

A: Where does C live?

B: Somewhere in the South of France,..., let me see,...oh, here it is: Aubenas.

(...indicates a pause, accompanied by the action of looking over the map)

In (10), the implicature B does not know exactly where C lives is suspended. It is not the case that this implicature is derived and later rejected when B points out the exact place; it seems to me rather that the assumption B does not know exactly where C lives is not implicated by B's utterance of *Somewhere in the South of France.* Note that in this case the utterance *Somewhere in the South of France* is what could be called a 'self-deliberating statement;' that is, a class of utterances with similar properties could be identified. Therefore a solution appealing to types of talk-exchanges in the spirit of Green (1995) seems plausible here.[2]

Consider now implicatures arising by exploitation of the first Maxim of Quantity, of type 1.2.1 in (9). I find it extremely hard to set up a context for Grice's example so that the supposed implicature does not arise. Perhaps the following might do:

(11) A: What do you think of X's paper?

B: It is good for bibliographical references on the topic.

In a situation where A and B are making up a list of readings for an academic course, and are working on the principle that papers with lots of bibliographical references are preferable, B will be taken to have implicated that X's paper should be included in the list. There is no exploitation of the first Maxim of Quantity. However, in other situations A would normally be understood as asking about the content of X's paper, and here B's utterance would be seen as less informative than expected, hence triggering an implicature that B thinks X's paper is no good. However, it could be argued that the situation in which the quantity implicature is suppressed is quite special and it is not obvious that there is a range of similar types of situation which would all suppress this type of implicature. In that case, an explanation appealing to types of talk-exchanges in the spirit of Green (1995) seems less plausible.

As for examples of the type 2.1 (various implications of indefinite descriptions), Grice himself noticed the failure of the supposedly generalised implicature to arise in utterances like *I have been sitting in a car all morning.* (Grice 1989:38). He suggested a solution in terms of intrinsic properties of transactions involving objects or information closely connected with the communicator(s), as opposed to objects or information remotely connected with the communicator(s) (Grice 1989:38). In other words, he does not suggest a solution linked to conversation type. The implication is that an account along the lines of Green (1995) is not necessarily called for.

I have not yet been able to find clear examples of implicatures linked to maxims other than the Quantity Maxims exhibiting a similar problem. Kitis (1999:652) asks why the Manner Maxim 'be brief' does not trigger an implicature in (12a) comparable to the one in (13a):

(12) a. She has gone to her final rest. (Kitis 1999:652)
b. She passed away.
c. She died.

(13) a. Miss X produced a series of sounds that corresponded closely with the score of 'Home Sweet Home.' (Grice 1989:37)
b. Miss X sang 'Home Sweet Home.'

In each case there are shorter alternative ways to express the same information (the b. and c. examples). It is not obvious that a speaker who chooses (12a) or (13a) violates the Maxims of Quantity, Quality or Relation. Hence, the obvious implicature *Miss X's performance was of minor musical quality* in (13a) must be attributed to the Manner Maxim 'be brief.' But then the question arises why this same maxim doesn't trigger an implicature in (12). At first sight this example may seem similar to the scalar implicature cases discussed by Green (1995). However, the Gricean might argue that in a conversation where (12a) is uttered, other options, such as (12b.c), are simply unavailable for social reasons, so that the maxim 'be brief' is not in fact violated.[3] So it is not clear whether this example does indeed show similar problems to the scalar implicature cases discussed by Green (1995).

To sum up the empirical conclusions so far, it seems that Green's observation about scalar implicature may carry over to quantity implicatures of type 1.1 (implicatures arising through a violation of the Quantity Maxims because of a clash with another maxim), and could therefore be generalised to at least another type of implicature. However, although similar observations can be made about the suppression of expected quantity implicatures in two other subtypes, it is not necessarily plausible that an approach in terms of types of talk-exchange is called for. Furthermore, the fact that the suppression of otherwise expected implicatures seems to be rare — if it exists at all — with non-quantity implicatures strongly suggests that Green's proposal cannot be generalised to all kinds of implicature. This provides evidence that genre, if it does have a role in an inferential account of communication, has a relatively narrowly defined function.

Notice in particular that Green's proposal is most plausible with just two types of quantity implicatures, and with exactly those two types which Sperber and Wilson (1995) admit were not adequately handled in the unrevised version of relevance theory.

9.5.2 The revised presumption of relevance and genre

Let us now look at the differences in predictions made by a relevance-theoretic account of genre based on the original version of the presumption of relevance, on the one hand, and on the revised version of this presumption, on the other. In order to explore these differences, let us consider the Kurdish folk story of *Memo*. Memo was a young Kurdish man sent off to serve in the Ottoman army. Once he got an unexpected home leave during his term and returned home. It was late at night when he returned, no one expected him, and he didn't want to disturb anybody. So he simply went in the house and lay down on his bed beside his wife. When his mother rose up early in the morning, she saw a man lying beside her daughter-in-law and immediately took a spear and killed him. Only afterwards did she recognise her son. Then she broke into a lament and in it she used the words:

(14) *ser* *rim* *giheşt* *hesti-ya*
head spear reached bones-OP
The spear has reached his bones'

This same expression could be used in a narrative about such events; indeed, the story actually does use a very similar sentence:[4]

(15) *ew* *remê* *girt* *il* *nîv-a* *sing-ê* *wî* *zelamî* *da*
that spear stuck in midst-of breast-of that man
***
'that spear went right into the breast of that man'

Arguably, however, this expression (14) carries a lot more weight and emotional impact in the poem (the lament) than within the narrative. This is obviously not due to any particular poetic form or rhetorical device in the utterance; it is solely due to the fact that it is used in a poem.

On the revised presumption of optimal relevance example this may be explained in the following way: although the recognition of the proposition *The spear swung by Memo's mother cut deep into Memo's body* is enough on its own to make the utterance relevant enough to be worth the audience's attention, the fact that it occurs in a poem raises expectations of a higher level of relevance on the effect side. The audience is expecting a rich reward in poetic effects, that is of a whole range of weakly communicated assumptions. Lots of such assumptions having to do with grief, the tragic results of a rash deed, remorse, and so on, are at hand.

Under the original version of the presumption of relevance, the account would go as follows: being part of a poem, the minimal level of relevance to be expected is rather high, including the promise of a rich harvest in weakly communicated assumptions. The same assumptions are manifest as shown above, leading to the same expectation of relevance achieved through many weak implicatures. However, the expected level of effects is always treated as the minimally adequate one: enough relevance to make the utterance worth the audience's while to process. Given the expectation that Memo's mother's utterance will be optimally relevant to the hearer in terms of giving rise to a range of weak implicatures, 'adequate relevance' must be interpreted in this case as achieving a level of effects which contains enough weak implicatures to justify this expectation for the hearer. This means that the unrevised version of relevance theory predicts that only a recovery of a range of weak implicatures (over and above the explicature and the strong implicature shown above) will make it worth the hearer's while to process. On the revised version, on the other hand, the expected level of relevance is derived from the combination of the presumption of at least adequate relevance and the presumption that the speaker produced the most relevant utterance compatible with her abilities and preferences. In the present example, the expected level of relevance will be higher than that of mere adequate relevance. It follows that the revised version of relevance theory predicts that the hearer will treat more implications as (weak) implicatures than on the unrevised version.

There is also another difference between the two approaches which becomes evident in what happens when a hearer for some reason does not recover the 'rich' interpretation of B's utterance, but nevertheless recovers the explicature and the strong implicature. On the original relevance theory approach, this hearer would be unable to understand how the speaker could have intended the utterance as relevant to the hearer. He should therefore abandon this line of interpretation, perhaps describing his intuitions in these words: 'I have not been able to find an adequate interpretation of this utterance.' On the revised relevance theory approach, the hearer only partly identifies the speaker's intention, but is still able to see how the speaker could have meant her utterance to be relevant for him. He would probably describe his intuitions in these words: 'I have been able to find an adequate interpretation of this utterance, though not a full, proper, one.' In other words: the hearer may be fully aware that he is unable to find an interpretation satisfying the expectation that the speaker produced the most relevant utterance (given her abilities and preferences), but able to find an interpretation which satisfies the expectation of mere adequacy, this time understood as giving enough cognitive effects to make it worth the hearer's attention — which in this case is probably a lower level than under the unrevised version (where special assumptions had to be made to adjust what 'adequate relevance' means).

Now the experience of being unable to appreciate the full poetic impact of poems is quite a common one, especially when reading poetry from other cultures. Yet it would be counter-intuitive to claim that such readers fail to understand the text at all, that is, fail to see what makes the utterance worth the audience's attention. I conclude that the revised relevance theory account describes the intuitions better than the unrevised one.

The consequences of this choice, that the role of genre in communication be best explained with the revised version of relevance theory, can be summarised as follows: the role of genre information is not invariably to provide special assumptions about what the speaker presumes to be adequately relevant; rather, genre information may merely provide assumptions about which level of relevance the hearer is licensed to expect from the presumption that the speaker produced the most relevant stimulus compatible with her abilities and preferences. This is not to say that genre information never can provide assumptions about what counts as adequate relevance in particular cases; indeed, I will turn below to cases where genre influences expectations as to the content of utterances in a discourse. These can be seen as instances where genre information provides assumptions about what counts as adequate relevance. But the revised version of the presumption of optimal relevance allows for a more subtle treatment of genre than the unrevised version would.

9.5.3 Conversation types and requirements of talk exchanges

As a third strand of this critical evaluation of Green's (1995) proposal, let us look at the precise place or role of conversation types in his account. A key statement is found in the author's abstract: 'Crucial to this explanation is an appreciation of how what a conversation, or a given stage of a conversation, requires, depends upon what kind of conversation is taking place' (Green 1995:83). In other words, the crucial point in this account is that knowledge of what conversation type (text type) is presently being employed plays an important role in determining what the conversation requires (at the present stage). Green argues that two parameters determine what is required at a given stage in the talk-exchange:

a. The current aim of the interlocutors, particular examples of which are exchange, debate and inquiry.

b. The state of the 'conversational score;' that is, what illocutions have been made, which questions are open, what the topic is, and so on (p. 106)

In an example, Green explains how this works (p. 107): Someone asks the question *How many children does Nigel have?* and the situation makes it clear that the questioner wants an answer in terms of an integer (rather than an interval *between n and m*). Furthermore, it is clear in the situation that the question hasn't been rejected nor the subject changed. Thus, the communicators are engaged in an enquiry and being as informative as required in the current state of the talk exchange means giving a complete answer to the question underlying the enquiry. When in this scenario the speaker says *Nigel has fourteen children,* then the addressee is entitled to infer that the speaker can't make the stronger claim that Nigel has fifteen or more children, since he knows (or believes) that such a claim would be false.

This can summarised as follows:

1. From the state of the conversational score it is inferred that an enquiry is taking place.
2. From the fact that an enquiry is taking place it is inferred what the requirements of the conversation are at its present stage: in this case, a (truth-)full answer in terms of a precise number should be given.

The question is: what does the intermediate step of conversation-type recognition add to the recognition of what the conversation requires? It seems to me that — at least in this example — the requirement of the present talk exchange (give a precise number) is inferable from aspects of the 'conversational score' alone, just as it is in the relevance-theoretic explanation(s). It therefore seems that this step of conversation-type recognition is superfluous. The problem is compounded by the fact that the requirements of a conversation may vary even within the same conversation type, as Green's next example shows. This is also a case of enquiry, but such that no scalar implicature results from a weaker statement:

> Suppose on the other hand that S and H are jointly inquiring into the question whether every adult male in the Shifflett clan has at least fourteen children. Here once again the speakers are engaged in an inquiry, but one that is driven by a different question from the one that drove the conversation in our last case. In response to

> the question whether every adult male in the Shifflett clan has at least fourteen children S may say, "Nigel has fourteen children, and so does Jed and so does Uriah." The claim that Nigel has fifteen children is conversationally relevant, since it straightforwardly implies that Nigel has fourteen. Yet from the fact that S does not make this stronger claim we cannot infer that he does not take himself to be in a position to do so. (Green 1995:108)

The fact that it is not only the conversation type (characterised by the aim of the interlocutors) which determines the current requirements of the talk exchange, but that other factors also come into play, undermines the explanatory power of this account.

The relevance theory accounts, on the other hand, do not require this intermediate step: relevance depends on the cognitive environment of the interlocutors, and by providing an account of context selection, Sperber and Wilson's approach is able to explain the inferences without having to appeal to type-information.

However, in the last subsection we have seen a genuine example of where some kind of type-information is important: the case of utterances in narrative or song setting, respectively. I take it that the utterance *ser rim giheşt hestiya* 'The spear reached his bones' in (14) above does receive a different interpretation than if it was uttered in a report. The hearer must be able to realise that the speaker's preferences included the desire to communicate many weak implicatures, that is, to create poetic effects. If we agree that this preference is inferred on the basis of textual or situational features (for example a tune; an explicit introductory statement), then the recognition of these features and their link to the preference for creating poetic effects is crucial. This link is presumably mediated by the concept SONG, which includes this information in its encyclopaedic entry: the recognition of a tune makes the concept SONG accessible, which in turn has the assumption *The communication of many weak implicatures is a common pattern in songs* as an encyclopaedic entry, making this accessible as a contextual assumption.

It therefore seems fair to conclude that text-type information is not always involved in judging 'what the conversation requires.' Thus

Green's Gricean account is not successful in many cases. However, there are cases where the recovery of implicatures is genuinely influenced by the type (or genre) of text in which it occurs. For these, an account along the lines suggested by Green seems plausible.

9.6 Genre in relevance theory

In the last section I argued that genre is best explained in relevance theory on the basis of the revised presumption of relevance. On this approach, genre information is seen as influencing the hearer's expectation of relevance by entering into an inferential process involving the mutual adjustment of content, context and cognitive effects constrained by the communicative principle of relevance, and is recognised by following the regular relevance-theoretic comprehension procedure. This contrasts with approaches to genre in Gricean frameworks such as Holdcroft (1979), Kitis (1999) and Green (1995). In all these approaches, the contribution of genre to utterance interpretation falls outside the inferential comprehension processes governed by Gricean communicative principles.

Recall that the approaches of Kitis and Green imply different claims about the hermeneutical function of genre: while Kitis (1999) amounts to claiming a strong hermeneutical function — that is, claiming that utterance interpretation depends crucially on discourse-type recognition, since it is the discourse type which determines which pragmatic maxims are operative — Green (1995) in effect argues for a weak hermeneutical function, claiming that genre influences understanding only insofar as it affects the recovery of implicatures in some cases.

Having rejected Kitis' approach and endorsed a relevance-theoretic re-analysis of Green's account, it appears that I should conclude that genre will always have a weak hermeneutical function. However, matters are not so simple. Recall my argument that genre information constrains the hearer's expectations of relevance. As expectations of relevance may be stronger or weaker, and more or less precise, different genres may encourage different expectations of relevance. It should follow that not all cases where genre information influences comprehension work in the same way. Consider the case of employers' letters of reference for employees in German. This genre is highly standardised, and there are books written about how different utterances within it are supposed to be understood. Here the reader's expectations of relevance are very detailed. Another example of a standardised genre may be that of business letters in English. The following encyclopaedic information about business letters is part of English cultural knowledge:

(16) a. A business letter begins with 'Dear Sir' or 'Dear Sir or Madam.'

b. After the greeting, a business letter concisely states the issue at hand.

c. A business letter ends with 'Yours faithfully' or 'Yours sincerely' and the signature of the sender.

There is common knowledge of how such a letter is likely to unfold. If the reader comes across appropriate indications of genre (for example the conventional greeting), he will have certain expectations about how the letter will proceed, and what kinds of inferences he is entitled or not entitled to make (for example he should not infer that the writer is being rude if she expresses her concerns concisely, stating the issue rather directly, without a personal introduction). This saves the hearer processing effort in arriving at the speaker's meaning.

Klinge (1998) gives another example of a highly standardised text type, that of legal contracts in English. He argues that a major force in the process of conventionalising the form of legal contracts has been considerations of relevance: legal contracts (like texts in general) are most successful when they create early assumptions about how the text will unfold, thus saving the hearer processing effort (see Blakemore 1992:99, 134). As the intents and purposes of contracts are quite stereotypical, the pressures arising from processing a text for relevance lead to a highly conventional schema for legal contracts. Klinge's account fits in well with the one I am proposing, and differs from mine mainly in perspective: he is mainly concerned with the motivations for the conventionalisation process, whereas I am focusing on the role of genre in comprehension. I would add that the conventional 'schema' for legal contracts creates rather specific expectations of relevance in the reader, which reduces processing effort and makes it desirable for the writer to conform to the schema.

Letters of reference from an employer in German, English business letters and legal contracts are thus examples of genres which (via encyclopaedic information about these genres) raise very specific expectations of relevance. In contrast, the expectations of relevance raised by (14) were more general, affecting the level of relevance to be expected rather than the types of cognitive effects to be achieved.

In other words, genre influences utterance interpretation in different ways. Genres differ in the kind of information with which they influence the hearer's expectations of relevance: information about the form of texts (that is, which utterance occurs where), information about standardised interpretations of utterances, information about the speaker's preferences, and so on. Correspondingly, in some cases genre has a strong hermeneutical function, in others a weak one. It is thus obvious that no one model of genre can explain how genre works in general. This should come as no surprise in the light of the overview given in Chapter 1 of the diverse criteria which have been brought to bear on the definition of genre. What is surprising, though, is that attempts to explain genre in a reductionist way prevail in the area of discourse studies (for example systemic-functional register and genre theory, feature-based systems such as Longacre's 1983; 1989a; 1989b; van Dijk and Kintsch 1983).[5]

However, genre knowledge need not contribute to determining the hearer's expectations of relevance. It plays no role in most of the (invented) dialogues between Peter and Mary in the relevance theory literature. Moreover, even in cases where the genre of a discourse is obvious, it need not always be brought to bear on utterance interpretation. Utterances exploiting unusual syntax and figures of speech make the speaker's preference for creating poetic effects obvious from properties of the utterance alone, and the hearer can form the appropriate expectations of relevance without having to take genre information about songs into account. Thus, genre does not always have a hermeneutical function; when it has, this function can be strong or weak, depending on the nature of the genre in question and how it may influence the hearer's expectations of relevance.

9.7 Conclusion

By way of conclusion, I will summarise my answers to the original questions raised in this chapter. The first question was: is the claim that the recognition of text type is crucial for utterance interpretation necessarily related to the adoption of a code model of communication? The answer is no, as the accounts of Holdcroft (1979), Kitis (1999) and Green (1995), which do have some initial plausibility, show. The answer to the second question is more complex: should a place for genre be included in an inferential theory of communication, and if so, how? The empirical data used in considering this question were connected with the (alleged) influence of genre on the derivation of implicatures. First it was pointed out that a place for genre could be found in four types of inferential theories of communication: a modified Gricean account (Kitis 1999; Holdcroft 1979), the original Gricean theory (Green 1995), the original relevance theory account (Sperber and Wilson 1995), and the revised relevance theory account in the postface of Sperber and Wilson (1995). I argued that the relevance-theoretic account based on the revised presumption of relevance is more adequate than the first three. However, it is doubtful whether a generalisation of Green's (1995) proposal in relevance theory terms would be adequate: first, the data with which Green is concerned are not that general. Second, I argued that not all cases of scalar implicature or its absence explained by Green in terms of conversation type (among other factors) can be adequately explained in that way. Nevertheless, I gave some examples which seem to require some kind of genre-information recognition, and showed how these might be analysed in the revised relevance theory approach. It follows that there are cases where genre has an influence on the derivation of implicatures, but these cases are quite restricted, more so than Green's (1995) account suggests, and they are best handled in the revised version of relevance theory. While Kitis (1999) and Holdcroft (1979) suggest that genre may have a strong hermeneutical function, and Green (1995) assigns it a weak hermeneutical function, the conclusion reached in the suggested relevance-theoretic account is that some genres may have a strong hermeneutical function and others a weak one. Moreover, genre does not always play a role in utterance interpretation. The main question is whether some genre information contributes to determining the hearer's expectation of relevance; since these expectations can vary in strength and precision, different genres are expected to influence comprehension in correspondingly different ways.

10 A re-analysis of genre and its implications for pragmatics

10.1 The role of genre in cognitive pragmatics

I would now like to summarise the main points made in this book and relate them to the wider field of pragmatics. I will do this in four steps: in Section 10.1 I will summarise my positive claims about the role of genre in cognitive pragmatics. In Section 10.2 I will highlight the consequences of these claims for pragmatics in general and relevance theory in particular. Section 10.3 will discuss the consequences for discourse analysis. Finally, in Section 10.4 I will outline some new research questions which the present account opens up.

In Chapter 1, I argued that only theories of genre which claim to shed light on utterance interpretation are of interest to pragmatic theory. Claims about the function of genre in comprehension can be classified into two main types: those assigning genre a linguistic function, and those assigning it a hermeneutical function. By the linguistic function of genre, I mean the claimed contribution of genre information to the semantics of certain linguistic forms such as tense and aspect. By the hermeneutical function of genre I mean the claim that genre information facilitates discourse comprehension by affecting the recovery of implicatures of the text. The major part of this book was spent in arguing that claims about the linguistic function of genre are not sustainable. However, genre can have a hermeneutical function, which may be either strong or weak. In cases where genre information leads to very specific expectations of relevance, the intended interpretation of a text is strongly influenced by genre information (as in the case of standardised genres such as business letters or letters of reference from an employer). In cases where genre information leads to rather weak expectations of relevance, comprehension is weakly influenced by genre (as in the case of 'narrative poetry' where it is expected that the author aims to achieve relevance by conveying many weak implicatures).

The way in which genre functions is by providing information that influences the hearer's assessment of what level of relevance to expect from the stimulus (which may be simple, for example an utterance, or complex, for example a text), and how relevance is to be found. The comprehension process is governed by the communicative principle of relevance, which says that every act of ostensive communication communicates a presumption of optimal relevance, that is, of at least adequate relevance, and as much more as is compatible with the communicator's abilities and preferences. This presumption of optimal relevance is merely a hypothesis which needs to be adopted as a working hypothesis and then verified. Utterance interpretation can be seen as the process by which this presumption of relevance is verified. By adopting the presumption as a working hypothesis, the audience generates expectations of relevance, which my be satisfied by following the relevance-theoretic comprehension procedure until an appropriate interpretation has been found.

Expectations of relevance can be more or less precise. Genre knowledge can play a role in generating these expectations. Genre information can moreover be of different kinds, thus influencing the expectations of relevance in different ways. It may specify typical ways in which a discourse of a certain kind will unfold. This happens primarily in conventionalised genres such as business letters, and so on, and creates rather precise expectations about what utterances (or kinds of utterances) are to be expected in which sequence. Besides such highly standardised genres with fairly specific expectations as to how they unfold, the expectations about the form of the discourse may be more or less precise, that is, more abstract, for example in the case of sonnets, short stories, weather forecasts, news bulletins, advertisements, linguistic articles, and so on. In this latter genre, for example, the expectations will not be so much about which utterances are expected when, but about the format of the text, about the sort of content that various parts of the text will have: that there will be an abstract, an introduction, the main argument, a conclusion and a bibliography. Genre can also provide information about the kind of cognitive effects to be expected: the love song genre in Hebrew, for example, contains information about what kind of figures of speech are used and how to interpret them. In this case, expectations of the overall relevance of the discourse are more loosely constrained and concern content rather than form. Furthermore, genre information can influence the level of relevance to be expected rather than the kinds of effects to be achieved. Narrative poetry is an illustration: recognition of the genre leads the audience to attribute to the author desire to communicate many weak implicatures, which in turn causes them to expect more weak implicatures than might have been recovered from the same utterances in a narrative context. Thus, genre is not a homogeneous notion, and it can function in various ways.

In this account of the cognitive pragmatic function of genre, genre information is implicitly treated as encyclopaedic information, which must be easily accessible to the inference processes involved in comprehension. In a relevance-based account of cognition, the implication is that this information must be used quite often in cognitive processes, otherwise it would not be easily accessible, for memory is organised so as to tend to maximise relevance (Sperber and Wilson 1996). Sperber (1996) argues that cultural information — that is the information which constitutes people's cultural knowledge — is epidemic in a society because it is often used successfully in understanding communicative behaviour. On this account, genre knowledge is seen as a type of cultural knowledge, as it is indeed often argued to be (for example in systemic-functional register and genre theory as discussed in Chapter 8, see Eggins and Martin 1997 and references therein; Swales 1990; Paltridge 1995; Kitis 1999).

The claim that genre information is part of cultural knowledge is not as simple as it may appear, for cultural knowledge can vary widely from culture to culture. If genre is part of cultural knowledge, it too can be expected to vary widely from culture to culture. This, of course, is indeed the case for many genres. Business letters, for example, follow different conventions even in different Western

European countries, and the inventory of genres may be different from culture to culture (Downing 1996). However, there are also genres such as 'narrative' or 'poetry' which presumably are found universally. It is implausible to treat these universally occurring genres in the same way as genres which are culture specific. Moreover, these genres are notoriously difficult to define: the most widespread characteristic of narrative, for example, is that it narrates events in temporal sequence. However, recognising whether two utterances are in temporal sequence is part of the inferential phase of utterance interpretation (Chapter 2; Wilson and Sperber 1998), and it is unlikely that knowledge attached to a general 'narrative' genre is involved in this process (Chapter 2). For these reasons I conclude that the general 'narrative' genre is not a genre which enters into pragmatic processes. However, subcategories of narrative — such as stories and tales — can be culturally specified. This point has also been made independently by Swales (1990:58–61).

My claim is therefore that only culturally-specified genres contribute to pragmatic processes. The question that then arises is how this can be explained. It has been generally accepted that the crucial issue here has to do with context: genre is obviously an aspect of the context of utterances (Downing 1996; Eggins and Martin 1997; Thibault 1999; Kitis 1999). In particular, the issue is whether the context is treated as given in advance of the interpretation process (the position taken in systemic-functional register and genre theory) or whether it is chosen as part of the inferential phase of utterance interpretation (the position taken in relevance theory). In Chapter 8, I have argued that only on the relevance-theoretic view — that context is chosen as part of the inferential phase of utterance interpretation — can the effect of genre on utterance interpretation be adequately explained. Here I want to point out another feature of relevance theory which helps to explain how cultural genre information affects pragmatic processes: that relevance is defined in cognitive terms and that a cognitive principle of relevance is proposed. This cognitive principle of relevance is strong enough to make human information processing somewhat predictable to other individuals (Wilson and Sperber 2002). It not only has the communicative principle of relevance as a consequence, but also allows an account of cultural (social) knowledge in terms of an epidemiology of mental representations (Sperber 1996). Thus, *pace* Kitis (1999), it is precisely the definition of relevance as a technical notion in cognitive terms which allows for an adequate explanation of how sociocultural information such as genre information can contribute to pragmatic processes.

Genre information is accessible to inference processes involved in fleshing out the audience's expectations of relevance because it is part of cultural information. However, cultural knowledge is not confined to genre information. The question then arises whether other kinds of cultural information can have a similar function to genre. Indeed there is no reason to suppose that genre information is unique in this regard. Phenomena connected with register are a case in point: register information can arguably also be regarded as cultural information affecting speaker's preferences ('do not say XY in situation AB'). Such information can also help to create specific expectations of relevance. It is interesting in this regard to recall the ambivalence within systemic-functional linguistics on the status of register in relation to genre (see Chapter 8). This ambivalence is precisely to be expected on my account, which treats the difference between register and genre phenomena in pragmatics as epiphenomenal.

Finally, on my account, genre information does not always play a role in comprehension. Where expectations of relevance arise from, and are satisfied by, other sources than genre information, there is no need for genre recognition (see the remarks above on narrative and poetry). This contradicts Lakoff and Johnson's (1980:83) claim — quoted in Chapter 1 — that comprehension necessarily includes the classification of experiences, including the classification of speech events (genres). The rejection of this claim on the basis of a relevance-theoretic account of genre is consistent with Sperber and Wilson's (1995) rejection of the claim that speech-act recognition is always crucial to comprehension. Rather, it is the pursuit of relevance which is crucial to comprehension, and genre or speech-act recognition may or may not be essential in this process.

10.2 Genre and pragmatics

Having summarised my account of genre and the cognitive role it plays in communication, I turn now to some of the consequences of this account for pragmatics in general.

10.2.1 Global coherence and relevance

A prominent theme in pragmatics is the enquiry into discourse coherence. Discourse coherence is most commonly seen as resulting from the presence of coherence (or rhetorical) relations between units (clauses, sentences, utterances, paragraphs and so on) of the discourse (Hobbs 1979, 1983; Samet and Schank 1984; Mann and Thompson 1986; Sanders et al. 1993; and others).[1] These local coherence relations are supposed to explain the connectedness of well-formed texts. However, it was recognised early on that local coherence relations cannot explain everything about the connectedness of discourse: they can't explain why good, acceptable texts do not normally drift off in any direction, displaying only local semantic connections (Samet and Schank 1984; Giora 1985a,b; see Chapter 2). Therefore, it is argued that the theory of coherence must include an account of global as well as local coherence. It has even been claimed that local coherence relations play no role in a proper theory of coherence, which is then exclusively a theory of global coherence (Giora 1985a,b).

Relevance theorists have engaged in a long-standing debate with coherence theorists, arguing that the notion of local coherence is defective and that the effects of local coherence are better explained as results of processing the text along the relevance-theoretic comprehension procedure(for example Blakemore 1987, 1988, 1992; Blass 1990; Wilson 1994, 1998; Wilson and Matsui 1998; Rouchota 1996; Unger 1996). However, the theory of global coherence has not yet been widely discussed within relevance theory. Approaching the theory of global coherence from a relevance-theoretic point of view has been a major concern of this book.

One possible reason for the lack of relevance-theoretic discussions of global coherence is that the notion of global coherence is not well defined within coherence theory. A number of suggestions have been made: for example, that global coherence should be defined in terms of topic-relevance (Giora 1985a,b, 1988, 1998), in terms of information grounding in discourse (Longacre 1989a,b), in ways similar to local coherence by appealing to dominant semantic relations (Samet and Schank 1984; Caenepeel 1995), or by appealing to different sets of (local) coherence relations in different discourse types (Asher and Lascarides 1998b). I have argued that all these approaches to global coherence are defective. The effects of topic-coherence and information grounding in discourse are better seen as by-products of the relevance-theoretic comprehension process. The other two approaches mentioned (dominant global coherence relations; different sets of relations in different text types) presuppose genre recognition, but because they allow embedding of genres they are psychologically implausible.

The main concern of the discussion about global coherence was: how to account for the fact that acceptable discourses (a) do not drift off the theme like the mock narrative in example (2) of Chapter 2, but (b) do allow for topic drift, and can even include locally unconnected sequences, as in example (7) of Chapter 2. This is similar to one of Grice's problems which he expressed in the following words:

> Under the category of Relation I place a single maxim, namely, "Be relevant." Though the maxim itself is terse, its formulation conceals a number of problems that exercise me a good deal: questions about what different kinds and focuses of relevance there may be, how these shift in the course of a talk exchange, how to allow for the fact that subjects of conversation are legitimately changed, and so on. (Grice 1989:27)

It is interesting to note that Grice expected the solution to this question to be intimately linked to the proper definition of relevance.

None of the approaches to global coherence surveyed in this book can deal with both aspects of this problem simultaneously; they often attempt to solve the first problem, that good texts do not drift off thematically. However, when the principles underlying these solutions are relaxed to allow for locally unconnected sequences in acceptable texts (that is, to allow for topic shifts within a unit of discourse), the solution to the first problem is usually compromised. The claim made in this book is that it is expectations of relevance raised by discourses on the basis of the communicative principle of relevance that provide the key to these problems. However, unlike in Grice's theory, relevance is seen as a cognitive property of inputs to cognitive processes (which are ostensive stimuli in the case of communication). I have argued in Chapters 2 and 5 that this relevance-theoretic approach is able to deal with both aspects of the problem simultaneously.

The conclusion reached in this book is therefore that the notion of global coherence cannot be properly defined, and that the facts that a theory of global coherence is designed to explain find an appropriate explanation in relevance theory. The relevance-theoretic notion of relevance, and the relevance-theoretic comprehension procedure are enough on their own to account for intuitions of global coherence. This conclusion suggests the possibility of accounting in alternative terms not only for pragmatic phenomena usually approached in terms of global coherence, but also for a number of psycholinguistic experimental results. In Chapter 6 I discussed a number of these results and proposed alternative relevance-theoretic explanations. While this discussion could not possibly be exhaustive, the range of data discussed suggests that the relevance-theoretic approach can indeed shed new light on these issues.

10.2.2 Expectations of relevance and the inferential theory of communication

Relevance theory has sometimes been criticised for underestimating the importance of genre (and register) in communication (Bex 1992; Goatly 1994; Thibault 1999). These criticisms have been seen as suggesting different conclusions: some say that relevance theory can and should be amended by the addition of a theory of genre, where genre theory is understood along the lines of systemic-functional register and genre theory (Bex 1992; Goatly 1994). Others conclude that relevance theory should be abandoned in favour of systemic-functional linguistics which fully integrates a theory of genre and other contextual dimensions (Thibault 1999). Given that systemic-functional linguistics (including register and genre theory) is a thoroughly code-based theory of communication, these arguments amount to the claim that the phenomenon of genre provides evidence against a thoroughly inferential theory of communication. Thibault (1999) is fully explicit on this claim, as was discussed in Chapter 8.

Seen against this background, the central argument of this book, that the influence of genre on comprehension is best explained via its influence on expectations of relevance which regulate the inferential phase of utterance interpretation, is then a direct dismissal of these claims. Rather than challenging inferential theories of communication, the role of genre in communication provides evidence in favour of an inferential theory of genre. Indeed, it does more than that: it provides evidence for a particular theoretical architecture of an adequate inferential theory of communication.

Recall that the main problem of systemic-functional register and genre theory is that it treats context as given in advance of the interpretation process (where genre is rightly seen as an aspect of context). Relevance theory, on the other hand, argues that the context is chosen as an integral part of utterance interpretation. The choice of relevant contexts is part of the inferential phase of comprehension, governed by the relevance-theoretic comprehension procedure. The derivation of cognitive effects, the choice of the contexts warranting them, and the recovery of explicatures are parallel inferential processes. The adoption of the presumption of relevance, and its consequences for the hearer's expectations of relevance, are also part of this parallel inferential process; thus, the role of genre information in communication can be fully integrated into this inferential account of comprehension.

There are other inferential theories of communication which have a different theoretical architecture: here genre is seen as influencing utterance interpretation via psychological processes which lie outside the scope of, and exist prior to, the maxim-guided inferential phase of comprehension (Kitis 1999; Holdcroft 1979). In these theories, recognition of genre is prior to, and independent of, other aspects of inferential comprehension. Thus, at least part of the context is said to be given in advance. But this is a hybrid theory which either has to concede to a code-based approach to social semiotics (the direction which Kitis 1999 seems to favour), thus compromising the inferential approach to communication, or has to propose an independent inferential phase of genre recognition. In this latter case, something would have to be said about the inference system governing genre recognition.

In short, observations about genre provide support for the relevance-theoretic view of context: that the context is chosen as part of the inferential phase of utterance comprehension. This calls for a theory of genre which sees the influence of genre on comprehension as part and parcel of this parallel inferential process involving mutual adjustment of cognitive effects, content and context (Sperber and Wilson 1998; Wilson and Sperber 2002; see Chapter 5). Thus, observations about genre also provide arguments against alternative inferential theories of communication which differ in their theoretical architecture in that genre recognition is seen as a process prior to the operation of conversational maxims or principles.

10.3 Genre and discourse analysis

A sizable part of this book has been devoted to discussing whether discourse properties such as grounding, which in turn depend on discourse type, directly affect the meaning of linguistic markers, most notably tense and aspect markers. In the literature on discourse analysis it has generally been argued that they do (Hopper 1979; Hopper and Thompson 1980; Reinhart 1984; Longacre 1989a,b; Caenepeel 1995 and others). It is further pointed out that the way grounding is marked differs cross-linguistically (Hopper 1979; Hopper and Thompson 1980; Reinhart 1984; Longacre 1989b). An interesting question is whether this evidence can support an argument similar to that of Prince (1985, 1988, 1997), who argues that syntactic devices of topicalisation, for instance, can differ arbitrarily from language to language, thus suggesting that topicalisation is part of the discourse component of grammar. Can a parallel argument be constructed to show that grounding is encoded in the discourse component of grammar?

Prince's argument turns on the point that the linguistic forms which give rise to discourse effects differ arbitrarily in different languages, and arbitrariness is typical of the relation between encoded information and the form used to encode it. She illustrates this by comparing topicalisation structures in English and Yiddish:

(1) a. They found Eichmann.

b. It was they who found Eichmann. (Carston 2000:98)

(2) a. ... zey hobn gefunen aykhmanen
... they have found Eichmann

b. ... *dos* hobn zey gefunen aykhmanen
... this have they found Eichmann
= it was they who found Eichmann (Prince 1997:169; quoted after Carston 2000:98)

The *dos*-construction in Yiddish — which is a single clause — is structurally quite different from the *it*-cleft construction in English — which involves a relative clause —, though they have the same discourse function (see Carston 2000:98).

On the question of whether the linguistic marking of grounding in different languages allows a similar argument that they are encoded in the grammar, notice first that the variation in the ways that grounding is marked in language does not seem to be arbitrary: all the data quoted in Hopper (1979), Hopper and Thompson (1980), Longacre (1989b, 1990b) and Hooper (1998) involve morphological marking of the tense-aspect-mood system of the verb. Word-order variation is also mentioned as a widespread means of marking distinctions in grounding, but it is nearly always intricately linked to the choice of verb forms (for example in Hebrew, where the standard narrative form — the *weqatal* form — is morphosyntactically restricted: it can occur only when the verb is in the first position in the sentence). Hence there does not seem to be enough cross-linguistic variation in the marking of grounding to warrant the conclusion that it is arbitrarily encoded in the grammar of languages.[2]

While this may not amount to a strong argument against the claim that grounding is encoded in a discourse component of grammar, it does cast some doubt on this claim. At least it raises the question why it is so often the morphological tense-aspect-mood marking of the verb that indicates information grounding in discourse. This question, I think, must be answered by any adequate theory of grounding.

However, there are stronger arguments against the conclusion that grounding is encoded in the grammar. These are discussed in Chapter 4. One of the strongest arguments is that the linguistic marking of grounding is apparently always based on a statistic probability relation between the use of certain linguistic forms and certain grounding levels (Hopper 1979; Hopper and Thompson 1980). Most theories of grounding therefore treat the relation between grounding levels in discourse and the use of certain grammatical forms (mostly tense-aspect-mode markers) in probabilistic terms (Hopper 1979; Hopper and Thompson 1980; Reinhart 1984). On the other hand, the only theory of grounding couched in terms of a strong code model, the theory of Longacre (1989b, 1990a,b), fails because it has to allow for embedding of discourse types (and other modifications of the norm) in order to explain the variation exhibited by the data; this undermines its explanatory power and leads to a psychologically implausible theory of comprehension.

The conclusion reached in this book is therefore that the effect of information grounding in discourse are a purely pragmatic phenomenon, a by-product of the inferential phase of comprehension. However, properties of the stimulus can be used to exploit the relevance-guided inferential comprehension process in subtle ways. This does not necessarily involve encoding: various options in language — such as grammatical word-order alternations, variable assignments of contrastive stress (Sperber and Wilson 1995), or the choice between alternative semantically possible aspect markers — may be used to point the audience toward a certain nuance of interpretation, much as a gesture in conversation can be used to highlight an object without explicitly referring to it. I argued in Chapter 7 that this not only explains the use of linguistic devices to create grounding effects in discourse, but also sheds light on why it is so often tense-aspect-mood markers that are used to create these effects: information grounding has to do with the way in which an utterance is perceived to be relevant, and this depends on the expectations of relevance raised by the discourse as a whole. In narratives, for example, the expectation is that utterances describing events are likely to be most relevant. Whether an utterance should be seen as describing an event largely depends on the aspectual properties of the predicate. If the language in question allows for morphological marking of aspect, this is then an obvious means for indicating grounding.

The fact that the effects of information grounding in discourse are a purely pragmatic phenomenon, not explainable in a 'discourse competence' component of grammar, has interesting consequences for the way we look at discourse analysis. Carston (2000) has suggested that the phenomena which Prince (1985, 1988, 1997) assigns to the domain of 'discourse competence' are in fact very similar to those which have been investigated in relevance theory under the label of 'procedural semantics.' Carston further suggests that little hinges on whether this domain of linguistic competence is to be called 'discourse competence' or 'procedural semantics.' This is certainly true as far as it goes, but it would become problematic if the area of 'discourse competence' were then equated with 'discourse analysis' (or 'discourse grammar,' to use Longacre's term). For grounding in discourse does get indicated by linguistic means, though not by being either conceptually or procedurally encoded. Discourse analysis therefore has a diverse subject matter, and includes the study of aspects of linguistic semantics such as procedural encoding, the study of how linguistic devices can be exploited to achieve pragmatic effects, and arguably also the study of how implicatures and relevance relations are managed in discourse (Blass 1990).

This issue ties in with another one: whether discourse should be considered a well-defined linguistic object. If it is, the observation that discourse analysis has such a diverse subject matter would be highly surprising. However, the claim that discourse is a well-defined linguistic object has been challenged on independent grounds by Blass (1990) and Reboul and Moeschler (1997). Their arguments are based mainly on the failure of discourse analysts to provide an adequate definition of discourse in terms of coherence: there are acceptable discourses which are not coherent, and there are coherent sequences of utterances which are not intuitively regarded as acceptable discourses (see Blass 1990; Wilson 1998). Thus, coherence is neither necessary nor sufficient for discourse well-formedness or acceptability. However, these arguments are developed primarily with the notion of local coherence in mind. Coherence theorists could counter many of them if a supplementary notion of global coherence could be developed which could be shown — perhaps in conjunction with local coherence — to be necessary and sufficient to account for intuitions of well-formedness or acceptability of discourse. The conclusion reached in this book, that there is no well-defined notion of global coherence, and that no such notion can be defined, forestalls such arguments. This gives further support to the claim that discourse is not a well-defined linguistic object, and that the diversity of the subject matter of discourse analysis is therefore not surprising.

I would like to close this subsection by pointing out that the diverse issues falling into the domain of discourse analysis are all included in the concerns of relevance theory. Wilson and Sperber (1993) have summarised the relation between coding and inference in utterance interpretation by highlighting different ways in which information can be conveyed by an utterance. Their summary shows how the different ways in which linguistic form can be exploited in verbal communication — by conceptual or procedural encoding, by exploiting relevance-guided inference processes while falling short of encoding — are indeed motivated by relevance considerations. Thus, while it does not fall squarely under either the headings of pragmatics or the heading of linguistic (procedural) semantics or 'discourse competence,' discourse analysis does fall squarely under relevance theory, in the sense that the interests of discourse analysis are shared by relevance theory, though the interests of relevance theory are wider (including, for example, questions of stylistics and rhetoric such as irony and metaphor).[3]

10.4 New questions

At the heart of the account of genre proposed in this book is a detailed account of how expectations of relevance are raised on the basis of the presumption of optimal relevance communicated by every act of ostensive communication (Chapter 5). I noted that the presumption of relevance is in fact a member of the set of assumptions which the communicator intends to make manifest or more manifest to the audience, that is, it is part of the information that the communicator intended to convey to his audience (Sperber and Wilson 1995:164). However, this information is presumably relevant only as long as the comprehension process unfolds. It would be an unnecessary burden on the cognitive system to transfer it to (long-term) memory along with other information made manifest by the utterance. Hence, by common considerations of cognitive efficiency, the conclusion must be that the presumption of relevance is discarded at the end of the interpretation process (Deirdre Wilson, personal communication).

This so far uncontroversial consideration has an interesting consequence: the result of the interpretation process is not identical to the representation of it which gets stored in memory. As pointed out in Chapter 6, this conflicts with the widely accepted view that the goal of discourse comprehension is to (re-)construct a mental representation of the discourse as intended by the communicator (van Dijk and Kintsch 1983; Graesser et al. 1997). On this latter view, the result of the interpretation process should be identical to the representation of the discourse which is stored in memory and which facilitates retrieval and recall.

If the presumption of relevance were the only piece of information conveyed by the utterance which is discarded at the end of the information process, it could be argued that this view differs only minimally from the standard view of the role of discourse representation in comprehension. However, I have argued in Chapter 5 that there is a lot more information which is made manifest or more manifest by the communicator, but which is relevant only as long as comprehension is in progress and should therefore be discarded at the end of the interpretation process: this includes all the information needed to establish more specific expectations of relevance in cases where the presumption of relevance cannot be adopted as is. If these arguments are on the right lines, then it follows that the goal of discourse comprehension cannot be the construction of a mental representation of the discourse which will be the one that is eventually stored in memory.

This conclusion raises questions about precisely how the eventual mental representation of discourse can differ from the result of the comprehension process, and what are the processes which transform the output of comprehension into the discourse representation eventually stored in memory. A suggested answer was implicit in the discussion above: the information which is discarded at the end of the comprehension process is discarded because it is relevant only to the process itself, by suggesting specific routes to verifying the specific expectations of relevance raised in the discourse. It is not foreseeable at this point that this information will yield further cognitive effects; hence, by the cognitive principle of relevance the mind should not be expected to process this information further. It is thus the cognitive principle of relevance which may guide the processes involved in transforming the outcome of comprehension into the discourse representation eventually stored in memory.

This suggestion, that the cognitive principle of relevance helps to determine which information will be discarded from the set of information inferred during the comprehension process, may have further consequences. In Chapter 6, I raised the question of whether the cognitive principle of relevance motivates the deletion from the eventual discourse representation of information closely resembling information stored under a genre concept, and replacing it in the same with a pointer to this genre information before storing it in long-term memory. In this way, the cognitive role of genre may go beyond merely constraining comprehension. Clearly, more research will be needed to clarify these issues, and that is beyond the scope of this book. However, I hope to have shown that the account of genre advocated in this book opens up new and interesting questions for further research.

Notes

Notes to Chapter 1

[1]Hatim and Mason (1997) illustrate this point with an example involving the English expression *what is lacking*. This expression implies a contrast. Leaving the contrast implicit creates an impression of subtlety in argumentation. In Arabic, where the contrast cannot be left implicit and must be made explicit by use of an expression roughly paraphrasable as *but what is lacking*, the effect of subtlety is lost.

[2]Lenk (1998:15 footnote 1), following Widdowson (1995), makes a related, but slightly different distinction: discourse is the actual use of text, that is, in speaking or writing the speaker or author produces discourse, as does the hearer or reader in interpreting a text. The text is the result of discourse production.

[3]Some authors have suggested further terminological distinctions between *Textsorte* (maybe translatable as 'text kind') and *Texttyp* ('text type') such that *Textsorte* would be a set of *Texttypen*. However, this distinction has not been widely used, and Lewandowski (1985) uses the terms synonymously without comment.

[4]Sperber and Wilson's position on these points will be reviewed in more detail below.

[5]These terms are introduced purely for expository reasons, and no theoretical status is claimed for them.

[6]For a discussion of the foreground-background distinction, and of Longacre's and Hays' analysis of the Hebrew verb in different discourse types, see Chapter 4.

[7]Since conclusions about the history of a text within a genre must rest on observations about the linguistic and hermeneutical interpretation of the text and its genre, this study may nevertheless have indirect implications for this approach.

[8]For discussion of the extent to which coding and inference play a role in verbal communication, see Sperber and Wilson (1998), Wilson and Sperber (2002). See also Wilson and Sperber (1993).

[9]Strictly speaking, whether or not the hearer will adopt the presumption of relevance depends on how much the hearer trusts the speaker (Sperber and Wilson 1995; Wilson and Sperber 2002). Also, the utterance may not be optimally relevant to the hearer for reasons which the speaker may not necessarily have foreseen. Relevance theory takes these factors into account by recognising different degrees of sophistication in the comprehension procedure (Sperber 1994): a naively optimistic hearer expects *actual* relevance, while in successively more sophisticated procedures the hearer expects *attempted* or *purported* relevance. I ignore these complications for ease of exposition in this short introduction.

Notes to Chapter 2

[1]The literature on intersentential coherence relations is vast, including Hobbs (1979, 1983); Mann and Thompson (1986, 1988); Fox (1987); Sanders et al. (1992, 1993); Lascarides and Asher (1993); Knott and Dale (1994); Knott and Sanders (1998) and the references cited therein.

[2]The term *eventuality* is a cover term for events and states.

[3]Actually, Caenepeel (1995) accounts for global coherence in narratives in terms of relations of consequentiality, which is considered

to have various sub-types, including causality. Since causality is probably the most important kind of consequential relations, I link Caenepeel's (1995) account to that of Samet and Schank (1984).

[4]I use square brackets [ ] to indicate descriptions of events or states to distinguish them from propositions and utterances.

[5]Together with assumption 5, this strengthens assumption 1.

[6]See Unger (1996:417–9, 425–36) for an elaboration of this point.

[7]'Titanic' here refers to a movie which in Germany was shown from January 8, 1998 in the cinemas.

[8]'Die Feuerzangenbowle' is a well-known movie classic in Germany which has been around for decades and has often been shown on TV.

[9]Needless to say, if other contextual assumptions are more prominent and more easily accessible to the hearer, the interpretation may be different.

Notes to Chapter 3

[1]Unger (2001) considers a fourth approach, van Dijk's (1977;1980; van Dijk and Kintsch 1983) theory of macroproposition. On this approach discourse topic is seen as a semantic notion, a statement which is uniquely entailed by all sentences of the discourse (segment). Since this early semantic notion of discourse topic has largely been superseded by pragmatic notions of discourse topic, I do not discuss this approach further in this book, but I will look at the psychological aspects of van Dijk and Kintsch 1983 in Chapter 6.

[2]While Giora (1985b:700, 714) makes strong claims about coherence being explained only with relation to the discourse topic, she also contends that 'it is nevertheless obvious that the interrelations between sequenced propositions must be somehow constrained ... it is clear that such an analysis [of local coherence relations, CU] is

needed to arrive at an adequate characterization of coherence' (p. 707). But these relations are to be explained not in terms of relations between sentences (or other units), but in terms of the relation between a proposition and a context set (p. 707).

[3]This point is underlined by the fact that Giora gives various examples of sets of parallel discourses, one incoherent but acceptable, one coherent and also acceptable (Giora 1997:26–7).

[4]This holds true despite Giora's (1997, 1998) claims to the contrary. But notice that while Giora argues against intuitions of relevance and takes intuitions of coherence for granted, she does not *argue* for the existence of intuitions of discourse well-formedness.

[5]It is worth noting that his notion of topic, because of the second claim about topics, does avoid (at least some of) Giora's problems (see above, section 3). I will have more to say about the third claim elsewhere in this book (Chapter 6, section 6.2.4).

Notes to Chapter 4

[1]In fact I will argue below that foreground marking is of just this kind. Gumperz' (1992) account of 'contextualization cues' is similar in spirit to Sperber and Wilson's (1995) account of focal stress. For Gumperz (1992:232), 'foregrounding or backgrounding of items of information' is a characteristic effect of contextualization cues, which are verbal or non verbal signals which do not encode meaning, but point the hearer to a certain interpretation in context of what has been said.

[2]Van Kuppevelt's argumentation is admittedly hard to follow at this point. I am not sure why sentences (c) and (e) should be intuitively 'important' to the foreground. Either of these sentences could have been left out without any impact on the quality of the text (witness van Kuppevelt's 1995b example (9) on page 824, which lacks these sentences). Furthermore, while I can see that (c) may

serve to strengthen the idea that the investigations really stopped, and in this way affect the validity of the foreground material, I don't see how (e) has a comparable impact on the foreground. Thus, one could argue that (c) and (e) are not even in the same category of substructure.

[3]Grosz and Sidner (1986) emphasise that the discourse segment purpose (or discourse segment intention) is a property of the discourse, not of the communicator(s). I find this point hard to follow since intentions are basically attitudes which an individual bears to some proposition (Grice 1989; Fodor 1987a,b, 1994, 1998; Sperber and Wilson 1995), hence the notion of intention cannot be separated from the individual which entertains them. To say that the discourse segment purpose 'is the intention with which the communicator standardly uses this segment in discourse' is my attempt to make sense of Grosz and Sidner.

[4]Van Kuppevelt (1995b:811) criticises Grosz and Sidner's (1985,1986) account for providing no criteria to distinguish different categories of side structure. See sub-section 4.2.7 above.

[5]The relation of discourse continuity and foreground is also dealt with in Fabb (1997:180–8).

[6]A similar approach to discourse typology has been proposed by Werlich (1982); see Renkema (1993:91–2) and the introduction to this book.

Notes to Chapter 5

[1]A phenomenon is manifest to an individual at a given time if he is capable at that time of representing it mentally and assign a (probable) truth value to it (Sperber and Wilson 1995:39).

[2]An assumption is mutually manifest if not only this assumption is manifest to the individual, but also it is manifest to this individual

that the assumption is manifest to another individual as well (Sperber and Wilson 1995:41–2).

[3]There are actually many more inferential tasks involved such as the narrowing down of the intended meanings of the preposition *lĕ*, resolving the meaning of construct nouns (the equivalent to genitive constructions in English), and so on. I discuss only the two sub-tasks mentioned since the contextual assumptions involved in these tasks turn out to be relevant to the discussion of genre.

[4]The following abbreviations are used in the glosses: ACC 'accusative'; HT 'hortative'; PCP 'participle'.

[5]Not all commentators agree on this interpretation, see Wildberger (1972) for a survey. Wildberger himself rejects this interpretation on the ground that the beloved could not be expected to say about herself that 'he did not bring good fruits,' and that later, the 1SG appears to refer to the owner of the vineyard. However, I hope to show in the unfolding analysis that these difficulties dissolve once one rejects the view that the genre is a rigid grid on interpretation which doesn't allow for context shifts.

[6]It probably would if it were a case of gossip or casual conversation; but then one would expect a continuation, which is blatantly missing, as the following verse shows.

[7]This is the possible result of contradiction resolution, not a conclusion of a deduction.

[8] *ʔāśîr* is the *Qerê* reading; the masoretic text's *Ketib* reads *hāśēr* 'to remove' (infinitive).

Notes to Chapter 6

[1]In the case of (4b), the most easily accessible interpretation of the second sentence on the basis of the first one is to assume that 'Imsbach' and 'Steinbach' are villages or towns located in such a way

that walking from one to the other amounts to hiking. This is independent of whether the hearer knows these respective locations or not.

[2]This is one aspect of Sperber and Wilson's account of focus. This account involves two major components: (a) the on-line construction of a set of successively more complete propositional schemas, and (b) a procedure for establishing a focal scale of logically ordered proposition schemas. In this section I discuss only the first component of their account of focus.

[3]That this is expected to be the case is part of the particular presumption of optimal relevance communicated by the utterance. The speaker must have believed that it would be manifest to the addressee that on some easily accessible assignment of reference, the utterance — on some interpretation — would seem relevant to him: otherwise the speaker should have rephrased her utterance.

[4]See Carston (1993) and Unger (1998a), as well as the remarks in Chapter 2 of this book. I distinguish sharply between cognitive causal relations and semantic causal relations.

[5]Note that Klein and von Stutterheim's (1987) account does not necessarily entail the claim that discourse is hierarchically structured. While they do suggest that complex discourses may have side-structures which in turn have their own *quaestio,* resulting in a 'hierarchy of *quaestiones*,' they do not formalise a hierarchical relation of *quaestiones* in a way comparable to van Kuppevelt's (1991, 1995a) proposal.

[6]It is actually difficult to see what conclusions Copman and Griffith draw from their findings. The paper ends with a summary of the results of the study and suggestions for an explanation of these, and with the call for further investigation: 'because text type yielded the greatest number of significant results in this study, further investigation of text effects on recall by children with disabilities is needed' (p. 243). It seems fair to say that their interest lies more in

investigating language impairment than in contributing to the development of pragmatic theories of genre.

[7]The well-structuredness of such a text is thus a consequence of the communicative principle of relevance, as argued in Blass (1990) and elsewhere in this book.

[8]This point will be crucial later in this book, when I discuss the role of schematic structures in more detail.

[9]It is in fact difficult to evaluate Kintsch and Greene (1978) as they do not quote examples of the stories used in their experiments in full. The published sources of these texts were not accessible to me.

[10]Van Dijk and Kintsch (1983:254) classify essays as 'descriptive texts.' It may be better to classify them as expository texts.

[11]According to van Dijk and Kintsch (1983:236) this assumption was a common one in cognitive science at the time their book was written. That this assumption remained common for some time afterwards can be seen in Eysenck and Keane (1991).

Notes to Chapter 7

[1]The semantics of the Biblical Hebrew imperfect consecutive form is still a matter of debate.

[2]The assumption that various indicators may be used for foregrounding or backgrounding information is shared by Gumperz (1992:232) who comments that '[f]oregrounding processes, moreover, do not rest on any one single cue.' For an illustration of the variety of 'contextualization cues' available in narrative, see Basso (1992).

[3]In these Greek examples, *participium coniunctum* is marked with italics. PCP is the abbreviation for 'participle'.

[4]Attempts to specify the overriding factors on default interpretation have been made on the basis of defeasible logic and commonsense entailment (Dahlgren et al. 1989; Lascarides and Asher 1993), but see Sequeiros (1995:compare comments in Chapter 2) for arguments against these approaches.

[5]Actually, the text in John 7:53–8:11 is absent from the oldest manuscripts and may therefore be of a later origin. However, this does not affect the argument at hand.

[6]Note that the participial clause follows the finite one here; thus it is expected that word order (clause order) has a 'neutralizing' effect on the labelling of parts of the sentence for backgrounding. Intuitively, this seems to be the case. For present purposes it is not necessary to go into the details here.

[7]Notice that this example shows more generally that neither coherence-based nor accessibility-based accounts can explain pronominal reference in discourse fully. Since relevance theory balances processing effort against cognitive effects, it may not only account for accessibility factors on the effort side, but also for other factors on the effect side.

Notes to Chapter 8

[1]See the remarks in the following section on the difference between the cultural and social setting in systemic-functional register and genre theory.

[2]Another recent analysis of genre within the systemic-functional framework is Whittaker and Martín Rojo (1999).

[3]Thibault (1999:592–3) makes this point in the context of summarising his criticism of Franken (1997). However, he explicitly states that in focusing on Franken's paper, he intends to discuss the theory behind her approach, that is, relevance theory in general: 'in responding to her paper and in confronting theory with theory, I

hope to be able to make explicit the differences between the two approaches and their wider implications for the study of human social meaning-making.' (Thibault 1999:558)

[4]There are other serious general objections to Thibault's non-cognitive theory. These have to do more generally with the validity of the Representational Theory of Mind and with the role of intentional states in communication, and are discussed in depth in the literature on these topics (for example Fodor 1975, 1987b; Carston 1998b, 2002. Note in particular Carston's (2002:56–64) argument that an adequate account of natural language semantics requires it to be a translation into the Language of Thought, and see Unger (2001) for a more detailed discussion of Thibault (1999).

[5]This, in turn, can be achieved in various ways: either by saving the hearer processing effort in arriving at a certain hypothesis, or by constraining expectations of the kind of cognitive effects to be achieved.

[6]Other examples (suggested to me by Deirdre Wilson, personal communication) supporting this conclusion are jokes and wit, which achieve their effects via a wide array of weak implicatures, but where comprehension is virtually instantaneous. Also, Gibbs' (1994) reading-time experiments show that most ordinary metaphors do not take longer to understand than 'literal' utterances.

[7]In Unger (1994) I looked at differences in the usage of preparatory questions in Behdînî-Kurdish on the one hand, and in English and German on the other. In Behdînî-Kurdish, preparatory questions such as *Isn't that Bêgova? Half of its inhabitants belong to the Berwarî tribe and the other half to the Gulî tribe* are used to a much greater extent than in German or English. I argued that this correlates with the fact that the cultural maxim *Don't show superiority to others* is much more prominent in Kurdish culture than in German or English culture, and that it is therefore more relevant for Kurdish speakers to communicate compliance with this cultural norm. One way of doing this efficiently is by using the question form, since (sincere) questions typically show that the communicator is not su-

perior in knowledge to his addressee. When the audience can easily infer the speaker's intentions behind the preparatory question (that is, when they are not likely to mistake the preparatory question for a real one), such a question will save the audience processing effort by giving concise evidence for the speaker's informative intention as well as his intention of communicating compliance to social norms.

Notes to Chapter 9

[1]See also Grice (1989:369): 'I take it as being obvious that insofar as the presence of implicature rests on the character of one or another kind of conversational enterprise, it will rest on the character of concerted rather than solitary talk production. Genuine monologues are free from speaker's implication.'

[2]In fact, there is another possible line of argument: a self-deliberating statement is not addressed to the hearer, so he is not intended to see the speaker as obeying the conversational maxims in the same way as in a real talk-exchange. On this view, the example is not analogous to the scalar implicature cases.

[3]Kitis (1999) acknowledges that (12) may pose a problem for her theory. She suggests that the social domain (institution) of death exorcizing may give the hearer access to the information that the speaker wants to avoid naming death in order to provoke death (Kitis 1999:652 footnote 13). However, no such elaborate explanation is needed for the Gricean.

[4]As it appears in my taperecorded version told by Mullah Nasir and quoted with his kind permission.

[5]Possible exceptions to this trend are theories of genre based on the notion of prototypes, such as Swales (1990) and Paltridge (1995). However, neither Paltridge nor Swales systematically address the function of genre in a theory of communication.

Notes to Chapter 10

[1]For somewhat different views on coherence see Charolles (1983); Grosz and Sidner (1986); Laux (1998).

[2]Hooper (1998) seems to come closest to claiming that there is some arbitrariness in the way grounding is marked cross-linguistically. He argues that the markers which encode functionally equivalent grounding levels in Tokelau and European languages are quite different. However, it is still the morphological marking of aspect which is the means of indicating grounding in discourse, not some other structural feature.

[3]The claims made in this paragraph (as well as in the whole subsection) are made mainly with a 'narrow' conception of discourse analysis in mind, one which does not focus on sociological aspects. Discourse analysis in this sense has also been called 'discourse grammar' (for example Longacre 1983) or 'discourse semantics' (Tomlin et al. 1997). However, since social aspects of communication are also of interest to relevance theory (Sperber and Wilson 1995:61–2, 279; 1997), this statement should also largely hold true for a broader conception of discourse analysis.

Bibliography

Abangma, S. N. (1987). *Modes in Dényá Discourse.* Dallas, TX: The Summer Institute of Linguistics and The University of Texas at Arlington.

Anderson, A. and N. Belnap (1975). *Entailment.* Princeton: Princeton Univeristy Press.

Ariel, M. (1985). *Givenness Marking.* PhD thesis, Tel-Aviv University.

Ariel, M. (1988). Referring and accessibility. *Journal of Linguistics 24*, 65–87.

Ariel, M. (1990). *Accessing NP Antecedents.* London: Routledge, Croom Helm Linguistics Series.

Ariel, M. (1994). Interpreting anaphoric expressions: A cognitive versus a pragmatic approach. *Journal of Linguistics 30*(1), 3–42.

Ariel, M. (1996). Referring expressions and the +/− coreference distinction. pp. 13–35. In Fretheim and Gundel (eds).

Asher, N. and A. Lascarides (1998a). Bridging. *Journal of Semantics 15*(1), 83–113.

Asher, N. and A. Lascarides (1998b). Questions in dialogue. *Linguistics and Philosophy 23*(2), 237–309.

Bailey, N. A. and S. H. Levinsohn (1992). The function of preverbal elements in independent clauses in the Hebrew narrative of Genesis. *Journal of Translation and Textlinguistics. 5*(3), 179–207.

Barsalou, L. W. (1987). The instability of graded structure: implications for the nature of concepts. pp. 101–140. In Neisser (ed.) 1987.

Barsalou, L. W., J. Usher, and D. R. Sewell (1985). *Schema Based Planning of Events.* Atlanta, GA: Atlanta, GA: Emory University. In Work in progress referred to in Barsalou (1987).

Basso, E. B. (1992). Contextualization in Kalapalo narratives. pp. 253–269. In Duranti and Goodwin (eds) (1992).

Bender, J. and D. Wellbery (eds.) (1990). *The Ends of Rhetoric: History, Theory, Practice.* Stanford, CA: Stanford University Press.

Bergen, R. D. (ed.) (1994). *Biblical Hebrew and Discourse Linguistics.* Dallas, Texas: Summer Institute of Linguistics.

Berger, K. (1987). *Einführung in die Formgeschichte.* Tübingen: Francke.

Bever, T., J. Kath, and D. Langendoen (eds.) (1976). *An Integrated Theory of Linguistic Ability.* New York: Crowell.

Bex, A. R. (1992). Genre as context. *Journal of Literary Semantics 21*, 1–16.

Birch, C. (1974). *Studies in Chinese Literary Genres.* Berkeley, CA: University of California Press.

Blakemore, D. (1987). *Semantic Constraints on Relevance.* Oxford: Blackwell.

Blakemore, D. (1988). The organization of discourse. pp. 229–250. In Newmeyer (ed.) (1988) volume IV.

Blakemore, D. (1992). *Understanding Utterances.* Oxford: Blackwell.

Blass, F., A. Debrunner, and F. Rehkopf (1984). *Grammatik des neutestamentlichen Griechisch, 16th edition.* Göttingen: Vandenhoeck and Ruprecht.

Blass, R. (1986). Cohesion, coherence and relevance. *Notes on Linguistics 34*, 41–64.

Blass, R. (1990). *Relevance Relations in Discourse.* Cambridge: Cambridge University Press.

Bodine, W. R. (ed.) (1992). *Linguistics and Biblical Hebrew.* Winona Lake, Indiana: Eisenbrauns.

Brown, G. and G. Yule (1983). *Discourse Analysis.* Cambridge: Cambridge University Press.

Caenepeel, M. (1995). Aspect and text structure. *Linguistics 33*, 213–253.

Caenepeel, M. and M. Moens (1994). Temporal structure and discourse stucture. pp. 5–20. In Vet and Vetters (1994).

Carruthers, P. and J. Boucher (eds.) (1998). *Thought and Language.* Oxford: Oxford University Press.

Carston, R. (1988). Implicature, explicature, and truth-theoretic semantics. pp. 155–182. In R. Kempson (ed.) (1988). Reprinted in Davis (ed.) (1991), pp. 23-51.

Carston, R. (1993). Conjunction, explanation, and relevance. *Lingua 90*, 27–48.

Carston, R. (1995). Quantity maxims and generalised implicature. *Lingua 96*, 213–244. Earlier version in UCL Working Papers in Linguistics, 2 (1990), 1-31.

Carston, R. (1997). Enrichment and loosening: Complementary processes in deriving the proposition expressed? *Linguistische Berichte Sonderheft 8*, 103–127.

Carston, R. (1998a). Informativeness, relevance and scalar implicature. pp. 179–236. In Carston and Uchida (eds) (1998).

Carston, R. (1998b). *Pragmatics and the explicit/implicit distinction.* PhD thesis, University of London.

Carston, R. (1998c). Relevance-theoretic pragmatics and modularity. *UCL Working papers in linguistics 9*, 29–53.

Carston, R. (2000). The relationship between generative grammar and (relevance-theoretic) pragmatics. *Language and Communication 20*, 87–103.

Carston, R. (2002). *Thoughts and Utterances.* Oxford: Blackwell.

Carston, R. and S. Uchida (eds.) (1998). *Relevance Theory: Applications and Implications.* Amsterdam and Philadelphia: John Benjamins.

Chafe, W. L. (1979). The flow of thought and the flow of language. pp. 159–181. In Givón (ed.) (1979).

Chafe, W. L. (1987). Cognitive constraints on information flow. pp. 21–51. In Tomlin (ed.) (1987).

Charolles, M. (1983). Coherence as a principle in the interpretation of discourse. *Text 3*, 71–97.

Chomsky, N. (1986). *Knowledge of Language.* New York: Praeger.

Cole, P. and J. Morgan (eds.) (1975). *Syntax and Semantics 3: Speech Acts.* New York: Academic Press.

Copman, K. S. P. and P. L. Griffith (1994). Event and story structure recall by children with specific learning disabilities, language impairments, and normally achieving children. *Journal of Psycholinguistic Research 23*(3), 231–248.

Dahlgren, K., J. McDowell, and E. P. Stabler (1989). Knowledge representation for commonsense reasoning with text. *Computational Linguistics 23*, 851–882.

Dancy, J., J. Moravcsik, and C. Taylor (eds.) (1988). *Human Agency, Language, Duty and Value.* Stanford, CA: Stanford University Press.

Davis, S. (ed.) (1991). *Pragmatics: A Reader.* Oxford: Oxford University Press.

Delitzsch, F. (1984). *Jesaja.* Giessen: Brunnen. Reprint of third edition, Leipzig: Dörflin and Franke 1879.

Downing, A. (1996). Register and/or genre? pp. 11–27. In Vazquez and Hornero (eds) (1996).

Dowty, D. (1986). The effects of aspectual class on the temporal structure of discourse: semantics or pragmatics? *Linguistics and Philosophy 9*, 37–61.

Duranti, A. and C. Goodwin (eds.) (1992a). *Rethinking Context.* Cambridge: Cambridge University Press.

Duranti, A. and C. Goodwin (1992b). Rethinking context: an introduction. pp. 1–42. In Duranti and Goodwin (eds) (1992a).

Duszak, A. (1994). Thematic progressions and global coherence. *Folia Linguistica 28*(3/4), 363–384.

Eggins, S. and J. R. Martin (1997). Genres and registers of discourse. pp. 230–256. In T. A. van Dijk (ed.) (1997).

Elliger, K. and W. Rudolph (eds.) (1983). *Biblia Hebraica Stuttgartensia.* Stuttgart: Deutsche Bibelgesellschaft.

Eysenck, M. W. and M. T. Keane (1991). *Cognitive Psychology.* Hove (UK), London (UK), Hillsdale (USA): Lawrence Erlbaum Associates, (USA).

Fabb, N. (1997). *Linguistics and Literature.* Oxford: Blackwell.

Fayol, M., M. Hickmann, I. Bonnotte, and J. E. Gombert (1993). The effects of narrative context on French verbal inflections: A developmental perspective. *Journal of Psycholinguistic Research. 22*(4), 453–478.

Fleischmann, S. (1985). Discourse functions of tense-aspect oppositions in narrative: toward a theory of grounding. *Linguistics 23*(6), 851–882.

Fleischmann, S. (1990). *Tense and Narrativity: From Medieval Performance to Modern Fiction.* Austin: University of Texas Press.

Fodor, J. (1975). *The Language of Thought.* New York: Crowell.

Fodor, J. (1987a). *Psychosemantics.* Cambridge, MA and London, UK: MIT Press.

Fodor, J. (1987b). Why there still has to be a language of thought. pp. 135–154. In Fodor (1987a).

Fodor, J. (1994). *The Elm and the Expert.* Cambridge, MA and London, UK: MIT Press.

Fodor, J. (1998). *Concepts.* Oxford: Oxford University Press.

Follingstad, C. M. (2001). *Deictic Viewpoint in Biblical Hebrew Text: A Syntagmatic and Paradigmatic Analysis of the Particle kî.* Dallas: SIL International.

Fowler, A. (1982). *Kinds of Literature: An Introduction to the Theory of Genres and Modes.* New York: Cambridge University Press.

Fox, B. (1987). *Discourse Structure and Anaphora.* Cambridge: Cambridge University Press.

Franken, N. (1997). Vagueness and approximation in relevance theory. *Journal of Pragmatics 28*(2), 135–151.

Fretheim, T. and J. Gundel (eds.) (1996). *Reference and Referent Accessibility.* Amsterdam, NL and Philadelphia, PA: John Benjamins.

Furlong, A. (1996). *Relevance and Literary Interpretation.* PhD thesis, University of London.

Gazdar, G. (1979). *Pragmatics: Implicature, Presupposition and Logical Form.* New York: Academic Press.

Gerhart, M. (1989). The dilemma of the text: how to "belong" to a genre. *Poetics 18*, 355–373.

Gesenius, W. (1985). *Hebräische Grammatik.* Darmstadt: Wissenschaftliche Buchgesellschaft. Reprint of the 28th edition (revised by E. Kautsch), Leipzig 1909.

Gibbs, R. (1994). *The Poetics of Mind.* Cambridge: Cambridge University Press.

Giora, R. (1985a). A text-based Analysis of non-narrative discourse. *Theoretical Linguistics 12*(2/3), 115–135.

Giora, R. (1985b). Towards a theory of coherence. *Poetics Today 6*(4), 699–716.

Giora, R. (1988). On the informativeness requirement. *Journal of Pragmatics*, 547–565.

Giora, R. (1997). Discourse coherence and theory of relevance: Stumbling blocks in search of a unified theory. *Journal of Pragmatics 27*, 17–34.

Giora, R. (1998). Discourse coherence is an independent notion: A reply to Deirdre Wilson. *Journal of Pragmatics 29*, 75–86.

Givón, T. (ed.) (1979). *Syntax and Semantics 12: Discourse and Syntax.* San Diego, CA and London, UK: Academic Press.

Goatly, A. (1994). Register and the redemption of relevance theory. *Pragmatics 4*(2), 139–182.

Graesser, A. C., M. A. Gernsbacher, and S. R. Goldman (1997). Cognition. pp. 292–319. In van Dijk (ed.) (1997).

Green, M. S. (1995). Quantity, volubility, and some varieties of discourse. *Linguistics and Philosophy 18*, 83–112.

Grice, H. P. (1989). *Studies in the Way of Words.* Cambridge MA: Harvard University Press.

Grimes, J. E. (1975). *The Thread of Discourse.* The Hague: Mouton.

Grosz, B. J. and C. L. Sidner (1985). *Discourse Structure and the Proper Treatment of Interruptions.* Proceedings of the 9th International joint Conference on Artificial Intelligence. Los Altos, CA: Kaufmann.

Grosz, B. J. and C. L. Sidner (1986). Attention, intentions, and the structure of discourse. *Computational Linguistics 12*, 175–204.

Gumperz, J. J. (1992). Contextualization and understanding. pp. 229–252. In Duranti and Goodwin (eds) (1992).

Gundel, J. K. (1996). Relevance theory meets the givenness hierarchy. An account of inferrables. pp. 141–153. In Fretheim and Gundel (eds) (1996).

Gundel, J. K., N. Hedberg, and R. Zacharski (1988). On the generation and interpretation of demonstrative expressions. In *Proceedings of the International Conference on Computational Linguistics*, Volume 12, pp. 216–221.

Gundel, J. K., N. Hedberg, and R. Zacharski (1989). Givenness, implicature and demonstrative expressions in English discourse. Volume 25, pp. 89–103. Chicago Linguistics Society.

Gundel, J. K., N. Hedberg, and R. Zacharski (1990). Givenness, implicature and the form of referring expressions in discourse. Volume 16, pp. 442–453. Berkeley Linguistics Society.

Gundel, J. K., R. Zacharski, and N. Hedberg (1993). Cognitive status and the form of referring expressions in discourse. *Language 69*, 274–307.

Gundry, R. E. and R. Warner (eds.) (1986). *Philosophical Grounds of Rationality.* Oxford: Clarendon Press.

Gutt, E.-A. (2000). *Translation and Relevance* (2 edn). Manchester: St. Jerome. (First edition 1991 Oxford: Blackwell).

Haegemann, L. (1993). *Introduction to Government and Binding theory.* Oxford: Blackwell. first edition 1991.

Halliday, M. (1978). *Language as a Social Semiotic: The Social Interpretation of Language and Meaning.* London: Edward Arnold.

Halliday, M. (1985). *An Introduction to Functional Grammar.* London: Edward Arnold. 2nd edition 1994.

Halliday, M. and R. Hasan (1976). *Cohesion in English.* London: Longman.

Halliday, M. and R. Hasan (1980). *Text and Context: Aspects of Language in a Social-Semiotic Perspective.* New edition as Halliday and Hasan (1985), Tokyo: Graduate School of Languages and

Linguistics and the Linguistic Institute for International Communication, Sophia University.

Halliday, M. and R. Hasan (1985). *Language, Context, and Text: aspects of language in a social-semiotic perspective.* Geelong, Vic.: Geelong, Vic.: Deakin University Press. Republished by Oxford University Press, 1989.

Hanauer, D. (1995). Literary and poetic text categorization judgements. *Journal of Literary Semantics 24*(3), 187–210.

Hanauer, D. (1998). The genre-specific hypothesis of reading: Reading poetry and encyclopedic items. *Poetics 26*(2), 63–80.

Harnish, R. (1976). Logical form and implicature. pp. 316–364. In Bever, Kath and Langendoen (eds.) (1976). Reprinted in S. Davis (ed.) 1991.

Harris, S. (1995). Pragmatics and power. *Journal of Pragmatics 23*(2), 117–135.

Hatim, B. and I. Mason (1997). *The Translator as Communicator.* London and New York: Routledge.

Hays, J. D. (1995). Verb forms in the expository discourse sections of ecclesiastes. *Journal of Translation and Textlinguistics 7*(1), 9–18.

Helm, J. (ed.) (1967). *Essays on the Verbal and Visual Arts.* Proceedings of the 1966 Annual Spring Meeting of the American Ethnological Society. Seattle: University of Washington Press.

Hirschberg, J. (1985). *A Theory of Scalar Implicature.* Department of Computer Science, University of Pennsylvania, PhD thesis.

Hobbs, J. R. (1979). Coherence and coreference. *Cognitive Science 3*, 67–90.

Hobbs, J. R. (1983). Why is discourse coherent? pp. 29–70. In Neubauer (ed.) (1983).

Hofmann, T. R. (1989). Paragraphs, and anaphora. *Journal of Pragmatics 13*, 239–250.

Holdcroft, D. (1979). Speech acts and conversation - I. *The Philosophical Quarterly 29*, 125–141.

Hooper, R. (1998). Universals of narrative pragmatics: a Polynesian case study. *Linguistics 36*, 119–160.

Hopper, P. J. (1979). Aspect and foregrounding in discourse. pp. 213–241. In T. Givón (ed.) (1979).

Hopper, P. J. and S. A. Thompson (1980). Transitivity in grammar and discourse. *Language 56*(1), 251–299.

Horn, L. (1984). A new taxonomy for pragmatic inference: Q-based and R-based implicature. pp. 11–42. In Schiffrin (ed.) (1984).

Horn, L. (1989). *A Natural History of Negation*. Chicago: University of Chicago Press.

Holy Bible. New International Version (1973, 1978, 1984). International Bible Society (ed.). Grand Rapids, MI: The Zondervan Corporation.

Jary, M. (1998). Relevance theory and the communication of politeness. *Journal of Pragmatics 30*, 1–19.

Joüon, P. and T. Muraoka (1996). *A Grammar of Biblical Hebrew*. Roma: Editrice Pontificio Istituto Biblico. Reprint of first edition (1991) with corrections.

Kamio, A. (ed.) (1997). *Directions in Functional Linguistics*. Amsterdam: John Benjamins.

Kamp, H. and U. Reyle (1993). *From Discourse to Logic*. Dordrecht: Kluwer Academic Publishers.

Kempson, R. (ed.) (1988). *Mental Representations*. Cambridge: Cambridge University Press.

Khalfa, J. (ed.) (1994). *What is Intelligence?* Cambridge: Cambridge University Press.

Kintsch, W. and E. Greene (1978). The role of culture-specific schemata in the comprehension and recall of stories. *Discourse Processes 1*, 1–13.

Kintzsch, W., T. S. Mandel, and E. Kozminsky (1977). Summarizing scrambled stories. *Memory and Cognition 5*, 547–552.

Kitis, E. (1999). On relevance again: From philosophy of language across "Pragmatics and power" to global relevance. *Journal of Pragmatics 31*, 643–667.

Klein, W. and C. von Stutterheim (1987). Quaestio und referentielle Bewegung in Erzählungen. *Linguistische Berichte 109*, 163–183.

Klinge, A. (1998). Context construction and conventionalization. Paper presented at the Relevance Theory Workshop, University of Luton.

Knott, A. and R. Dale (1994). Using linguistic phenomena to motivate a set of rhetorical relations. *Discourse Processes 18*, 35–64.

Knott, A. and T. Sanders (1998). The classification of coherence relations and their linguistic markers: an exploration of two languages. *Journal of Pragmatics 30*, 135–175.

Kotthoff, H. (1995). The social semiotics of Georgian toast performances: Oral genre as cultural activity. *Journal of Pragmatics 24*, 353–380.

Koutoupis-Kitis, E. (1982). *Problems connected with the notion of implicature.* PhD thesis.

Labov, W. (1972). *Language in the Inner City. Studies in Black English Vernacular.* Philadelphia: University of Pennsylvania Press.

Labov, W. and J. Waletzky (1967). Narrative analysis: oral versions of personal experience. pp. 12–44. In Helm (ed.) (1967).

Lakoff, G. and M. Johnson (1980). *Metaphors We Live By.* Chicago: Chicago University Press.

Lascarides, A. and N. Asher (1993). Temporal interpretation, discourse relations and commonsense entailment. *Linguistics and Philosophy 16*, 437–493.

Laux, B. D. (1998). Diskursrelationen. Paper presented at Sommerskolen i semantikk og pragmatikk - avhandlingsseminar, University of Trondheim.

Lenk, U. (1998). *Marking Discourse Coherence.* Tübingen: G. Narr Verlag.

Levinsohn, S. H. (1992). *Discourse features of New Testament Greek.* Dallas: Summer Institute of Linguistics.

Levinson, S. C. (1983). *Pragmatics.* Cambridge: Cambridge University Press.

Lewandowski, T. (1985). *Linguistisches Wörterbuch, 3 volumes.* Heidelberg and Wiesbaden: Quelle and Meyer.

Longacre, R. E. (1979). The paragraph as a grammatical unit. pp. 115–134. In Givón (ed.) (1979).

Longacre, R. E. (1983). *The Grammar of Discourse.* New York: Plenum Press.

Longacre, R. E. (1989a). *Joseph: A story of Divine providence. A text theoretical and textlinguistic analysis of Genesis 37 and 39-48.* Winona Lake, Indiana: Eisenbrauns.

Longacre, R. E. (1989b). Two hypotheses regarding text generation and text analysis. *Discourse Processes 12*, 413–460.

Longacre, R. E. (1990a). Introduction. pp. 1–17. In Longacre and Shaler (eds) (1990).

Longacre, R. E. (1990b). Storyline concerns and word-order typologies in East and West Africa. *Studies in African linguistics Supplement 10.*

Longacre, R. E. (1992). Discourse perspective on the Hebrew verb: affirmation and restatement. pp. 177–189. In Bodine (ed.) (1992).

Longacre, R. E. (1994). Weqatal Forms in Biblical Hebrew Prose. pp. 50–98. In Bergen (ed.) (1994).

Longacre, R. E. and D. J. Shaler (eds.) (1990). *Indian Textlinguistic Sketches*, Volume 4.

Lyons, J. (1981). *Language, Meaning and Context.* London: Fontana.

Mandl, H. (ed.) (1981). *Zur Psychologie der Textverarbeitung.* Munich: Urban and Scharzenberg.

Mann, W. C. and S. A. Thompson (1986). Relational propositions in discourse. *Discourse Processes 9*, 57–90.

Mann, W. C. and S. A. Thompson (1988). Rhetorical structure theory: toward a functional theory of text organization. *Text 8*, 243–281.

Matsui, T. (1995). *Bridging and Relevance.* University of London, PhD thesis.

Matsui, T. (1998). Assessing a scenario-based account of bridging reference assignment. pp. 123–159. In Carston and Uchida (eds) (1998).

Moeschler, J. (1993). Relevance and conversation. *Lingua 90*, 149–171.

Morrow, D. G. (1986). Grammatical morphemes and conceptual structure in discourse processing. *Cognitive Science 10*, 423–455.

Moser, H. (ed.) (1974). *Jahrbuch Gesprochene Sprache.* Düsseldorf: Schwann.

Motyer, A. (1993). *The Prophecy of Isaiah.* Leicester: Inter-Varsity Press.

Neisser, U. (ed.) (1987). *Concepts and Conceptual Development, Emory Symposia in Cognition, 1.* New York: Cambridge University Press.

Nestle, E., E. Nestle, B. Aland, K. Aland, J. Karavidopoulos, C. M. Martini, and B. M. Metzger (eds.) (1993). *Novum Testamentum Graece.* (27th edn). Stuttgart: Deutsche Bibelgesellschaft.

Neubauer, F. (ed.) (1983). *Coherence in Natural-language Texts.* Hamburg: Helmut Buske Verlag.

Newmeyer, F. J. (ed.) (1988). *Linguistics: the Cambridge Survey.* Cambridge: Cambridge University Press. Four volumes.

Niccacci, A. (1994). On the Hebrew verbal system. pp. 117–137. In Bergen (ed.) (1994).

Nicolle, S. and B. Clark (1998). Phatic interpretations: Standardisation and conventionalisation. *Revista Alicantina de Estudios Ingleses 11*, 183–191.

Nuti, M. (1998). The Carey-Ann situation. Paper read at the Second Relevance Theory Workshop, University of Luton, September.

Orta, I. V. (1996). Register, genre and linguistic choice. pp. 29–50. In Vazquez and Hornero (eds) (1996).

Paltridge, B. (1995). Working with genre: a pragmatic perspective. *Journal of Pragmatics 24*, 393–406.

Pilkington, A. (1992). Poetic effects. *Lingua 87*, 29–51.

Pilkington, A. (2000). *Poetic Thoughts and Poetic Effects.* Amsterdam: John Benjamins.

Polanyi, L. (1988). A formal model of the structure of discourse. *Journal of Pragmatics 12*, 601–638.

Prince, E. (1985). Fancy syntax and "shared knowledge". *Journal of Pragmatics 9*, 65–82.

Prince, E. (1988). Discourse analysis: a part of the study of linguistic competence. pp. 164–182. In Newmeyer (ed.) (1988) Vol. II.

Prince, E. (1997). On the functions of left-dislocation in English discourse. pp. 117–143. In Kamio (ed.) (1997).

Ramos, F. Y. (1998). Relevance theory and media discourse: A verbal-visual model of communication. *Poetics 25*, 293–309.

Reboul, A. (1992). *Rhétorique et stylistique de la fiction.* Nancy: Presses Universitaires de Nancy.

Reboul, A. and J. Moeschler (1997). Reduction and contextualization in pragmatics and discourse analysis. *Linguistische Berichte Sonderheft 8*, 283–294.

Reinhart, T. (1981). Pragmatics and linguistics: an analysis of sentence topics. *Philosophica 27*, 53–94.

Reinhart, T. (1984). Principles of Gestalt perception in the temporal organization of narrative texts. *Linguistics 22*, 53–94.

Reiss, K. (1981). Type, kind and individuality of text: decision making in translation. *Poetics Today. 4*(2), 121–131. Trans. Susan Kitron. Reprinted in Venuti (ed.) (2000), pp. 160-171.

Renkema, J. (1993). *Discourse Studies. An Introductory Textbook.* Amsterdam/Philadelphia: John Benjamins Publishing Company.

Rouchota, V. (1996). Discourse connectives: what do they link? *UCL Working papers in linguistics 8*, 199–212.

Sacks, H., E. Schegloff, and G. Jefferson (1974). A simplest systematics for the organization of turn-taking for conversation. *Language 50*, 696–735.

Samet, J. and R. Schank (1984). Coherence and connectivity. *Linguistics and Philosophy 7*(1), 57–82.

Sanders, T., W. Spooren, and L. Noordman (1992). Towards a taxonomy of coherence relations. *Discourse Processes 15*, 1–35.

Sanders, T., W. Spooren, and L. Noordman (1993). Coherence relations in a cognitive theory of discourse representations. *Cognitive Linguistics 4*, 93–133.

Schiffrin, D. (1981). Tense variation in narrative. *Language 57*(1), 45–62.

Schiffrin, D. (ed.) (1984). *Meaning, Form and Use in Context: Linguistic Applications.* Georgetown University Roundtable.

Schiffrin, D. (1987). *Discourse Markers.* Cambridge: Cambridge University Press.

Schnotz, W., S. Ballstaedt, and H. Mandl (1981). Kognitive Prozesse beim Zusammenfassen von Lehrtexten. In Mandl (ed.) (1981).

Sequeiros, X. R. (1995). Discourse relations, coherence and temporal relations. *UCL Working Papers in Linguistics 7*, 177–195.

Smith, N. V. and D. Wilson (1992). Introduction to the special issue on relevance theory. *Lingua 87*(1/2), 1–10.

Sperber, D. (1985). *On Anthropological Knowledge.* Cambridge: Cambridge University Press.

Sperber, D. (1994). Understanding verbal understanding. pp. 179–198. In Khalfa (ed.) (1994).

Sperber, D. (1996). *Explaining Culture.* Oxford: Blackwell.

Sperber, D. (ed.) (2000a). *Metarepresentations.* Oxford: Oxford University Press.

Sperber, D. (2000b). Metarepresentations in an evolutionary perspective. pp. 117–137. Oxford: Oxford University Press. In Sperber (ed.) (2000a).

Sperber, D. and D. Wilson (1986). On defining relevance. pp. 243–258. In Gundry and Warner (eds) 1986.

Sperber, D. and D. Wilson (1990). Rhetoric and relevance. pp. 140–156. In Bender and Wellbery (eds) (1990).

Sperber, D. and D. Wilson (1995). *Relevance* (2 edn). Oxford: Blackwell. (First edition 1986).

Sperber, D. and D. Wilson (1996). Fodor's frame problem and relevance theory. *Behavioural and Brain Sciences 19*(3), 530–532.

Sperber, D. and D. Wilson (1997). Remarks on relevance theory and the social sciences. *Multilingua 16*, 145–151.

Sperber, D. and D. Wilson (1998). The mapping between the mental and the public lexicon. pp. 184–200. In Carruthers and Boucher (eds) (1998).

Stainton, R. (1993). *Non-Sentential Assertions.* PhD thesis, Massachusetts Institute of Technology.

Stainton, R. (1994). Using non-sentences: an application of relevance theory. *Pragmatics and Cognition 2*(2), 269–284.

Stark, H. (1988). What do paragraph markings do? *Discourse processes 11*, 275–303.

Steger, H. et al. (1974). Redekonstellationen, Redekonstellationstyp, Textexemplar, Textsorte im Rahmen eines Sprachverhaltensmodells. Begründung einer Forschungshypothese. pp. 39–97. In H. Moser (ed.) (1974).

Swales, J. M. (1990). *Genre Analysis: English in Academic and Research Settings.* Cambridge: Cambridge University Press.

Thibault, P. J. (1999). Communicating and interpreting relevance through discourse negotiation: An alternative to relevance theory - A reply to Franken. *Journal of Pragmatics. 31*, 557–594.

Thomson, G. and B. Adnan Zawaydeh (1996). A search for inflectional priming reveals an effect of discourse type on the lexical access of inflected verbs. *Work Papers of the Summer Institute of Linguistics, University of North Dakota Session 140*, 111–125.

Todorov, T. (1990). *Genres in Discourse.* Cambridge: Cambridge University Press. Translated from the French original of 1978 by Catherine Porter.

Tomlin, R. S. (ed.) (1987). *Coherence and Grounding in Discourse.* Amsterdam: Benjamins.

Tomlin, R. S., L. Forrest, M. M. Pu, and M. H. Kim (1997). Discourse semantics. pp. 63–111. In Teun A. van Dijk (ed.) (1997).

Toole, J. (1996). The effect of genre on referential choice. pp. 263–290. In Fretheim and Gundel (eds) (1996).

Trotter, D. (1992). Analysing literary prose: the relevance of relevance theory. *Lingua 87*(1/2), 11–27.

Unger, C. (1989). Die Verwendung des Partizips im Biblisch-Aramäischen. Master's thesis, Freie Theologische Akademie Giessen.

Unger, C. (1994). Aspects of the Dialect of Behdinan. Paper read at the Kurdistan Forum of the School of Oriental and African Studies, London.

Unger, C. (1996). The scope of discourse connectives: implications for discourse organization. *Journal of Linguistics 32*, 403–438.

Unger, C. (1998a). Causality and relevance. Paper read at the Autumn meeting of the Linguistics Association of Great Britain, University of Luton.

Unger, C. (1998b). On the influence of genre on the deduction of implicatures. Paper presented to the 2nd Relevance Theory Workshop, University of Luton.

Unger, C. (2001). *On the Cognitive Role of Genre: A Relevance-Theoretic Perspective.* PhD thesis, University of London.

van Dijk, T. A. (1977). *Text and Context.* London and New York: Longman.

van Dijk, T. A. (1980). *Macrostructures.* Hillsdale, New Jersey: Lawrence Erlbaum Associates.

van Dijk, T. A. (ed.) (1997a). *Discourse as Structure and Process.* London: Sage Publications.

van Dijk, T. A. (1997b). *The Study of Discourse.* In van Dijk (ed.) (1997).

van Dijk, T. A. and W. Kintsch (1983). *Strategies of Discourse Comprehension.* Orlando, Florida: Academic Press.

van Kuppevelt, J. (1991). *Topic en comment: expliciete en implicite vraagstelling in discourse.* PhD thesis, University of Nijmegen.

van Kuppevelt, J. (1995a). Discourse structure, topicality and questioning. *Journal of Linguistics 31*(1), 109–147.

van Kuppevelt, J. (1995b). Main structure and side structure in discourse. *Linguistics 33*, 809–833.

van Kuppevelt, J. (1996). Inferring from topics. *Linguistics and Philosophy 19*, 393–443.

Vazquez, I. and A. Hornero (eds.) (1996). *Current Issues in Genre Theory.* Zaragoza: MIRA editores.

Venuti, L. (ed.) (2000). *The Translation Studies Reader.* London and New York: Routledge.

Vet, C. and C. Vetters (eds.) (1994). *Tense and Aspect in Discourse.* Berlin: Mouton de Gruyter.

von Stutterheim, C. (1997). *Einige Prinzipien des Textaufbaus.* Tübingen: Niemeyer.

Werlich, E. (1982). *A Text Grammar of English.* Heidelberg: Quelle and Meyer.

Werth, P. (1999). *Text worlds: Representing conceptual space in discourse.* Harlow, Essex: Longman, Pearson Ltd.

Westermann, C. (1977). *Lob und Klage in den Psalmen.* Göttingen: Vandenhoeck and Ruprecht.

Whittaker, R. and L. Martín Rojo (1999). A dialogue with bureaucracy: Register, genre and information management as constraints on interchangeability. *Journal of Pragmatics 31*, 149–189.

Widdowson, H. (1995). Discourse analysis: a critical view. *Language and Literature 4*(3), 157–172.

Wildberger, H. (1972). *Jesaja, 1. Teil.* Neunkirchen-Vluyn: Neunkirchener Verlag.

Wilson, D. (1992). Reference and relevance. *UCL Working Papers in Linguistics 4*, 165–191.

Wilson, D. (1994). Truth, coherence and relevance. Paper delivered to the European Society for Philosophy and Psychology.

Wilson, D. (1998). Discourse, coherence and relevance: A reply to Rachel Giora. *Journal of Pragmatics 29*, 57–74.

Wilson, D. (1999). Relevance and relevance theory. pp. 719–722. In Wilson and Keil (eds) (1999).

Wilson, D. (2000). Metarepresentation in linguistic communication. In Sperber (ed.) (2000), 411-448.

Wilson, D. and T. Matsui (1998). Recent approaches to bridging: Truth, coherence, relevance. *UCL Working Papers in Linguistics 10*, 173–200.

Wilson, D. and D. Sperber (1993). Linguistic form and relevance. *Lingua 90*, 1–25.

Wilson, D. and D. Sperber (1998). Pragmatics and time. pp. 1–22. In Carston and Uchida (eds) (1998).

Wilson, D. and D. Sperber (2002). Truthfulness and relevance. *Mind 111*, 583–632.

Wilson, R. A. and F. Keil (eds.) (1999). *MIT Encyclopedia of Cognitive Science*. Cambridge, MA: MIT Press.

Žegarac, V. and B. Clark (1999a). Phatic communication and Relevance Theory: a reply to Ward and Horn. *Journal of Linguistics 35*(3), 565–577.

Žegarac, V. and B. Clark (1999b). Phatic interpretations and phatic communication. *Journal of Linguistics 35*(2), 321–346.

Index